SIGNALS

SIGNALS

What Your Child
Is Really Telling You

PAUL R. ACKERMAN, PH.D.,
and
MURRAY M. KAPPELMAN, M.D.

The Dial Press/James Wade   *New York*

PUBLISHED BY
THE DIAL PRESS / JAMES WADE
1 DAG HAMMARSKJOLD PLAZA
NEW YORK, NEW YORK 10017

Part of the material in this book was excerpted, with permission, from *Sex and the American Teenager* by Murray Kappelman, M.D., published by Reader's Digest Press, New York, 1977.

Manufactured in the United States of America

First printing

Design by Francesca Belanger

Library of Congress Cataloging in Publication Data

Ackerman, Paul R., 1934–
Signals.

Includes index.
1. Parent and child.   2. Children—Management.
3. Child psychology.   4. Adolescent psychology.
I. Kappelman, Murray, 1931–   joint author.
II. Title.
HQ755.85.A26   301.42'7   78–15272
ISBN 0–8037–8151–2

To
Joan, for her support
Miriam, for her help
Mary, for her friendship

Contents

PREVENTION

THE PROFESSIONALS

PARENTING BY SIGNALS

A Letter to
Our Fellow Parents

This is a book for any parent, with children of any age. It is about children, not problems. It is about how they (and *you*) communicate.

Taken as a whole, this is a book about how to be an aware, receptive, effective, and compassionate parent. Its objective is to help you assert your own natural skills, authority, insight, and common sense to help your children become happy and free adults.

Signals is not "selling a method"; it tries to show how you can build on your own instincts, knowledge, and concern to form your unique and individual approach to the most important job you will ever hold in your life.

It is, most of all, a book about listening, seeing, evaluating, and acting.

True attention is the beginning of love!

Paul Ackerman
Murray M. Kappelman

1978

SIGNALS

WHAT
YOUR CHILD
IS REALLY
TELLING YOU

1

Signals: What They Are and How They Work

All of us have moments when our children do things we don't understand. These moments frighten us. We are baffled, and we often want to reach out for help, advice, and counsel. We search for answers, not always sure of the questions, aware only that our child and our family are in the midst of a troublesome time. We look around desperately for easy labels and quick remedies when we find our child doing things like these:

* Our three-year-old daughter has temper tantrums during which she holds her breath so long that she passes out.
* Our youngest, a four-year-old, is beginning to stutter.
* Our five-year-old son plays by himself and talks under his breath to "Chester," his fantasy friend.
* We find our six-year-old son with the box of Christmas candy under his bed; he has both stolen the candy and, when it was found, lied about it.
* Our eight-year-old daughter is so shy that she seems to have no friends. We watch her closely and notice that she spends more and more time alone.
* Our three children play well together. Put them in a car for a long trip, however, and they drive us crazy with their bickering and fighting.
* Our beautiful thirteen-year-old daughter is eating so little

and getting so thin that everyone thinks she is malnour-
ished and ill; but when we shove food at her, she refuses
to eat.
* Our teenage son is failing in school.
* Our fourteen-year-old son is beginning to act like a girl.
* We have heard through a chance remark that our sixteen-
year-old daughter is "sleeping around."

From this point on, these actions will be known as *signals.* They
are the child's way of telling you something that he or she cannot
express in normal words or through the usual family conversations. They are messages from your child to someone else—usually
you—that convey a feeling or a need too complex or too frightening to talk about in the usual way. A signal is an alternate way of
communicating, a method that usually says: "Please stop! Listen!"

This book is about those signals. The chapters are labeled by the
names most people give to childhood signals, i.e., "Lying," "Temper Tantrums," "Bedwetting," and so on. The book describes and
explores these signals. Some of them, you will find, only herald
"normal" growth, while others forecast much more serious problems. Age will make a difference; a signal frequently used by
young children might be innocent then but much more serious in
older children. Many signals carry more than one message; perhaps they are being sent to more than one person. The various
types of signals and their common use among children of all ages
will be found described carefully in the following chapters.

"Naming That Signal," however, is neither the game nor the
aim of this book. That act alone does not necessarily help you to
be a better parent. In order to help your child effectively, you
must first discover the *message* contained in the signal and then
act on that message. You will want to know the most probable
message that various types of signals might contain. You will want
to know how other parents and professionals perceive and then
deal with the messages contained in such signals. You will want to
know the successes and failures others have had when "answer-

ing" these messages. This book will offer you that information, often through anecdotes from our own experience. Through it you can unravel the mysteries of the signals that stand as barriers to your ability to help your child.

In determining the shape your child's signals take, and then discovering their inner meanings, you will be asked to engage in one very important exercise. You will be asked to think *as if you were your child.* As you read these first two chapters, learning how to be a detective by catching the signals and uncovering the messages, you will always be asked to translate what you learn into this question: "What does this mean to *my* child?"

Try to construct your child's world for yourself. It will not come easy, for you will find that it is colored by your own adult values. It will be hard for you to think with the immature perspective of your child. But you *can* enter his world deeply enough to solve some of his problems. To illustrate this, we ask you to engage in that kind of exercise right now. The purpose of this exercise is to explore how signals operate in the minds of children. Pretend *you* are the child described in each case, and answer the questions as that child might. See if you don't produce signals.

CHILD 1

Think of yourself as a four-year-old. You are an only child. You live in a neighborhood where there are few other children. Your company is mostly Mommy and Daddy and, infrequently, cousins or friends at family parties. You are unsure of how to make friends. You have had some unhappy experiences trying to play with friends your own age; children often make fun of you and don't stay around you very long. Now Mommy and Daddy are about to enroll you in a preschool class with fifteen other children, none of whom you know. The whole idea of that many strangers at one time really frightens you.

How can you let your parents know that you are frightened? How can you make them understand that inner fear? How can you tell them that you would rather stay at home and play with them—or play alone?

Would you:

(a) Tell them that you just aren't ready for school?

(b) Determine to use the preschool experience to learn how to make and hold friends?

(c) Worry a lot and probably get sick on enrollment day so you won't be able to go?

(d) Become shy and withdrawn in class, hoping to avoid contacts with the other children that might be unpleasant or hurtful?

(e) Throw a noisy, angry temper tantrum on the first day of school, thus showing your parents your rage at their lack of understanding?

Check your ability to get into the mind of this four-year-old. You have probably ruled out answers (a) and (b); they are far too sophisticated for the usual four-year-old. These answers are, however, the answers that the parents of this child *wish* he or she could give. The real answers to this quiz are (c), (d), and (e)—one or all of them. Which of these options the child selects will depend on two things: the degree of fear and insecurity, and the child's basic temperament. Obviously a child cannot directly relay his fears to his parents; he does not have the adequate or appropriate vocabulary. So, he must act out this message in a *signal*. Either (c), (d), or (e) is that signal. Each carries the *message:* "I want to be with you rather than in school."

CHILD 2

Now we are going to ask you to try something a bit harder: deciphering the signals of an older child. In this exercise, imagine that you are a ten-year-old girl who feels that she is clumsy, awkward, and too big for her age. You feel even more awkward when family friends constantly compare you to your "beautiful" older sister, Shirley—Shirley, the talented one in the family—the cheerleader, member of the student government, and now the lead in the class play. You have tried to tell your parents how inadequate these comparisons make you feel, but they merely shrug it off, saying, "You'll probably change in a few years. Shirley did." You know you can't change that much. And now your parents are giving the cast party for Shirley. All of the "in" kids in her school as well as your parents' close friends have been invited. You have been asked to serve the punch.

Isn't this a set-up for another comparison session? How can you tell your parents that their adult friends can be unintentionally cruel? When will your parents stop emphasizing beauty and achievements? How can you tell Shirley to stop ruining your life?

If you were ten years old, what signals would you send?

(a) Run away to a girlfriend's house the evening of the party.
(b) Feel ugly, be ugly; look and act unattractive at the party—on purpose.
(c) Act as charming as possible, watching Shirley closely so you can learn how to be as gracious and lovely as you think she is.
(d) Ruin Shirley's party with spiked punch, dropped food, spilled drinks; make it look like an accident.
(e) Go to bed with stomach pains; let those who really care come to see you.

Didn't you feel that you were capable of anything but (c)? You are right. This girl needs desperately to tell her parents that things in her life are very wrong; but she cannot. Something dramatic has to happen to get that message across, so watch out for (a), (b), (d), or (e). If she has the temperament to be aggressive or angry, (a), (b), and (d) are possible. If she is more passive, the physical complaints in (e) are most likely. It is obvious that she has to tell her parents—but in the language of signals.

CHILD 3

One more exercise may help you understand the complexities of signals. We have selected an exercise from that most confused period of childhood, adolescence. This time, you must try to enter the mind of a fifteen-year-old boy. You are shy and awkward, very painfully aware of your rapidly growing body. You are usually quiet, and you have a secret: you are also very bright. You try to keep your intelligence under cover, however, because you don't want to be identified with those "brains" at school who are made fun of by your crowd. Only you know how much satisfaction you get from reading at home—novels, newspapers, magazines, anything. And your life is complicated, in a wonderful way, by Glenda. You think you're really in love with her. You would do anything to keep her interested—anything. Since she also hates "brains" and only makes "C's" and "D's," you're afraid she'll drop you if she finds out you are an "A" student.

How can you hide from her the fact that you really are a "brain"? At the same time, how can you meet your parents' expectations (and your own) about high grades? Which is more important to you, good grades and adult approval, or the attentions of this very important girl?

What will happen at school? What signals will you send?

(a)   Decide that Glenda will see your high grades and realize you are OK after all.

(b)   Fail your semester exams, by choice, playing sick that week.

(c)   Tell your parents about your dilemma, continue the good grades, and then lie to the girl about your report card.

(d)   Lower your grades systematically by late papers, poor test scores, and sloppy work, letting no one know why you're slowly slipping in school.

How did you score this complex adolescent problem? A teenager's mind would not have picked (a). Other kids don't change overnight. The (b) choice might work, but not for long. You'd soon have to make up the work and get high grades once again. The (c) option might work with the parents, but is this any way to start a relationship? It isn't fair to the girl—or to you. Probably, (d) will be selected as the choice. Your parents will have little control over it. It keeps the girl. The signal is complicated; it has several messages for several people. Yet it is not an uncommon adolescent signal. Can you imagine how hard a teenager's parents will have to work to understand *that* one?

These exercises have been designed to teach you something about why children send signals rather than straight communications to their parents. You have entered the mind of a child, and you saw how choices were made. You saw how communication had already been blocked so that the child *had* to formulate another method of getting a message across. You have seen the "hows" and "whys" of signals. Now you can apply some of that insight to your own experiences as you seek to enter the mind of your own child.

But before you start entering your child's world, allow yourself a parental point of view. Think through what you have learned about signals. Here are some pointers that will help you later on in your detective work in finding your child's signalled messages:

* Signals occur when a child does not have the words to express his feelings or his predicament to his parents. Child 1, the four-year-old, simply could not talk meaningfully about his "insecurity" in making friends. He had to *show* his parents through his actions, his signal.

* Signals occur when the child thinks her parents *cannot* or *will not* listen to her words. Child 2, our "ugly duckling," had the vocabulary to talk about her feelings. She tried, but her parents did not really hear her or help her. She therefore felt that she had to try an alternate method of communication. She had to signal.

* Signals substitute for words when a child feels he must get an action or response that words will not produce. The teenage boy, Child 3, could not have told his girl that he

was a "brain" and still expect to continue their relationship. He thought he had to signal by actions—lower his grades.

* Signals are sometimes *learned.* In each of our examples, the child could have used a signal of physical complaints. Often when this is done, it is rewarded by attention and sympathy and becomes a learned signal. As in our examples, a physical complaint could have postponed the preschool experience for the reluctant four-year-old; it could have commanded the attention of the parents to the less attractive child. An illness could have provided a convenient excuse for lowered grades in the teenage boy. Parents have to be careful of the signal that they fix into the lifestyle of the child by paying too much attention to it.

* Signals are sometimes sent by the child as messages to himself. The child is trying to fool himself into thinking he has one problem and not another. A young child may not eat; it's easier to say, "I'm not hungry," than it is to admit, "I need the undivided attention of my Daddy and Mommy because I am afraid they will leave me." Likewise, the older child who simply cannot make friends may feel it's easier to admit, "I'm shy," than, "I'm unattractive, or have poor social skills."

Signals have other characteristics that you should know, dimensions that you will not have learned from these simple exercises, but will learn throughout the lifetime of your child.

* Signals almost always make a parent uneasy, anxious, or angry. They are challenges. They are puzzles, representing a different and unexpected action from a child. They do not "fit" with your expectations of your child. They make you think that they are personally directed at you,

even when they are not. Such signals put your parenting on temporarily shaky ground because they appear to come from nowhere and go in no particular direction.

* Signals quite often represent a challenge to the family rules and values. The unexpected actions of children often unerringly hit the soft spots within parents. If you label these signals by words like "lying," "stealing," "promiscuity," "male effeminate behavior," you will shudder with the negative feelings aroused by such labels. You can recognize a signal by the label, but you must try to look beneath that name to discover the real reason behind it. The more a signal gets you "uptight," the more important it is to your child. He or she is *trying* to command your attention!

* There are no limits to the ways in which children signal. Signals can be physical or mental; temporary or permanent; verbal or nonverbal; directed against family or self-directed; subtle or obvious; simple or complex; and just about any other combination of opposite adjectives you can invent. Their only commonality is their substitution for conversation and their initiation by the child. Look for the signals that are becoming a general lifestyle as well as the temporary signals of childhood growth.

* Signals vary in children of different ages. A signal such as bedwetting deserves one set of explanations in a four-year-old and an entirely different interpretation in a four-teen-year-old. Some signals almost never occur in childhood, and some childhood signals become a great deal more serious when they occur in adolescents. A signal cannot, therefore, be generalized. It must always be interpreted within the knowledge of the age and maturity level of the child who sends it.

* Signals are not easy to perceive. You have to work very hard at receiving them correctly, no matter how perceptive you are as a parent. No adult is immune to the clever signal that provokes his or her guilt. Your child intuitively hits your "nerve center" and makes you want to cry out in anger or frustration, "Why are you doing this to me?" You forget that he may be doing "it" for entirely different reasons than you suspect.

There is small comfort in the knowledge that *all* children signal. When a parent confronts a signal in his or her child, it is *always* difficult—the message behind the signal *always* takes some effort to understand. This is why this book was written. To help parents perceive, understand, and act intelligently when they receive the signals from their children. This book promises no easy trip, but an insightful one, a trip guaranteed to help a parent know his child—and himself—better, with more depth and more understanding. Reading this book and exploring the world of your child, determining his or her hidden message as well as listening to his or her open communication, watching his or her signals appear and then disappear as you help him or her along the pathway to normal growth and health—these are the joys and the rewards of parenting. These are the responses that can make a very real difference in your child's life. These actions can reward you with the truly satisfying feeling of being a successful parent.

2

Finding the Message

Your child has signalled. You know it because you feel and see it. Something vague, undefined, unpredictable is happening in your child's behavior and it worries you. Your child is in some kind of personal distress. But what? What is he trying to tell you? How can you help him? What is the message that lies buried somewhere in what your child is doing or saying?

You are now engaged in the search for the message hidden inside the outward signal. It is a search that may proceed easily, or perhaps may take every bit of your intelligence, patience, and ingenuity. You must enter your child's mind as a detective enters the mysterious world of the unknown. You must reconstruct your child's world, consider your child's actions, and try to uncover what made him act the way he did. What you want to come up with is the message *in the manner in which your child thinks and feels it.* You will do an injustice to your child if you explain his message by saying, "He wants more attention," when he is really saying, "I feel nobody pays any attention to me because I'm quiet." These last three words are so important. They present a totally different challenge that requires you to search deeper and act accordingly if you want to help him. A perceptive parent must discover which is the real message—the *child's* message—if the end result is to be a happier, healthier child.

How can you start your detective work to find the message(s)

15

behind your child's signal? Reading about the signals in this book will help, of course, but you will ultimately have to interpret the advice contained here to fit your child in your specific situation. How? Start by asking yourself some of the basic questions about the signals, questions which are suggested below. Be systematic in your search. Ask yourself all of these questions and make certain that you are covering every point. Do not stop until the signal and the message fall into a meaningful pattern.

When does the signal occur? Look to see if the signal repeats itself. Does it happen at a certain time of the day? Each day? If you find, for example, that a child signals every night just before bed, perhaps that child is trying to postpone bedtime and put off his real fear: the dark. That child may be saying a lot more than the quick conclusion that he merely wants to watch more television. In your observation of the timing of the signal, try to notice if it occurs after some particular event. Does some person seem to provoke it—to "trigger" it? Are *you* the trigger?

In what setting does the signal occur? Have you noticed that your child's signal occurs outside as well as inside the house? Signals often occur in school and not at home, and signals often direct a message to peers rather than parents. When your child signals, are people generally around or is the child alone? Are there any unusual aspects to your child's surroundings—family chaos, sibling rivalry, and so on—that may be present when your child is sending her signal? A child may only throw temper tantrums during the tense arguments between her mother and father. The message is not the tantrum but her desire to divert her parents' anger at each other. Does the signal occur in settings where it will embarrass your child—or you? In other words, what is the stage upon which the signal is being played? A good psychological detective spends many hours reconstructing that stage setting.

Who is generally most affected by the signal? To whom is the message really being sent? You, as a parent, may think that all messages are sent to you. You want to be responsible for your child's development and you want to share all of his or her communication. But some messages are meant for others. Sibling rivalry, for instance, may truly be directed at another envied child in your home and not be directly related to you. Stealing from another may be a method of "getting even" for another child's insults and not represent a rejection of parental values. By searching for the person to whom the signal is being sent, the parents may obtain a clue about the message and find, happily or otherwise, that the message may *not* be for them.

Does my child have the vocabulary to send me a "straight" message? How many children can really express themselves on the subject of their loneliness, rejection, failures, or insecurities? They can talk about insults, fights, rewards, injuries, or material wants, but values, philosophies, longings are often beyond their abilities to express. If they have problems about which they cannot adequately speak, they must signal. You will, therefore, often find more signals coming from younger children than older ones. But be cautious about overestimating the vocabulary of the older child; remember that the adolescent has different kinds of problems from the younger child, problems which are also very difficult to talk about. An adolescent can often talk adequately about loneliness, but cannot talk so easily about sexual strivings, about the awkwardness of his or her bodily changes, or about his or her fears of the future. The signal to you then, like that of the younger child, may be based upon an inability to find the right words.

What is the response given to the signal? Do you respond to your child's signal with anxiety, fear, punishment, concern, attention, conversation? The signal is meant to evoke one or more of those responses. Your honest analysis about your responses to your child's signal will help you to find this important clue by playing by the rules of the child's game: "Here's the answer; what is the question?" *Why* does my child want that response? What is missing in his life that he wants attention, punishment, or anxiety from me? When he repeats the signal, does it always provoke the same response? If so, then you are "onto something." Do you always overreact when he is ill? In that case physical complaints will be the best signal to attract attention to a hidden problem. Find out what he wants by using this "game" and you will be able to hypothesize several reasons for his wanting it. Don't let your automatic response blind you from looking at the underlying cry for help. Work backwards from response to signal so you can find his motivation for his actions.

Is my relationship with my child open and comfortable enough to allow the child to send me a "straight" message without signals? Play this one calm, "cool," and objective. If your child is having trouble communicating with you, he or she may have to signal. That does not necessarily mean that you are in any way to "blame" for his having to signal. Almost all children have trouble at some time communicating with parents. This is a fact of life. Do you remember the acute embarrassment with which you had to ask your own parents those first basic questions about sex? Or your problems in discussing with them one of your school or social failures? Ask yourself this question about your own past so you can get a clue about the messages contained in your child's signal. *After* you have gotten the message, then you will have time to contemplate the positive and negative parts of your relationship with your child. Then you can ask yourself if your child has enough time with you to communicate or if your relationship with him or her allows the freedom needed to talk openly with you. First, however, you must discover the message and act upon it.

How uncomfortable does the signal make me feel? A characteristic of a signal is that it often hits a point of vulnerability in you. Perhaps the child is making fun of church in a religious family. Maybe his manners are atrocious and his eating habits sickening. If dinnertime is a cherished time, then this is a good "battleground." Are you offended by her appearance or lack of cleanliness? The dirty child upsets the orderly, neat parent. In trying to find the message, you may ask yourself, "What was it about the signal that made me angry, resentful, or hurt me?" In other words, "What was my child trying to provoke in me? And why?" If the child hit a "bull's-eye" in emotion, the message is probably quite important to him. He or she is telling you: "Stop! Pay attention to me." If the signal does not strike at your particularly sensitive areas, it may be meant for someone else. Use this clue to try to discover both the recipient of the message and the emotion that lurks behind it.

Once you have all the clues, you must put the pieces together to find out what your child is really telling you. Try a tentative diagnosis—put your ideas about the message into words and state what could be the "answer" to the problem. Think through what the child truly means by what he says or does and how you can help him. Perhaps you will need the help of a friend, mate, or a professional to devise a plan of action. But try phrasing it in the *child's* language. This will prove very useful. Once you have done this, you will be ready to talk to him about the problem in words you both can understand. You have prepared yourself to reach the point where you can help him find a solution to his own problems. Your detective work has paid off.

The process of helping your child does not stop with finding a message, however. One more vital question remains: Is the message you have discovered the *only* message contained in the signal? Perhaps not. Often signals carry more than one message. A parent can frequently miss a more important cry for help by stopping the search after finding only a whimper of discomfort. Make sure that your detective work is as thorough as possible, leaving no stone unturned in the search for all the possible messages contained within your child's signal.

As we conclude our discussion of the framework of signals and messages in parent/child relationships, it is time to put the search for signals into a perspective that offers some hope. In our explanation about the importance of looking for signals and messages, we hope we have not given you the idea that huge amounts of time must be spent in the process of observing your child's behavior, analyzing signals, looking for messages, and planning ways of offering help. This could be true for certain crisis periods in a particular child's life, when his or her problems are quite serious or chaotic. But for most of the signals given during your child's life, intelligent observation aided by a few well-placed questions will be sufficient for you to discover and interpret the signals and messages. "Parenting by signals," as explained in the final chapter of this book, or "preventive parenting," as explained in Chapter 26, can easily become your styles of parenting. Both styles offer you open communication with your child and minimize the need for signalled messages.

We end this chapter with a story illustrating the process of discovering signals and messages in the case of Chuck. Chuck's story illustrates a signal sent to cover a message he felt his parents were not ready to receive. He was wrong, as the following case history shows:

Of all the four children in Chuck's family, Chuck was the most "responsible," a fact of which his parents were extremely proud. He was the oldest child, and had been able to babysit for the other children since he was seven years old. He was entrusted with the job of making bank deposits for the family, and all of the tellers at the neighborhood branch knew him. If his brothers or sisters asked him to take them downtown on the bus, he would give up an afternoon. Chuck was given a small allowance which often did not cover his personal needs. Yet he banked all the money he earned from his newspaper route, saving "for college." Even his newspaper customers regarded him as the most "responsible" newsboy in memory. He never missed a day's delivery. Chuck was only twelve years old, but a "model" child.

One night, when Chuck's mother was driving past the corner where her son picked up his papers for delivery, she noticed him emerging from a record store with a record album. Later that night, when she questioned him about it, he replied that a customer had "tipped" him, and he had used that money to pay for the record.

A week later, his mother noticed another new album on top of his phonograph. The answer to her query this time was, "I found the money in the street."

When the third record appeared in his room, Chuck's mother said nothing. But she knew, instinctively, that there was something very wrong. She was perceiving a signal that she could not—did not want to—understand.

She went to the kitchen cupboard and counted the loose change which she always stored in an old teapot. She waited until the next shiny record appeared on Chuck's phonograph before she re-counted the money. Several dollars were missing.

When she confronted Chuck that evening, she repeatedly asked *"Why?"* He could not answer. He could not explain why he took the money. He could only tell his parents that he wanted to "be like the other kids." Chuck wanted to be able to talk about the records with his friends. But his confession did not explain why he had to steal the money to buy the records. And he had his own newspaper money, still untouched, in his top bureau drawer.

When Chuck's mother finally talked over the incident with her best friend, she was surprised by the woman's words: "Aren't you always expecting too much of Chuck? Of course, you can't let him steal and lie. But are you letting him be a normal twelve-year-old? Or are you expecting him to be as responsible as you are?"

Chuck, through his signal, was telling his parents *to stop.* "Stop pushing me into premature adulthood. Let me be normal. Let me be like my friends. Don't make me into your model child. Let me make a mistake just once in my life. Let me be me—a twelve-year-old ME!"

Chuck's signal, as with many children, was destined to be dis-covered. He probably wanted to be caught because he could not express himself openly. He had not hidden the records. The change had been stolen, and he knew his mother regularly counted her money. His cover-up lies were artificial. Chuck was signalling. He was trying to state a message which he felt his parents did not want to hear—that he was a child and not an adult.

What would you have done if you were Chuck's parents? Punish him for stealing? Yes, with privileges withheld and money repaid. But Chuck's parents also had interpreted the message hidden in his signal. They knew that Chuck needed much more than imme-diate punishment. Chuck was helped to rebudget his money so that he could afford more records. His parents offered him options of additional work around the house and yard to earn more pocket money. He was encouraged to take time to socialize with his friends and permitted to hire a substitute newspaper carrier when he had an important social event. He was allowed to give up "playing father" to his younger brothers and sisters. Chuck's parents were beginning to treat him like a normal twelve-year-old boy. He had successfully signalled his message. His parents had just as successfully perceived it and correctly interpreted it.

Chuck's story illustrates the importance of signals in the process of communication between parent and child. It offers an example of good parenting and, at the same time, issues a warning to other parents to keep alert and sensitive. Helping children mature will require knowing them as people and learning about their world. That can only be done by assuming that not all communication is verbal, that some communication is going to be transmitted by actions—at times surprising, disturbing, symbolic, or painful.

The process of discovering signals and messages often requires additional help. That is what this book is for. It offers you an objective exploration of the common signals of childhood and adolescence in a chronological, developmental order. These signals can either be potentially serious problems or simple "phases" of child growth. Use the book to help yourself "short-cut" your investigations into the signals and messages of your child. Find the advice and counsel that best helps you plan remedies for *your* child. Read and consider the methods of good parenting presented in this book. Then try to work out your *own*, unique methods.

By reading and using this book, you will be signalling your child that you care—that you will help and guide him or her into maturity. Your child's future adjustment as an emotionally healthy adult will be his message to you. He will be signalling "thank you."

THE
SIGNALS

3

Temper Tantrums

You have just told your three-year-old son, Billy, that he cannot have another piece of candy. He pouts and says belligerently, "But I want it." Shaking your head, you cover the candy dish and say firmly, "No." All of a sudden, he hurtles his small body to the floor, screaming in a loud, unintelligible voice, kicking his legs and arms, and rolling his body. Billy is having a classic temper tantrum. What does this overreaction to a simple denial mean? What is the signal?

Understanding the signal behind the temper tantrum in the young child helps the parent react sensibly to such sudden, wild behavior. The natural tendency on the parent's part is to attempt to soothe the child or talk him out of the temper tantrum. The sight of your child writhing on the floor in fury can be very disturbing and, to many parents, frightening. The normal parent intuitively would try to do something to put a halt to the unpleasant sights and sounds of the child's tantrum. However, this would be the *wrong* approach to the problem. Doing something means that the parent has received the signal of the temper tantrum but has not interpreted and acted upon the child's actions in the most appropriate and educational way.

The message in the temper tantrum that Billy is throwing is uncomplicated and very straightforward. He is trying to force his parent to bend to his wishes by the most outrageous form of behavior he can muster. A child who uses the temper tantrum signal often correctly perceives that the parents would be upset by the tantrum and do something to calm him down. Children reared in homes where discipline is relatively clear-cut know that a tantrum will not work. Their messages have already been answered. But the youngsters whose parents are still a little tentative and unsure of how strong and forceful they should be with their children will be the ones on whom the tantrums will be played. The message of the temper tantrum signal in these children is purely and simply manipulative in nature. That must be realized by the parents before they can take the next important step.

The word "play" was used as a verb to describe the temper tantrum. We could use the same word as a noun, meaning that the temper tantrum is a full-fledged dramatic performance by the child, usually before a select audience, the parents. Normally the child is not nearly as angry or upset as the kicking and screaming would suggest. But to make the point and force the parents to change their minds, the drama must be played at the highest pitch. Remember that no actor wants to perform before a completely empty house. Billy is an actor; his temper tantrum is a performance. His audience is one or both parents. Therefore, having received Billy's signal through his temper tantrum, his mother can break the cycle by removing the audience. If she leaves the room where Billy is banging on the floor in rage and walks out quietly, without a word about the boy's display of anger, she will be leaving the young boy to perform his temper tantrum only for himself. Very quickly, the screaming and the kicking will cease. The signal will be over; the message has been received and intelligently rejected.

Billy will probably try the temper tantrum tactic again. Young children often try the same signal several times until it is very clear that the manipulative ploy will not work. With older children, a failed manipulative signal is usually replaced by another. They learn the tricks of the trade quickly. But the temper tantrum is the signal of the very young child and may be repeated. If the parent quietly and without comment leaves the room each time, the signal will fade into memory and the temper tantrums will cease.

Temper tantrums may take other forms as the child grows older. Not only is the form different but so is the meaning of the signal. Six-year-old Karl repeatedly came in from the yard where the other children were playing and would stand in the kitchen crying and banging his fists on the kitchen table. His impulsive behavior, his seemingly unreasonable anger, and his loud abusive language at the inanimate objects in the kitchen gave him the uncomfortable appearance of a much younger child having a classic temper tantrum. He seemed unreachable by his parents. The physical aspects of his anger and frustration had to ebb before he could be questioned. Then he would start to cry and run into his room. His parents were confused. What did it all mean? What was the signal?

Karl's parents sat down and discussed the problem together. Clearly, the episodes occurred after their son had been playing outside with the other children in the neighborhood. He never became as physically upset when he was with them in his own home. The message obviously was contained in something that was happening outside. His father stationed himself in the corner of the yard the next day to watch as Karl tried again to play with the other children in the back yard next door. The cause of Karl's signal, his angry tantrum, became obvious in a very short time. As the other six- and seven-year-olds gathered, they selected teams to play ball. Karl was excluded. His father watched as Karl pleaded to be included on one of the teams, but the other boys said he would have to be the referee again. Within minutes, Karl had fled the play area and was back in the house, furious, beating his fists against the kitchen wall and crying. Karl's signal was one of complete frustration about a situation that he felt he could do nothing to change.

Now his father understood and could help his son. He approached the youngster and told him that he noticed the other boys would not include him on the team. "Why?" he asked with obvious concern. The boy looked away, embarrassed. Finally he stuttered, "Because I can't throw the ball so good. They don't want me messing up the game." His father nodded. "That must make you very angry," he said gently. Karl looked at him with appreciation. "It does, Dad." His father put his arm around the boy's shoulders. "How about if you and I practice throwing and catching the ball until you're good enough to be on the team?" His father squeezed his son tightly. "We're friends. I don't like to see you angry. And I remember having to practice with my own dad until I was good enough."

Karl's father had not only perceived the signal and interpreted the message, but he had reacted in a most compassionate and meaningful way. He had offered his son a solution to his problem and stressed that it was not one about which Karl should be ashamed. As the days went by and the practice between father and son continued, Karl became a better ball handler and the father-son relationship grew into one of deep mutual affection and respect. The other children began to watch Karl play ball with his dad and soon he was invited to play in the neighborhood games. There were no more fist-banging temper tantrums in the kitchen. The signal had worked.

Children become more physical as they mature. Their aggressive tendencies rise. Often boys, usually more than girls, attempt to handle problems by physically acting out against them. This is the basis for the increasing number of physical fights between boys as they grow older. However, when confronted by the desire to strike back, and being unable to do so, the older youngster may explode and display a signal similar to a temper tantrum either at home or at school. Boys who are harassed or bullied by bigger boys may come home and bang relentlessly upon the walls. Some youngsters have been taught "never take a fist to another child." These young people try to obey the family rules but find them increasingly difficult to live with when they are attacked by other children. Not fighting back when it is indicated and often living with the consequential label "sissy" may force the young person to act out in a temper tantrum within his home.

It is true that physical violence is to be abhorred and cautioned against by all parents. However, there are times when self-defense becomes essential for both boys and girls in the growing-up years. Indeed, self-defense methods can often *prevent* temper tantrum behavior in older children. Teaching the youngsters the concept of holding off as long as possible, challenging to a fair fight when necessary, and holding back from serious physical injury to the other person at all times should be parenting precepts. Boxing lessons will help the small, the frightened, the poorly coordinated, the shy male to defend himself properly if and when that time should occur. We live in a very real world where "turning the other cheek" is not always possible.

The mother of one of our friends called and begged for help. Her son, a college student, had violently wrecked all of the furniture in his bedroom and was locked inside the room crying. A serious temper tantrum signal, indeed! The overt violent temper outbursts of the adolescent or older person usually signify that the message within the signal is highly significant. What was going on with our friend that had forced him to use such an inappropriate, violent signal?

Stan, the only son among the three children in the family, had a very demanding and forceful father. All of the father's displaced dreams and aspirations had been thrust upon his older teenage boy. He had not been allowed to go away to the college he so desperately desired, but had been forced to attend his father's alma mater, which was near home. In order to keep a close eye on his son and his studies, the father had demanded that Stan live at home. The tension in the house had grown to unbearable heights. Stan had to report daily on his accomplishments. He was allowed to go out socially after getting his father's permission and then only after the older man had satisfied himself that Stan had completed all of his homework. Stan had been reared to be respectful, obedient, and compliant. He could not emotionally refuse to go along with his father's unreasonable demands. But as the stresses of school increased, the suffocating restraints at home became unbearable. Finally one Saturday afternoon, Stan exploded into a signalling temper tantrum of a serious nature. He lost all control and wrecked his room, a desperate message for help.

It was very difficult to convince this family that the signal was

not as important as the message it conveyed. Finally they agreed
to allow Stan to receive psychiatric help. Within a few weeks, the
psychiatrist was counselling the father to allow Stan to move
into the college dormitory. Watching Stan's grades plummet, the
father felt he had no other choice. Stan moved out, got a part-time
job, and helped pay for his apartment. He finished college with
honors, and was admitted to medical school. But as soon as he was
financially independent, he moved out of the city, and returns to
see his family only occasionally. Stan's signal came too late to save
the family relationships; but the tantrum did serve to announce his
impending emotional collapse as nothing else could have. *Stan's
signal saved him.* It served its purpose. How tragic that the signal
had to be so destructive, so violent, before anyone would pay
attention. As we think back through our years with Stan before
that explosive day, we can remember other signals which, if
heeded by his parents, would have prevented the major tantrum
and probably preserved the parent-child relationship.

Teenage tantrums can be a sign of serious trouble in the child
and in the family. They also represent the final attempt to send a
desperate signal to a family that has ignored all previous signals.

4

Fantasy Friends and Fantasies

Gwen's mother is working in the kitchen. The house is very still. Suddenly she hears the small voice of her three-year-old daughter chattering away in the child's bedroom. She puts down the dishcloth and listens. Gwen is holding a conversation with someone, talking excitedly and then pausing as if listening for an answer. But her mother knows that Gwen is alone in her room. Who could she be talking with? She moves quietly out of the kitchen, through the living room, and tiptoes in to look at her little girl. Gwen is sitting in the center of her room on the floor, knees crossed, arms outstretched. Seated in a circle around her are three stuffed animals, a teddy bear, a panda, and a reindeer. Gwen's small head bobs back and forth as she turns to face each of her mute friends, her mouth moving as she speaks happily to each in turn. She asks questions, listens for answers, then pauses and talks back. Gwen's mother is amused and she grins. But then she stops for a second, leans against the wall in the hallway, and ponders. Is it normal for her daughter to actually be talking to these stuffed animals? Doesn't she understand that they are not alive and will not answer? Why is she making up their responses in her head? Should she be worried about her daughter's fantasy friends? Is there a message hidden within this delightful signal?

There is indeed a message and Gwen's mother's first amused and tolerant reaction was the correct one. Fantasy friends are a

normal part of many young children's lives. The world around
them is so new, so exciting, that they want to share their delight.
The sounds of words coming from their mouths and getting responses from others are newly discovered miracles. The young
child wants to experiment with her words and her conversation,
as much and as often as possible. Because other children her own
age may not always be available, Gwen has chosen the solution
used by so many other young people. They create their companions from the toys, dolls, and stuffed animals around them.

It is particularly common for an only child or the first child in
a family to create imaginary friends with whom to talk and share
experiences during their very early years. These children do not
have other young children in the family and are living in an essentially adult world. When they cannot be with their playmates,
there are no other children around to share the exquisite joys of
childhood. The youngster perceives correctly that adults will not
be able to share in the excitement the way that another child
could. And these unexpected pleasures *must* be shared. They
can't be stored until a later time. Children bubble over with the
need to express themselves—at once—without a moment's delay.
Only another child (or an imaginary friend as a substitute) can play
that immediate, excited, unrestrained role. As a result, the only or
first child will often create these fantasy friends as perfect substitutes for the missing playmates. This does not necessarily mean
that this child feels lonely or left out. It merely signifies that the
moment of sharing cannot be delayed; the fantasy friend must
serve that purpose.

Unfortunately, the fantasy friend can sometimes be the signal
that a child is too lonely. The parent whose child has a fantasy
friend can decipher the message of too much loneliness by considering the following factors:

1. How available are children of the same age, and how
    often does your child have the opportunity to play
    with them? If the answer is "too few" (less than three)
    and "too seldom" (twice a week or less), then a

message of loneliness is probably being signalled.

2. How well does your child play with other children? If there are other children laughing and playing outside the young child's window, but your child prefers to play with the imaginary animal friends—then the messages of alienation and loneliness are real concerns.

3. Is your child really happy in substituting these imaginary friends for the real thing? If she is a silent, unhappy child, who holds her imaginary friends tightly against her as she yearns for the company of other children, then the fantasy friends are an inadequate cover for her isolation.

Other signals of a full fantasy life that could prove of concern to the parent do exist and must be heeded. The child should not carry the fantasy into her real life by insisting that her parents and other childhood friends join her imaginary world. The major part of the child's daily activity should not consist of communicating with fantasy friends. The child should not reject actual communication with the real world. Primary friends who are fantasy friends should not extend beyond the first three years of the child's life. When this happens, parents are seeing potentially serious messages in the otherwise benign signal.

When we daydream, we usually fantasize. To daydream occasionally is normal, even expected, in all of us. Like Candide, each of us, including children, often fantasizes about the best of all possible worlds. But when daydreaming overtakes our ability to deal with routine daily tasks, we are in trouble. Children fall into the same category. The daydreaming child is emitting a signal. What is the message?

George spent most of his school day staring out of the window daydreaming. He could tell his parents and his teacher what he was dreaming about: weekends at his grandparents' summer home, Christmas vacations in the mountains, afternoons after school riding his bike. What the eight-year-old boy would not tell them was why he chose to daydream, to fantasize and neglect his schoolwork. The signal was George's daydreaming. The message was that he was avoiding his schoolwork. But the key question was Why? Until this was discovered, the signal and the message would continue without relief and George would fail in school.

The boy's teacher solved the problem. She kept George after school one day to talk about his work. She started her conversation by telling him how bright she thought he was and how well he could do if he tried. George made a face. Picking up on the visual clue, the teacher asked, "Don't you believe you're a smart boy, George?" The boy grimaced and sat silently. The teacher was not going to give up. She prodded gently, "Why don't you think you're smart?" Finally George hissed in exasperation: "I'll never be as smart as Harold." George's teacher had taught his brother, Harold, two years before. She knew that the older brother was also very bright and had received exceedingly good grades. She had begun to unlock the secret behind George's message. "But nobody expects you to be Harold. I only expect you to be yourself—to do your best." He frowned. "Then you're not like my father. He does." The teacher understood. She closed the discussion by commenting softly, "I'm not comparing you to anybody, George. Be yourself and you'll make me very happy."

George's teacher called his parents to the school. She outlined her conversation with the young boy and repeated her final comments as a guide for them to follow. She asked them to help her make George understand that he didn't have to be just like his older brother, that he had many special qualities all his own. This sensitive and perceptive teacher alerted George's parents to the subtle competition they had been fostering at home—a competition that had forced the young boy to see himself as second-best. As a result, he gave up in school. His signal was his daydreaming. George's fantasies were clearly used to get out of a situation in which he felt he could never succeed. Many children use the world of fantasy and daydreams as their buffer in these frustrating situations. It is an obvious signal. But the message may be murky and unclear without careful and gentle investigation.

As our children grow older, they develop a set of wants and needs. Not all of them are realistic or possible. But they want certain things *so* badly. Often they cannot understand why we cannot give them everything they want. To make the point as sharply as possible, a child may put the wish or desire into fantasy play. Children may spend days "playing camp" in their back yards, sending the parents into fits of guilt because they had to deny the requests for summer camp because of tight finances. The signal is the fantasy play. The message is the "I want badly" plea. The reaction should be one of realistic evaluation by the parents of the wisdom of their original decision and the subsequent discussion with the child about why the decision had to be made.

To deal with difficult home problems, children may create fantasy situations, and so work through the problems. In the home of a professional colleague, a separation and impending divorce was evident. The children were sensitively told. Within a week, the young daughter created a divorce situation for one of her dolls, asked her brother to act as lawyer and judge, and together the two children lived through the future family split satisfying each other that they could understand and cope with the sudden and disruptive change in their lives. Here the signal of fantasy play contained the message of using inanimate objects to simulate the real world and allow the solution of problems that might not have been as easy with the grown-ups involved.

Our lives are constantly bombarded by fantasy through our devotion to television and films. Children sit glued to the television screen, surrounded by impossible and fantastic situations that are made to seem very real. Films are moving more and more away from reality into the realm of science fiction. Rated "G," we hurry to take our youngster to them. One thing must be remembered. The young child is a literal creature. He has little ability to deal with the abstract and, therefore, puts everything into the concrete, the actual. Much of the fantasy that he sees is interpreted as real unless we intervene and tell him otherwise. If such overstimulation produces a fantasy-ridden young child in your home, who lives his hours as a space cadet or Fred Flintstone, do not become alarmed. Become active. Watch television with him and help him separate the fantasy from the actual on the television screen or in the movies. Do not contribute to a next generation of adults who intrinsically believe that total escape from reality is better than coping and living in the real, but sometimes painful, everyday world. Today's science fiction may become tomorrow's reality. But let us teach our children to accept it only when it arrives, not to wait in unreal anticipation for the fantastic voyage. Parents have to put the world back into "real" balance by recognizing the signals.

Adolescents also fantasize. They imagine themselves as their favorite record or movie idol. These fantasies only become a problem when the teenager actually tries to emulate the "star" in looks or behavior. Then the fantasies become a dangerous part of the adolescent's real world. Considering the lifestyle and appearance of some of today's rock stars and screen idols, it becomes extremely important for parents to be alert for the subtle signs of over-infatuation with the fantasy and the gradual slipping of the adolescent into the patterns of the idol. Bringing the real world of the family back into perspective may help convince the adolescent that the unusual lifestyle being copied will not work in the context of the world in which the young person is expected to live. Looking like Elton John or living like Mick Jagger usually will prove disastrous for the adolescent. "Stars" are commodities, who frequently bank their success on being bizarrely different from everyone else. The adolescent must be helped to realize that that "differentness" is not acceptable in his or her everyday world. The signals of fantasy identification are rather easy to spot. The message is universal: "Accept me and give me status." But the ability to interpret reality to the teenager without making him angry will take the gentlest and most intelligent of parental communication.

Infrequently, the fantasies of children are the signals of serious mental illness. When the young person drifts from his real world into a world of the imaginary and believes that the unreal is as concrete as the factual, then schizophrenic behavior is evidenced. Childhood mental illness has no favorite age. But the chances of mental illness are much greater for the adolescent than the child, since this time of life holds the greatest stresses of responsibility, decisionmaking, sexual problems, and career and school issues. If the signal is a child lost in a fantasy world, who cannot be easily retrieved back into reality, the message is mental illness. The followthrough must be quick and correct. Consult your family doctor for the name of a competent mental health professional. Your child needs help—and fast!

We have been told that "We are such stuff as dreams are made of." Fantasies are part of those dreams. They may be the signals of an imaginative mind, an avoidance attitude, or a schizophrenic youngster. The range is wide; the signals are obvious. The interpretation of the message is up to you. But it cannot be ignored. Otherwise, your own fantasy as a parent that nothing is happening may result in disaster or despair for both you and your child.

5

Lying and Stealing

LYING

* When you come home from work, Larry, your seven-year-old, is not there. He arrives late for dinner, telling you he was at the next door neighbor's house. Later that week you meet a woman who lives several blocks away who tells you that your son was at her house that evening and ate an early dinner with them.
* Amy, your fourteen-year-old daughter, does not come home in time to set the table. She tells you that she has been at a school play rehearsal all afternoon. On the way home from work, you saw her outside the local drive-in restaurant with her friends.
* You overhear your eight-year-old daughter, Sharon, telling the little girl in the next apartment that her daddy is the chief of police. Actually your husband is a motorcycle patrolman.
* "I didn't lose my tennis shoes, Mom. They were taken from my locker." You find the shoes underneath Matt's bed the next morning.
* "Not me." You are standing in front of Dave, your six-year-old, pointing to the purple chalk marks on the pavement outside your front door. As you take his hand to go into the house, colored chalk dust rubs off onto your palm.

These are your children, and they have signalled you with a lie. Should you do something right away or wait until you feel calmer and less angry? What about punishment? Is it warranted and, if so, what kind and how severe? Maybe you should ignore it completely. Worrying you the most is the fear that lying means there is something really wrong with your child's character.

During those first few moments of anger you must remain "cool" and wait until you can think and reason carefully. To settle on the correct plan of action, you must discover the answer to the "why's." Once you understand some of the possible messages behind childhood lying, you will be able to put into operation the most appropriate method of dealing with the specific lie. On some occasions, the punishment is for the lie; other times, you will discipline *the action* that brought about the lie. You *and your child* must know the difference between the lie itself and the reasons for the lie.

A frequent cause of childhood lying during the early years is the exploration of the unknown. Your youngster may lie, as do most children when they are young, to discover the other side of truth and find out what might be hiding there. Young children believe the rules and regulations that parents lay down. They accept the consequences—until that special day when each one of them wants to explore and find out if the rules are really firm. What will happen to me if I break the rules? What would it feel like to actually tell a lie? The "exploratory" lie represents your child's first hesitant step toward independence. This could well be called "lying for lying's sake." The young child is clearly testing the limits to find out what lying is all about.

It is unlikely that we can prevent a child from telling that first lie of exploration. Somewhere along the road of growing up, each one of them has to test the truth. Most of us told these exploratory lies when we were youngsters. We survived, and we learned from the punishments we received. Your young child needs that same experience. *Telling* him about the consequences will never replace experiencing real discipline.

Expect the "exploratory" lie. As a parent, you can feel relatively comfortable when it occurs. Its message usually points to a normal stage of child development.

Another very common reason for lying among the younger child is the "cover-up" lie, which throws a smokescreen over something he or she has just done and knows is wrong. The youngster tells this lie as protection against discovery. Discovery means punishment, the child knows, and he must try to avoid the consequences of misbehavior.

As our children grow into adolescence, the cover-up lie takes on more significant proportions. Often it is not a spontaneous lie, but more calculated and planned. Most parents of teenagers have experienced the teenage cover-up lie. Why is this act of lying so prevalent among the adolescent population? Teenagers are constantly being faced with the pressures of "being with it," of conforming to the unwritten code of their peer group. "Being with it" often requires that teenagers act in ways they know will not be condoned nor accepted by their parents. What are some of these pressures that are felt almost daily and that force teenagers into the "cover-up" lie? Dating, nighttime curfews, smoking, drinking, experimenting with drugs, and cutting classes are group pressures that surround teenagers today as inviting temptations. If and when they accept the peer group challenge to participate, they end up by coming home to us with the cover-up lie. How many of us have heard that "Jim's dad's car broke down," when our sixteen-year-old daughter arrived home one hour after curfew? Many of us face this problem daily.

Parents who understand the reasons behind the cover-up lie can minimize these lies by asking their teenagers to explain the pressures (not the lie) that bring about the undesirable actions. Understanding such peer pressures does not make lying acceptable. But this insight may help your teenager to reduce the social pressures, which will, in turn, reduce the lies that are used to "keep peace" in the family.

Occasionally the cover-up lie hides a more important message than misbehavior. The "lost" report card may be the first valuable signal that a child is having serious school difficulties. The "late from school" lie may mean that your child has taken a very long route home from school to avoid being harassed by bullies on her usual route. These are cover-up lies of embarrassment or failure. Digging more deeply into the reasons that brought them about will uncover the hidden problem. Only when you find these problems can you as a parent help your child overcome the cover-up lie.

Lies can produce results! Children know this; you must be prepared to ask yourself a very sensitive question after your child has lied to you: "Is my child looking for something from me? Attention? Praise? Recognition? Have I given this 'something' in the past, when my child has lied to me?" We, as parents, often keep lying alive when we respond to a lie by overlooking it or not recognizing it. As a consequence, we actually *reward* our child for lying. So a lie becomes a way to get the upper hand, to achieve a goal, to gain the psychological reward. If this manipulative lie is allowed to go unchallenged in the home, lying will gradually infect the child's life outside the family. When this happens, serious trouble is in store for the youngster. A parent should never reward a child's lie by allowing it to persist.

The "whopper" lie, as exemplified by the "chief of police" story at the beginning, is another frequent lie told by the young child. The message behind the whopper lie is that the child wants to make himself look better in the eyes of friends, relatives, and/or parents. Very often, this looks like an extreme form of bragging or exaggeration. Not uncommonly, the youngster tells his whopper lie because of pride or delight. By expanding the truth, the story seems even better. There may be something quite innocent in this type of storytelling. But the child who tells the whopper lie to win friends and influence people may be trying desperately to buy friendship with the tall tale. Here the parents can help by discovering the basic problem behind this lie—loneliness—and then help their child to fill empty moments with real friends, not friends won by lying.

Related to the exaggerated whopper lie is the blatant lie. This is the lie that is totally obvious. The lie is told even though the child knows full well that the parent is aware of the truth. The first thing most parents ask in bewilderment after being struck by the blatant childhood lie is "Why?"

The message behind the blatant lie is that the child, whether for the right or wrong reasons, is seeking the attention of the parent. The child does not care if the attention is negative or positive. Why would a child, whom a parent had thought to be comfortable and loved, suddenly begin to tell a blatant lie? Is there a new baby in the house getting the attention of the family and neighbors, waking up to be nurtured in the night, crying for attention and receiving it constantly? Is an older brother getting honor grades in school, or mentions in the newspaper about his varsity performance on the soccer or baseball team? The dinner conversation may be shifting away from the youngster toward other children in the house or parents who have work or home problems. The child may feel that he is living in a shadow and needs the coveted sunlight of parental attention. Often the child seeks this attention by telling the blatant lie.

Punishment for this lie is *not* the answer. Indeed, it may be punishment the child is seeking. Why? Because punishment is sometimes better than no attention at all, at least in the reasoning of a child who thinks that he or she is ignored or unloved. What the child finds in that moment of the parents' exploding anger is concentrated attention—a brief moment of illumination and focus.

The parent of the child who tells the blatant lie must first begin to probe for messages behind the behavior. They must discover what it is the child wants, determine if it is really needed, and then attempt to meet the challenge. Planning together for activities shared by parent and child will usually eliminate the need for the blatant lie.

An often delightful but also confusing problem is posed by the fantasy lie. "Jiminy Cricket did that, Daddy," was the wide-eyed explanation given to one of the authors by his three-year-old daughter every time she broke a rule or committed some act of misbehavior. This was the fantasy lie, the lie which bubbled up from the make-believe world and which the youngster did not or could not distinguish from the real world. Her bright little face and shining eyes glowed as she repeated over and over again that her imaginary friend continued to misbehave. How could she have left that door open when "Jiminy" came in after her?

The fantasy friend can seem quite real to the very young child. But the fantasy lie cannot be accepted or encouraged; the parent will have to point out the difference between the imaginary and the real when these become blurred into a fantasy lie.

The author and his daughter talked seriously about her friend, "Jiminy Cricket." He was HER special friend, he pointed out, and not known to others in the family. "Jiminy" had to follow all the rules of the family—no exceptions. "I hope your friend doesn't do that any more," her father cautioned. "He is your responsibility because he is special just for you. You will have to be the one who will be punished next time." She screwed up her face. "But he did it," she insisted. "To you, he did it. To me, you are responsible," was the reply, gentle but firm. It was not long after that conversation that "Jiminy Cricket" went to live with some other imaginative boy or girl.

When a lie is discovered, you, as parents of the lying child, have to face the challenging problem of punishment. Should you make the punishment particularly harsh? How should the discipline be explained to the child? What kind of punishment will keep the lying from happening again?

Each family usually has consistent punishments that are used to correct misbehavior, and these punishments range from light "reminders" such as a missed television program to major confrontations resulting in spankings or revoking of important privileges. The forms of punishment should fit the child *and* the incident. Parents need to understand exactly what they are punishing when they are reacting to the childhood lie. Are they punishing the act of lying or are they punishing the reasons that caused the lying? In the minds of both the parents and the child, these differences must be made unmistakably clear. The effectiveness of the punishment in preventing future lying depends upon the understanding of the child about *what* is being punished.

If a child is being punished for a cover-up lie, he or she should be punished *both* for the act of lying and for the misbehavior that prompted the lie. Two punishments may be appropriate in this case; perhaps two different sets of privileges should be lost, or a double punishment inflicted. Whatever your decision, it is important that the child know that he or she is being punished for the misbehavior *apart from* the lying. If this understanding occurs, then the child may know that the next time he misbehaves in a similar fashion, he may receive less punishment by telling you the truth about the act. This encourages better communication between parent and child. Furthermore, the child also will know that he will continue to receive punishment for misbehavior regardless of cover-up lies. Both problems, the misbehavior and the act of lying, need to be dealt with separately by the parents each time.

When administering punishment to a child for a cover-up lie, remember that an older child is more aware that he has lied. The lie is more deliberate. But the older child also has a greater ability to control his lying behavior. Try to find out what outside pressures have been placed on your child. You will have to understand these pressures to help prevent recurrences of the misbehavior.

When you feel your child is telling you an exploratory lie, you should punish him for the act, even though you know he is simply testing independence. The child is asking about how far he or she can go, and your response needs to say "go no further." You know the reasons for the exploratory lie—the child wants greater independence—and perhaps you should determine if the time has come in your child's life to expand some of the rules to allow the youngster greater independence. But those rule changes should be discussed *after* you have meted out the punishment for the exploratory lie. They are separate issues.

A parent who deals with the whopper or manipulative lie must also analyze the reasons for this type of lie. It can be a message from the child that something is wrong in his or her relationships with other people. Parents must ask themselves, "Does my child really *need* the attention he is getting from those lies, or is he merely finding out how to be more important?" If the child is truly feeling neglected or alone, parents must take steps to build activities that will bring attention and gratification into the child's day. Yet the whopper or manipulative lie itself must be punished because it is an inappropriate way for the child to get attention and praise. The need for attention and approval must be separated from the act of lying and dealt with as a separate problem. If not, the whopper and manipulative lie could become a way of life for the child—a way of adjusting his environment and his world to his needs.

Punishment for the fantasy lie can be gentle, since it usually happens in early childhood, but also firm, since the lie cannot be allowed to continue. An explanation of what is real about household rules should accompany it. The fantasy lie does not usually last beyond the early years.

Some parents will encounter the child whose lies will not cease, no matter how firm the punishment, how understanding the parent, or how consistent the family rules. In these cases, the child may be "marching to a different drummer": he or she may have some serious confusion about reality. The young person may have a grave act of misbehavior to cover up. He or she may be getting the wrong advice from friends. If lies are persistent, cannot be readily explained, or recur despite proper punishment and understanding, the child may need professional help. Give the first lies a chance to diminish, but if they continue, or increase over a period of time, seek help. Lying is a natural consequence of growth and maturity, but should stop within a reasonable period, particularly if standards of truth are maintained within the home.

STEALING

Stealing, like lying, can also be an expected part of growing up.

Discovering that a child has stolen something usually shocks parents badly. This reflex response is filled with reactions similar to those of parents who find their children are lying—questions about the child's morality, anger, fear, and disappointment. Lying and stealing are often used in the same context by adults who want to describe "bad" behavior in children. Both are seen as acts of disobedience. They are flagrant rejections of known family rules.

An analysis of the messages behind the signals of lying and stealing will often show, in fact, that the two acts might be telling the parents the same things. A comparison between the exploratory lie and the exploratory theft can be illustrated by the following story:

One of the author's sons had never been known to lie to his parents. When he misbehaved, he would try to avoid talking about it but, if pressed, would admit to the misdeed in detail. He never tried an exploratory lie.

One evening, after a routine shopping trip, the seven-year-old boy was playing his favorite solitary game, model cars, when his sister asked him about the newest addition to his set. The boy ignored her. She asked again, and her brother suddenly left the room. To his parent, this action was a tip off of trouble. The young boy was brought back into the room and asked directly about the new model car. He admitted that he had stolen it that evening.

This was his exploratory act. He did not need the toy; he could have bought the car with his allowance. The youngster had not asked for nor been denied the car; therefore, his act was not rebellious. His stealing was an act of impulsiveness, done with the full recognition that he might be caught. He was exploring, by this signal, the solidness of the family rules and the consistency of his parents in enforcing them.

As a form of his punishment, the child had to return the car to the store manager. The lecture given to him by this stranger in the store was harsh, angry, and punitive, far more severe than his parent would have administered. The child learned about the rules and reactions of his family as well as the stricter, harsher rules and reactions of the outside society, a valuable lesson indeed.

The exploratory act of stealing has certain clues that can easily be recognized by the parent. Usually it is done at an early age when the child first begins to test his own independence. The act is often done clumsily, without forethought or finesse. The object stolen has little value to the store or person from whom it was stolen. As in the case of the exploratory lie, the child awaits or even expects discovery. The consequences of the act are far more important to him than the stolen object.

As in the signal of lying, stealing can also be a message that the child needs and craves more attention. Blatant stealing, which is easily detected and at times flaunted by the child, is like blatant lying. The child wants to be the center of his family's focus, even if the attention is negative. The clues to this type of stealing are many: the child usually steals from a member of his family, and does so clumsily; he admits the stealing with very little prompting and will repeat the behavior if the attention is not paid or is minimal in response.

The remedy for this type of stealing is similar to the remedy for blatant lying. The act must be punished, but the underlying cry for attention must be responded to by the family. The child must be shown how to best achieve his goal of getting more recognition and attention by more acceptable and positive actions.

Another similarity between the stealing signal and the lying signal is the recognition that stealing also becomes more prevalent during adolescence and often represents a direct response to peer pressures. Adolescents, as part of their exploration of the adult world, often feel a need to test the limits of adult laws. Stealing is one of the common experiments. The message of adolescent stealing is one of exploration outside the family rules. Stealing also tends to bind groups of teenagers into a cohesive "gang," friends held together by a shared secret act of breaking the law.

If you discover that your adolescent is stealing, you must, as in the adolescent lie, sort out cause from action, preferably with the help of your teenager. The act of stealing must be punished, but you must also strengthen your youngster's ability to withstand the mischievous pressures of his or her friends. Moral lectures are not sufficient deterrents. When your young person once again passes the local drugstore with four friends who are daring each other to steal "something, just for the fun of it," your words of what is "right and wrong" will be forgotten. What the teenager must know and believe is that he has the right and the obligation to say "No." This is tough for a kid today faced by a group of his closest teen-aged friends. But he can be encouraged to give it a try. Balancing the possible scorn of his friends will be his understanding that this act of group defiance will be rewarded by the quiet but evident pride and praise of his parents, who can appreciate the maturity necessary to make that response at that time, and by the inner satisfaction of having made a "right" decision.

The stealing signal also has important *differences* from the lying signal. Stealing involves property or money. Therefore, the act may impose a hardship upon another person. Stealing also may go undetected by parents if the objects are stolen from outside the family and cleverly concealed. In addition, stealing when it does not represent an exploratory phase or a period of adolescent testing may carry the message that there is something seriously wrong in the young person's world. What happens when you, as a parent, discover that cache of objects hidden in the back of your child's dresser drawer? How do you manage to control the quick anger you feel when you suddenly realize that your child has been stealing these objects over a period of time? How do you deal with the unanswerable question of "Why?" when the stolen objects appear so valueless to you? In order to decipher the messages behind stealing, you must ask yourself several questions about the stealing before you confront the child. First you must ask yourself, "From *whom* did my child steal?," followed immediately by a second question, "What would the loss of these objects mean to the person from whom they were stolen?" If the objects were stolen from another child in the family or from a child's "friend," the motivation behind the theft might have been to hurt that other person —to give the stealing child a form of revenge from an earlier hurt. Stealing can also permit the youngster to "win" secretly from another child, whether inside or outside the family, against whom he has trouble competing.

But if the person or store from whom the object(s) or money was stolen has no known relationship to the child, the parents must then ask themselves the following question: "What is my child trying to tell me about his own unfulfilled needs when he steals?" Another important but difficult question may unearth the hidden message behind the stealing signal: "What does the act of stealing mean to my child?" When the parent can find no motive, no message behind the youngster's stealing, it is time to seek outside professional help to discover the cause.

Parents can be certain that the child who steals has a message! The child may be signalling that he or she feels there is something painfully wrong about his personal life—that something is missing or something must be changed. The stolen objects sometimes symbolize areas of the child's concern. For example, a girl who steals jewelry or cosmetics may be signalling messages of feeling ugly or unattractive. Her parents may not feel that she is ugly, but to this girl, her negative feelings are very real. A child may steal candy or trinkets to give to other children because he feels that the only way he can make friends is to *buy* their affection. In a family seen by the authors, a thirteen-year-old girl was caught one day shoplifting a scarf from the local department store. The girl did not need the scarf; she had five of them at home. She did not need to steal for social acceptance. There was only one other frightened girl with her at the time and the other girl had refused to participate in the act. The stealing seemed purposeless and futile, a whimsy that would result in endless anguish to the young girl and her parents because of the legal complications and the social stigma.

The reasons for her stealing become clear, however, if one contemplates the circumstances within the girl's life at that time. Four months before, her parents had separated after several years of psychological combat so vicious that it preoccupied the battling adults to the point of excluding and ignoring their children. The young girl would often have to babysit for two younger brothers when the parents consulted lawyers, marriage counsellors, or ministers. Finally her father moved out, and the girl was left with an uprooted family and a bitter, ineffective, devastated mother who retreated to mourn the failure of her marriage.

The teenage girl, by her stealing, forced her parents into joint action to provide her assistance. Her stealing made them take the time to sit down with her and consider *her* problems. The teenager also achieved a degree of revenge for their many months of neglect by heaping guilt about her stealing behavior directly upon them. She *forced* a parent-child confrontation and so finally managed to communicate with the two most important people in her life. She had used the signal of stealing to deliver a very complex message that she felt her parents could not perceive in any other way. This family obviously needed professional help to work through a minefield of bad feelings. The young girl's stealing brought the family to this very necessary helping place. This was her subtle message.

Whenever the answer to a child's stealing behavior is not clear, or when that stealing persists despite attempts to understand and help, then a professional must be consulted. Most complex messages of stealing are not as easy to decode as those of the girl in the above case history. Many suggest deep-seated and highly personal negative feelings unknown to the parents. These need the expertise and objectivity of the psycho-social therapist.

Lying and stealing are two commonly expected "sins" of childhood. They cannot be overlooked because they are expected, nor can they be easily forgiven because they are common. Each incident of lying or stealing is a signal that cannot be ignored. Analyzing the messages behind the lying or stealing gives parents an opportunity for rare insight into the child's world—and how parents can fit most comfortably into a part of that world.

6

Bedwetting and Soiling

When the frustrated mother of the five-year-old strips his bed of the wet sheets, folds them in her arms, and carries them down to the basement for washing, as she has done as an almost daily ritual, she feels that her son's signal is very clear. He refuses to control his bladder at night, and she has the aggravating job of cleaning up after him. As she stuffs the stained sheets into the washing machine, she keeps repeating to herself, "What can I do to make him stop?" She tries to repress her feelings of anger and resentment toward her son as she wearily throws the laundry powder into the machine and starts the wash cycle. Watching the sheets begin to spin in the machine, she realizes that she blames her son because of all the inconvenience and bother he is causing her. She tries to rationalize his behavior but finds it difficult to forgive him for something that she feels he should be able to control.

In reality, this mother is reacting to the *consequences* of her son's signal of bedwetting rather than to the signal itself. This is a natural tendency which we, as parents, find ourselves doing very often. We react to the results of what our children do rather than to the causes which made them do it in the first place. Parents are human beings, and negative reactions to an unpleasant situation are normal human behavior. But these reactions get in the way of our ability to perceive and analyze the signals of the behavior. Our angry responses cloud the basic issues.

The basic issue in this case is the bedwetting of a five-year-old boy. What could it mean? Why is it happening? What is the underlying signal that needs to be understood before the parent can act and react intelligently and effectively?

In medical terms, bedwetting is known as *enuresis*. This fancy name in no way minimizes the bother to the mother, the frequent shame on the child's part, nor clarifies the causes. In addition, giving bedwetting a medical term does NOT signify that all children who wet their beds are having a medical problem, or that the signal can only be interpreted by a physician.

There are several key questions that the parent must ask when confronted with the common problem of bedwetting. And "common" is the appropriate word because almost 10 percent of all children (more often boys than girls) experience the problem of bedwetting at some point in their growing-up period. What are these important questions?

1. Has your child ever been dry at night?
2. Is there daytime wetting as well?
3. When was toilet training completed?
4. How difficult was the toilet training process?
5. Does your youngster have any other symptoms with urination?
6. Does your child suffer from abdominal pains, unexplained fevers, anal itching, or failure to grow and gain properly?
7. Has your child had any recent problems in the home, neighborhood, or school?
8. How healthy is the current parent-child relationship in your home?
9. How old is your child?

Nine questions? So many answers for something as common as bedwetting? But bedwetting may not be as uncomplicated as a parent might believe. Simply "stopping it" may not be possible for the child. Why? Because the signal of bedwetting may have a number of causes, all of which must be familiar to the parent if the proper interpretation of and subsequent action around the problem are to be undertaken.

Many children may not develop the necessary control of their nervous system when they are toilet trained to allow them properly to retain a full bladder when they are asleep. This is a normal variation in the growth of the nervous system in children. There is nothing physically wrong with the child who has only the developmentally delayed nervous system. Time is the healer in these youngsters. Usually by the age of five, all children will have reached the point of proper nervous system balance so that nighttime bladder control is possible. If the child has never been able to go through most nights without wetting the bed, and if there are no indications that other physical symptoms are occurring (see questions 5 and 6 above), then the parents must be patient. The signal of the wet bed may simply mean that the child is moving more slowly toward bladder control than usually expected. The signal has absolutely nothing to do with the child's intelligence, motivation, or emotional health. The brightest, most determined, well-adjusted four-year-olds can still wet the bed because of delayed bladder control. The signal of the nightly bedwetting may be as upsetting to the child as it is to the parent. Therefore, understanding the innocence of the bedwetting signal in the very young child will enable the sensitive parent to reassure the embarrassed child that within months the problem will be solved. The parents should encourage the child to limit fluids at bedtime to keep the load on the kidney-bladder system at a minimum. Sensitive handling of a slow physical maturation will motivate the child to the degree that when the nervous system control finally occurs, the child can be prepared to present the parents with a dry bed proudly in the morning.

Unless there are other signs or symptoms in the medical history to go along with bedwetting in the child five years or younger, the pediatrician rarely puts a child through any investigative tests. Occasionally medication, which helps to firm the muscle tone of the bladder at night, may be prescribed mainly as a way to help the child overcome the shame and relieve the parent of the inconvenience. But basically we are dealing with a "normal" child giving off a "normal" signal.

Parents of six- and seven-year-olds come into the office and sometimes state, forcefully, "But he's not trying." They may be right. The signal may be the fact that the child has not emotionally determined to be dry. There is an element of conscious control of the full bladder at night after the nervous system is in balance. We all know that we awaken when the pressure in our bladders tells us we must go to the bathroom. The failure of the over-five-year-old child to heed that message may be due to a lack of conditioning on the child's part to feel, interpret, and act on his need to urinate during the night. Is this a signal that the child is "lazy"? It could be misinterpreted that way but, in reality, what the child needs is the parent's help to assist in learning the responses to his own body. Punishing, threatening, waking the child up in the middle of the night are not the answers. Who is being conditioned when parents act this way? Actually, it is the parents who are responding, not the child. But it is the child who must learn to control his bladder and keep his bed dry.

Often the young child needs stimulation and encouragement to overcome this signal. Parents can use a reward system to accomplish the goal. What is a "reward system"? Simply rewarding a youngster for a job well done—always, methodically. The system will reap its own harvest. The child will continue trying and delight in success. He can give up the reward system quickly once the nighttime control of the bladder has been mastered because he will have developed his own rewards—a dry, comfortable, satisfied feeling. A popular and often successful reward system is the use of the gold star on the calendar for each dry morning. When a specified number of gold stars appears on the calendar, the child receives the reward. The sight of the gold stars and the pride that the child feels in his success are often reward enough. However, special treats and privileges such as a weekend visit with a grandparent, a ballgame with father, a shopping trip with mother, a movie with both parents, will punctuate the child's "gold star" success with a family reward. The limitation of fluids again can assist the child. This should be the child's responsibility, as is the whole problem of solving the bedwetting signal. The parents act as helpers, not policemen. Occasionally medication is used initially to give the youngster the sense of success, but it is usually soon withdrawn so that the child can "do it on his own." The misinterpretation of the bedwetting signal, when a parent becomes aggressive and punitive rather than positively helpful, will only result in a frustrated child, an angry parent, and a continually wet bed every morning.

Mrs. Stein brought seven-year-old Judith into the office because the girl had started to wet her bed over the preceding months. The mother was honestly perplexed. "She was so easy to train. She was dry from the time she was eighteen months old. And now . . . every morning. . . ." Mrs. Stein did not have to go on. Her tone and her set jaw conveyed her intense feeling of resentment. Together we tried to look carefully at Judith's signal. She had been trained. She was over five. The bedwetting was of very recent duration. She had no other urinary or physical symptoms. She was a cute, active, seemingly happy little girl with no school or social problems. No answers to the baffling signal could be found in those questions. But when we probed for any changes in the home, Mrs. Stein reminded us that she had a relatively new baby boy in the house, one year old. "Judy loves the baby. She helps me all the time with him," Mrs. Stein quickly added when the subject was explored. "Tell me, what do you and Judy do together these days?" was the next question. Mrs. Stein thought for a long time. Finally she smiled, somewhat embarrassed, and answered, "We do a lot of things around the house, but mainly for the baby." To make the point of what the signal was telling Mrs. Stein, we asked the next question, "But what do you do with Judy alone . . . just the two of you?" Judy's mother shook her head. "Not much. The baby takes up so much of my time."

Judy was sending the "regressive" signal of bedwetting. She was losing the companionship and, she feared, the love of her mother since the baby's arrival. Her response was a clear signal of need.

"I am still a very little girl. I still need you," was the message on those wet sheets every morning. How appropriate that Judy used the most applicable signal to tell her mother that Tod's diapers were getting in the way of their relationship. Judy's sheets had to be washed along with the baby's diapers. Not subtle? Not at all. Children often are direct with their signals. And yet Mrs. Stein, in her busy, hurried day, had overlooked the obvious meaning behind Judy's actions. This concerned mother was able to eliminate Judy's signal of bedwetting by fulfilling the young girl's needs. She set aside two hours each day to devote to the types of mother-daughter activities that would support and nourish a seven-year-old. Changing diapers was obviously not one of these.

Frequently, the parent-child problems are not as clear-cut as they were in Judy's case. The bedwetting signal may be the wrapping on a package of more complex family problems. Parents must carefully inspect and analyze their relationships with their child when bedwetting suddenly occurs in the older child and appears to have no physical basis. If the parents can feel reassured that there are no real, important problems between themselves and their child, then a thorough assessment of possible school or neighborhood problems must be made. The signal is coming from some well of concern within the child. The bedwetting is not a capricious signal, to be ignored. The parent must uncover the child's worry or anxiety that has precipitated the problem.

Occasionally, bedwetting is an "independence" signal. The child is delivering the following message, in no uncertain terms: "You may be able to control every other part of my life but this is mine and cannot be controlled by you." Are children so sophisticated that they can think in these terms? The presence of daytime and nighttime wetting in a healthy child often expresses his hostility and frustration over too stringent parental rules and discipline. Whether the child is correct in his assessment that the parent's expectations of his good behavior are too great or too demanding is not as important as the fact that he feels as he does. And he signals these feelings by refusing to come under control in the one area that probably frustrates the strict parent the most—

toilet training and cleanliness. Often a history of too early toilet training (six to twelve months), which requires great parental pressure, can be uncovered. Every parent whose child has an unexpected signal of day or night wetting, or both, must analyze his relationships and problems with control of the child. If the shoe fits, the parent must start immediately to work with his child on the understanding of the family expectations and possible relaxation of home rules and punishments.

A smaller percentage of children are delivering a very important medical signal by bedwetting. Children with urinary tract infections, recent or long-standing, can become bedwetters. However, the parent will generally remember that the youngster had episodes of unexplained fevers, abdominal pain, difficulty in holding urine, frequency of urination, or failure to grow or gain weight properly. Such signs, when put together with bedwetting, are usually very clear. Diseases of the urinary tract can be "silent" in children and go unrecognized for long periods of time, causing irreparable damage to the kidneys. This must be avoided at all costs. In addition, children can be born with abnormalities of the urinary tract, which progress insidiously but continuously to a final stage of serious kidney impairment, threatening the child's life. Again, these congenital abnormalities of the kidneys may announce their presence via the signal of bedwetting, often along with one or more other serious symptoms. Diabetes may cause bedwetting because of the increased urine output in this metabolic disease. The perceptive parent must put together various signals that strongly suggest any disease and seek professional advice as early as possible. The wise parent of a bedwetting child should have a baseline urinalysis done on the child no matter what the possible cause of the bedwetting signal may appear to be. Being wrong and misinterpreting this signal could be very serious to the child's health. If the initial urinalysis is normal in all respects and no other physical symptoms exist, then the parent can return to another interpretation of the bedwetting with a calmer, safer attitude.

Little girls can have a special medical reason for bedwetting.

The cause is relatively innocent and can be eradicated without delay. Too few parents *and* physicians think of this cause when confronted with the bedwetting signal in a young girl. The cause is pinworms. Many children harbor tiny pinworms in their intestinal tract at some time during their childhood. These worms are easily passed from child to child. Usually the worms give the youngster very few symptoms and are an incidental finding in blood counts or stool exams. The pinworms, however, have an unusual habit that makes them uncomfortable for the children. During sleep, the tiny worms migrate to the anal area, where they deposit eggs that can cause constant itching. This is why many people called these little parasites seatworms. The pinworm may deposit the eggs also in the vulvar and vaginal area of the little girl. This area becomes irritated and itchy. The more inflamed and uncomfortable the area, the more likely the girl will wet the bed at night. Parents can often spot these wiggly worms at night by spreading the youngster's buttocks apart and flashing a light over the anal opening. Finding the worms is no cause for alarm. Medicine by mouth will eradicate the infestation and remove the cause for the bedwetting. Did you think of that message when the signal, bedwetting, was mentioned? Probably not. But as you can see, one signal can come from a very wide and dissimilar range of causes.

The problem of soiling is another matter. The signal is unpleasant and frustrating, but the causes can be even more disturbing. Soiling is defined as the elimination of fecal material by the child into the clothing *after* the successful toilet training period has passed. This occurs more often during the day than during the night. Fortunately few children suffer from this problem, many less than suffer bedwetting. But those that do are giving off a serious and important signal, which parents must not ignore.

Occasionally the youngster who soils does so only infrequently and when absorbed in play. This can occur to the young child between two and four who forgets the conditioning of toilet training because of the excitement of play or distance from home. It is not an ominous signal; it merely needs the gentle reinforcement of training principles, without shaming or punishing the child.

We have seen cases of youngsters who have soiled themselves because of teachers who have laid down unreasonable, rigid rules of bathroom privileges for young children. This signal trumpets the need for the parent to visit the school and demand a relaxation of such unhealthy rules. If the teacher refuses to modify the rules, the parents must go to the principal—or higher—until the unrealistic restrictions on bathroom privileges are rescinded.

While medical reasons for soiling do exist, they are uncommon. Diseases of the lower gastrointestinal tract associated with serious, chronic constipation may result in soiling. The parent who is aware that his youngster has bowel irregularities of a major nature should consult the pediatrician. Neurological problems may impair the sphincter muscle that tightens the anus and allows the child to hold back the fecal matter. Other neurological signs such as leg weakness, back pain, absence of feeling in the genital area, or dribbling of urine may accompany this soiling signal and alert the parent to the need for medical attention for the child. As with bedwetting, soiling due to medical reasons usually has many signals.

But where there are no medical reasons, the youngster who sends his message of "independence" by soiling, particularly after age five, is very often a child with far greater emotional problems than the "independent" bedwetter. Soiling as a signal must be taken very seriously by the parents when it becomes a persistent condition. Some children will flaunt their signal, depositing their messy pants in the middle of the living room, while others will "hide" it in places where the odor will quickly bring the message home to the parents. What is important is that the signal of soiling is usually a desperate call for help from a young person with deep and painful emotional wounds. Parents should not attempt to analyze and interpret this message by themselves. They should seek professional help as soon as the soiling signal is recognized. The first person for the parents to consult would be the child's doctor,

7

Stuttering

The kitchen door flew open as Jeff exploded into the room, his face flushed with the exertion of running, his eyes darting around. He was obviously looking for his mother, his arms leading the way, reaching for a dress to tug or a hand to grasp. Clearly Jeff had something important to tell his mother, something exciting, something rare. His mouth was already beginning to move as he stopped, suddenly, in front of her and touched her arm.

"Mmm . . . Mmmmmm . . . Mmmmo . . . Mommmmmm . . . Mmmmommy!" The effort to say "Mommy" had been very great for four-year-old Jeff. It was clear to his mother that he was really straining to speak. His facial muscles were tense and his eyes were clouded with frustration.

"Yes, Jeff, what is it?"

"Mmmm . . . Mmmmmm . . . Mmmmmmm . . . Mmmmmm!"

"Mommy?"

Jeff shook his head violently. Tears began to fill his eyes, tears of anger.

"Mmmmm . . . Mmmmm . . . Mmmmm . . . Mmmmm . . . ah . . . ah . . . Mmmmah . . . Martha . . . fff . . . ffff . . . found . . . sssss . . . sssss . . . Martha ffff . . . ffff . . . Martha found a ss . . . sss . . . sssnnnn . . . snake!"

Jeff's mother grabbed him and gave him a hug. She was ashamed that she had unintentionally made his speech harder by finishing the word for him too quickly. She knew that he was excited and was trying to calm down. And she wanted to comfort his fright at finding the snake. She listened as he told her the details, his speech flowing more easily with each word. Finally when he had finished his story, had been comforted and given a glass of lemonade, he went back outside. His mother quickly went to the phone and called her niece, who had just started graduate school to study speech pathology.

"Donna, I think Jeff is a stutterer," were her first alarmed words. She explained what had just occurred. Donna listened carefully and patiently. Then, gently, she said: "Relax, Aunt Marion. I've heard Jeff and he's OK. He's just learning how to think and speak like an older child. He is certainly *not* a stutterer," she paused slightly, ". . . yet."

What Donna explained was that at Jeff's age, many children talk as though they stutter. This problem is an expected phase to speech clinicians, who call it, in fact, "normal non-fluency." The problem usually is caused by dynamic differences in growth and development. The child is learning complex words and sentence structures too fast to be able to put them together easily. He or she may be thinking faster than the vocal muscles can react. Perhaps the child is also trying to think or speak in one of two languages spoken at home. Any of these problems in learning how to speak fluently can trigger the interrupted communication that occurred with Jeff, the kind of talking that parents fear is stuttering.

Donna had listened to Jeff, so she knew that he was undergoing a period of normal non-fluency. Her diagnosis that Jeff was not a stutterer was sound. But what did she mean by that ominous little word at the end of her sentence: "Jeff is not a stutterer . . . *yet*"?

Donna told her aunt that parents, in their concern for the child's proper growth and development, often "freeze" a symptom in their child by paying too much attention to the problem. Stuttering behavior can develop from normal non-fluency if the parents become too anxious and overattentive to this natural phase of speech development.

Parents hear what sounds like stuttering, a prolonged series of repetitions and hesitations. They become alarmed and diagnose the problem themselves, convinced that they have a child with a speech defect. Constantly they try to "help" the child, their voices betraying anxiety and fear that their child will continue with his dreaded handicap unless they can "cure" it. They overreact, finishing sentences for the child, making him repeat sentences or words, telling him to remain calm and relaxed, even when the youngster cannot slow down his excitement. But they manage to infect the child with their feeling that he is a stutterer—and so, in fact, he becomes one. As the child anticipates talking to his parents, he will feel the same fear and anxiety experienced by them. He will become tense when he tries to talk. And this tension will, by itself, hamper his speech. In an overwhelming desire to speak correctly, he will hesitate or repeat himself, acutely aware that his talking is imperfect. And as his words persist in the halting delays and stammers, his anxiety increases, so his speech becomes worse. The cycle has started: talk = tension = poor speech = stuttering.

The parent's best defense against a stuttering child is a relaxed attitude based on the realization that every child may face this puzzling stage of development. When the phase happens to your child, you can remember some rules of behavior that will help both you and your youngster:

1. Do not finish sentences for the child.
2. Do not talk about "speech problems" with the child.
3. Wait patiently for the child to finish his or her talking and try not to fidget while waiting for the final word.
4. Prevent other children from teasing your child about his or her speech.

In other words, treat the problem for what it is—a phase of development much like the growth spurts or voice changes in adolescent boys. You and the child can outwait the signal.

Some stuttering, however, is not the result of a developmental phase, but rather the result of complex problems between the brain, speech organs, and general abilities or perception. If a child's communication problem lasts beyond six months, seek aid and diagnosis from a speech clinician.

If the child's "stuttering problem" persists, or if it begins in later childhood, parents generally are facing a far more serious problem. They must start the process of helping the child, in cooperation with a professional speech clinician, by answering one very important question: Does the child stutter constantly or infrequently?

If the child stutters infrequently, then the parent should look behind the signal for the underlying reasons—messages. These messages often can be interpreted by asking the questions of time and place about the stuttering behavior. In other words, for periodic stuttering, the parent should observe the child and ask, "Under what conditions does my child stutter? Is it just in front of adults, or is it also with his playmates? Is it during periods of activity, during calm periods, or both? Does the child seem upset or anxious before or after the stuttering behavior? Are there any activities that usually precede the stuttering?"

You are investigating whether the message contained within your child's temporary stuttering is an expression of anxiety. Most parents have, themselves, suffered through these temporary periods of stuttering when excited or upset. It is not difficult to see that anxiety can cause temporary, periodic stuttering in children.

Jason had that problem. A tow-headed nine-year-old, Jason's great love—and his great sorrow—was baseball. Every morning, he could be found playing catch with his friends on his way to school. Recesses were his favorite time in school. Jason invariably faced a playmate, tossing the ball toward him, wearing a baseball glove he had bought with the money he saved diligently for six months.

Yet when he played baseball on the school team, he could hardly speak. Teammates would yell a greeting, and Jason could not answer them. He would catch a "grounder" but could not verbally signal the player to whom he was going to throw the ball. When his coach asked him a question, his face twisted into one huge mask of frustration as he tried, unsuccessfully, to answer him quickly.

The reasons for his stuttering were not hard to perceive. Jason came from a family of six children, where competition was fiercely valued, and where each family member was encouraged to "do his very best." To excel in baseball meant that Jason could have his special niche in his family. He knew his parents wanted him to be "really good at it," even more than he did himself. So success in playing baseball was very important to Jason—so important that he became very anxious about the game.

Jason felt that *all* his rewards came from baseball. He *had* to succeed there. He felt an overpowering inner drive as he put on his baseball glove. When playing in an actual game, he crouched on the field with a body dripping wet from sweat. His hands shook; his mind raced relentlessly. He was suffering a classic case of anxiety, which came to the surface when he tried to speak. His vocal chords would not obey him; his mouth wouldn't form the words. Then, and only then, was Jason a stutterer.

When his parents analyzed this signal, they realized that they would have to take the anxiety out of baseball for Jason. They looked for other areas in which he could get involved and be self-satisfied, and encouraged him to participate in them. They subtly indicated that it was more important to them if he enjoyed the activity rather than if he became the "best" in the game. Jason began to collect coins. His father joined him in the hobby. Jason's parents stopped coming to some of the baseball games. Both spent more time with him on a relaxed, informal basis. His baseball coach was urged to place less pressure on Jason—to emphasize the game and not his performance. Jason himself was encouraged to adopt a more casual attitude toward baseball. As he picked up his parents' messages, he relaxed; and his stuttering during baseball games ceased dramatically within four weeks.

Clarke, however, was not so lucky. At about seven years of age, he began stuttering *constantly*. Each month his speech flow grew worse, until he became almost totally uncommunicative. When we saw him in the office two years later, he was a severe stutterer. A sentence had become agony for him. Many words that ordinarily should have been in his vocabulary were simply impossible for him to pronounce. When he tried, his face became contorted as he valiantly tried to command both his mouth and his mind to work together. His complexion would turn beet red, and perspiration would form on his forehead from the exertion of trying to be understood. Clarke simply could not hold an intelligible conversation.

Five years later Clarke is still in speech therapy and has made little progress. This is a case where the stuttering is not a signal—it is a serious problem in itself. There are no messages except "Get help!" Stuttering is one of the problems about which modern science has woefully insufficient knowledge. It does not know all the causes. Clarke may grow into adulthood with a better speech pattern only because speech pathologists are learning how to treat stuttering, and because Clarke is diligent in trying to control his speech. This youngster faces the consequences of impaired friendships, lack of confidence in his ability to communicate, and the intense feeling that he is quite "different" from his playmates.

What can Clarke's parents do to help him? They can stay in close touch with his speech clinician. Clarke, if he follows the pattern of many stutterers, will become quite discouraged with his therapy and attempt to discontinue it. His parents need to encourage him to keep trying. As a persistent stutterer, Clarke will have a lot of pent-up anger—anger at himself because he feels different, anger at his insensitive classmates, and anger and frustration at having to live and cope with this severe communication problem. His parents can help him with his anger by providing him with outlets to vent his feelings—punching bags, physical sports, or creative manual skills such as art or carpentry. And, finally, Clarke may have to adopt some new speech-related actions in order to control his stuttering, actions like controlled breathing, pausing, or hand motions, that may appear foolish or unusual to his friends. These actions are therapeutic, however, and should be explained to both Clarke and his parents. By understanding the unusual maneuvers, Clarke's parents can encourage him to continue in the face of possible peer ridicule. In addition, an expression of sincere optimism about his progress and pride in his dedication to improve will make the difficult task seem somewhat easier.

Stuttering is a tricky signal. It can be a false signal in a young child, a signal of other contributing intense emotional strain in an older child with temporary stuttering, or a severe communication problem in a permanently impaired stutterer. No stuttering should be taken lightly. If a parent has any questions, he should talk to his pediatrician and seek an evaluation by a speech clinician if indicated. Stuttering can be one of the most uncomfortable and disabling of all childhood problems.

Your child is struggling to voice his distress through a faltering word flow. The signal is stuttering. The message may be as hard to perceive as his inadequate speech. Listen calmly—until you unmistakably understand the message. Already you have begun a process of communication—healthy communication—that will enable you to help your child while at the same time communicating your own message: "I hear. I understand. I care."

8

Hyperactivity

It is a rare day when a pediatrician does not face an exhausted
parent who gestures toward her frenetic child and whispers desperately, "He's so active, doctor. He's driving me crazy. There has
to be something wrong." On the first day of school, the concerned
elementary school teacher's eyes search the class and she wonders,
"Which ones will be the overactive children and disrupt my class
this year?" Parents, physicians, teachers—all receive the signals of
childhood hyperactivity with alarming frequency. As a tired nurse
in a doctor's office commented one evening after a full day of child
visits, "The whole world must be made up of overactive children."
This is an overstatement, to be sure. However, if you are forced
to cope with even one hyperactive child for a full day in the home,
the school, or the office, you will forget all the children who were
normally responsive and recall with dismay and fatigue only those
few whose energy and activity seemed never to let up, who appeared to be racing their way through their lives and yours.

"Hyperactivity" is a signal: something else is happening inside
the rapidly moving child. Parents must be prepared to take a very
hard look at the reasons behind overactivity and to interpret the
signals given by the child's impulsive, frantic behavior. To call a
child hyperactive is simply not enough. Unless the signalling behavior of hyperactivity is looked into by parents, the child will
continue the restless motion, missing many of the important edu-

cational and social lessons in life as well as alienating himself from the adult world around him.

The Warners brought their daughter, Amy, who was four years old, into the office. Amy was their third child, ten years younger than their second child. The mother and father were in their early forties. Both were professionals, actively working at important jobs every day while Amy stayed at home with an elderly babysitter. "It's not just us, Doctor," they commented. "The babysitter says she's ready to quit. Amy is into everything. She just won't stay still."

Amy was an absolutely delightful child. Her blond head moved tirelessly as she explored the world around her. She chatted continuously, laughing and excited as she discovered new and wondrous office machines. As one watched and listened to the ebullient four-year-old, one could tell she was a very bright little girl.

In talking with the Warners, the doctor learned that she seemed much more active to them than did their previous two older children. And yet, as the conversation continued, it became obvious that they did not recall the early years of the older two very well. "What does Amy do that makes you think she is hyperactive?" the doctor asked. When Mrs. Warner started listing Amy's activities, she was enumerating the normal exploratory ventures of a highly imaginative, intelligent four-year-old. "If you tell her to slow down, does she listen?" was the next question. "Yes," was the reply. "But in no time at all, she's off again—roaming around, chattering, demanding attention."

The signal of Amy's hyperactivity was very evident. Amy was a normally active four-year-old child with a great natural curiosity and adventurous nature. Her parents were "underactive." They were older; their jobs made them tense and often overtired, and they needed time to themselves to recover from the day's trials and tribulations. The babysitter was even older and less able to tolerate the effervescent activity of a vibrant four-year-old. Into all of these lives had erupted the normal activity of the very young and it was being misinterpreted as "hyperactivity."

Having analyzed the Warners' incorrect reception of Amy's signal, we were able to assist them to understand why this youngster wore them out and how to cope with the problem so that the older parents and young child could truly enjoy each other. For part of each day, Amy was sent to a preschool environment where her youthful energies could be released and properly channeled into creative play. A younger babysitter was hired. Each evening, the Warners decided which of the parents most needed "private time"; the other would take over the parenting of Amy for that evening. This became a shared activity. Weekends saw the family doing things together. The Warners were also encouraged to get evening babysitters and go out by themselves. In essence, the message was not that Amy was hyperactive but that she was seriously interfering with the usual activity of this older couple's existence. They had not developed the correct handle on how to cope with the problem. With the above adjustments, some of the "hyperactivity" disappeared, although Amy in no way slowed down in her wonderfully imaginative world.

During the same week Teddy Phillips, who was also four years old, was brought into the doctor's office with the same complaint. "He seemed to be a normal little boy until about six months ago, and then all hell broke loose. He became like a wild boy. We can't trust him to be alone for one minute. He forces us to be in his presence every moment. We can't trust him. He's so active." There was very real resentment in Teddy's mother's voice when she told her story. There was no question that Teddy was overly active. He fidgeted. He roamed the office almost continuously, seemingly without purpose. Occasionally he would slow down to come close to his mother or father, cling tightly to them for a brief period, then hurtle away into more restless activity. Yes, Teddy was hyperactive, but what was the signal that he was sending by his unceasing movement?

Several key questions had to be asked of Teddy's parents to help them unravel the reasons behind their son's new, frenetic behavior. Did he sleep well? "No. He very frequently has nightmares." About what? "He won't tell us. But he insists that we stay with him." Does he seem to be as happy and contented as he was a year ago? A pause. "No, he cries a lot. And he seems rather nervous and frightened." Has anything been happening at home that might have caused him to be upset?

Obviously this was the trigger. Mr. Phillips asked if the nurse could take Teddy out of the room. Finally, after much embarrassed silence, the parents haltingly began to tell the doctor about the serious marital problems that had been growing over the past months. Loud fights and tentative separations had been frequent occurrences within the Phillipses' home. The doctor leaned forward and asked quietly, "Isn't Teddy aware of all this?" The parents looked at each other, frowned, and almost simultaneously nodded. "Yes. I guess he must be," was his father's whispered reply.

Teddy's hyperactivity was a flashing signal that he was acutely upset, disturbed by the possible loss of his family structure. Yet the Phillipses—like so many parents—were unaware that tensions within the home are seen, known, and processed by their children, even the very young. The meaning of Teddy's sudden flight into restlessness was twofold: the expression of his troubled mind over his parents' anger at each other and his manipulation to bring them closer and tie them more permanently to him. He was attempting to prevent the loss of his family through the frantic signal of anxious, hyperactive behavior.

Hyperactivity can be the cue to an acute childhood reaction to stresses either at home or in school. The death of a close relative or pet, marital tensions, severe sibling rivalry, school failure, bullying by other children—all of these can disturb the mind of the child sufficiently so that they are expressed as hyperactivity. Receiving the signal and correcting the cause is the only way to alleviate the symptom of hyperactivity.

Before any attempt at correcting the hyperactivity could be successfully undertaken, it was important for the Phillipses to deal with their marital problems as quickly as possible and outside of Teddy's awareness. The same would be true of the other underlying causes. Helping a child deal with death, resolving problems of sibling rivalry, investigating school problems—these are some of the first steps that must be taken after the signal of acute anxiety hyperactivity has been received and correctly processed by the perceptive parent.

The kindergarten teacher told Calvin's mother flatly: "I don't know what to do any more with your son." Then she continued as calmly as possible: "He does what he wants when he wants. He won't listen to any suggestions. Calvin talks back and the other children are beginning to do the same. He seems so restless, as if he's never had to sit in a seat for any length of time before." The last remark contained the message behind Calvin's signal of hyperactivity.

Calvin's mother seemed somewhat embarrassed. The teacher asked very gently, "How do you discipline Calvin at home? Maybe I could learn from that." The boy's mother turned away for a moment, then, hesitantly, turned her head back toward the teacher. She spoke in an apologetic tone: "We don't. He has free run of the house." The teacher nodded. "You mean you don't discipline him if he disobeys?" Calvin's mother swallowed and replied softly, "No. We just overlook it."

Calvin's overactivity was based upon his failure to receive any home rules and regulations. He had been allowed to be a totally free spirit at home without any restrictions or limitations. School presented him with a strange environment. He was being asked to do things he had not been trained to do at home: obey, share, restrain, and take instruction.

Having interpreted Calvin's hyperactivity signal correctly, the teacher suggested some of the same forms of discipline and behavior control for the home that were being used in school. Parent and teacher became a team, attempting to channel the unbridled energies of the little boy so that his hyperactivity would diminish. Calvin's mother had not seen and understood the signal. Fortunately for Calvin, he had a teacher who could interpret child signals as a means of understanding children and not condemning them.

Very often the parent of the hyperactive child will bring the youngster to the physician searching for a medical cause for the restlessness. It is essential for the parents AND the physician to make certain that all of the other possibilities that create overactivity have been ruled out before a medical label is placed on the child's hyperactivity. Even when the hyperactivity has a medical basis, the other emotional, social, and educational factors must be kept in mind since they often go hand in hand with the medical causes.

Jerry had been hyperactive for as long as his parents could remember. Even as a baby, his mother recalls that he "thrashed around endlessly in the crib, getting his head caught between the railings." "When he started walking," his mother remarked ruefully, "that was the sorriest day of my life." He ran almost endlessly, without purpose or destination, and his mother or father had to chase after him, exhausted and frustrated. "He seemed bright enough," Jerry's mother remarked, "but he was so late in dressing himself and learning to tie his shoes." The family dismissed the frantic activity by declaring that Jerry was "all boy"—until he entered school, where his hyperactivity and his failure to learn became serious problems both for the teacher and the young boy.

Jerry's teacher wrote the following report after he had been in school for several weeks: "Jerry is constantly on the move. He can't sit in his seat longer than five minutes. He has great difficulty holding a pencil or crayon and rarely finishes any of his papers. He gets frustrated easily, and either cries or takes it out on one of the other children. Please get Jerry some help." Jerry's teacher was expressing the message very clearly: "These are the signals. Help your son by recognizing them, accepting them, and answer his message by getting professional help for him."

A visit to the pediatrician revealed that Jerry had some signs of central nervous system impairment. He had random muscle movements without direction. He could not determine objects when they were placed in his hand with his eyes closed. He had difficulty hopping and could not walk a straight line without stumbling. His fine motor coordination, as in buttoning buttons, was impaired. When asked to draw a circle, he gripped the pencil incorrectly and could not make the figure without wavy lines and repeated tries at closing the circle. The pediatrician correctly diagnosed Jerry as having the syndrome of minimal brain dysfunction (MBD) with hyperactivity. He placed Jerry on medication (methylphenidate-Ritalin) to control the impulsive muscular movements. Jerry responded dramatically. His hyperactivity lessened. The teacher was then able to focus on his learning problems and work with the special educators and Jerry's mother to program the best education for this bright but educationally impaired youngster. By picking up the signals at this early age and acting upon them quickly, Jerry's teacher and then his parents had given him a headstart toward attaining the best school performance possible despite his hyperactivity and specific learning problems. But, it must be noted, Jerry's signals were there from "almost as long as I can remember." Picking up these signals in the preschool years is an even better guarantee that the youngster will be able to work through the medical and educational problems of hyperactivity.

Jerry's signals were not just his restless overactivity. More than one signal was coming from this young man at the same time. Jerry was also sending the message that he had learning problems as well as his deep frustration at his own lack of self-control and learning failures. Being sensitive to the overlapping messages becomes extremely important if parents are going to be capable of helping the hyperactive youngster with minimal brain dysfunction (MBD) to the fullest degree.

The basic causes behind the MBD syndrome with hyperactivity still remain obscure. Research continues at a maximal pace in order to attempt to unravel the confusion around this syndrome, which probably affects as much as 1 percent of our child population. Boys are affected twice as often as girls. Maternal nutrition during pregnancy, dietary causes such as food additives, infections during the prenatal and infant period, trauma, biochemical abnormalities within the body systems, and genetic and family tendencies are all under serious consideration as potential causes. It is highly likely that more than one causative problem will be uncovered. MBD with hyperactivity may well be the "fever" of the behavior world—a single symptom with many and varied causes. The main issue is that the signal must not be overlooked by parents. The knowledge that hyperactivity may be treatable as a multiple medical problem makes the recognition of the signal vital to the emotional and educational health of the child.

Infrequently, hyperactivity signals a much more serious problem. Longstanding emotional illness of a significant degree may be present, and the child is restless and uncontrollable. In this instance, the parents and the professionals are led to look more deeply into the emotionally scarred areas within the child. What are the signals that would lead a parent to suspect deepseated mental illness? Severe changes in the child's behavior, unexplained withdrawals and acting-out periods, inability to relate to other people, inexplicable anger, destructive behavior, and inappropriate responses to normal life situations should alert the parent that the signalling hyperactivity may be only the tip of the iceberg. When this is revealed as the parent analyzes the overactive message, then the advice of mental health professionals should be sought. Remember, this is the rare rather than the common cause of childhood hyperactivity.

Another rare possibility is that the hyperactivity may signal a significant degree of mental retardation and even brain damage. All parents watch the development of their children and can usually detect the sluggish progress of a mentally retarded child. Overlooking failure by the child to reach the normal levels of attainment is a denial of the problem by both parent and teacher. Fortunately this happens only on rare occasions.

Hyperactivity can be one of the most exasperating childhood conditions with which a parent must deal. Often the parent ricochets, like the child, between frustration and anger, chasing the child, apologizing for his misdemeanors, explaining his behavior to neighbors and teachers. The child may create such a chaotic environment that parents wonder if they even truly love the child. Parents of the hyperactive child must pause and retreat long enough to analyze the signal and work through the many possible messages contained within the frenetic behavior. Only then can they become the intelligent, sensitive, and objective advocates for a child who seems to be hurtling through life and dragging the parents along. Although the signal may be chaotic, the process of working through the meaning of the message must not be. An article in a popular magazine years ago which referred to the hyperactive child was entitled "Is There a Monster in Your House?" How tragic to pin that label on any child! Parents must fight that tendency, no matter how difficult the situation. Give the hyperactive child a fair chance. Hear and see his signal, then interpret it by getting the proper help. Your home will harbor no "monster," but a child who is being understood, appreciated, and helped.

9

Shyness and Withdrawal

You hear the sound of children's excited voices from the next yard as you move about the kitchen. When you walk into the living room, you see your son, Johnny, sitting quietly in the windowseat, oblivious to the happy sounds from the outside, absorbed in a book, reading intently. "Why don't you save that for tonight, son, and go out and play next door?" you ask cautiously. He looks up at you, his face determined. "I don't want to," he says simply, and his head bends and his eyes return to the book. You are bewildered. What is the matter with your child? Why is he so different from the other children? What does it mean?

When a youngster separates himself from the other children on frequent occasions and seems to prefer to remain alone, he may be sending several very different messages. Each requires its own appropriate response from the sensitive and sensible parent. A parent must take a very thorough look at the behavior behind the shyness and withdrawal of the child so that worry and concern will not result in a hasty and destructive response.

Let us take a careful look at Johnny and see if we can uncover why he is reluctant to join the other children. You can help by remembering his earlier years. Johnny has never been comfortable in groups. Since the time he was three years old, you have noticed that he enjoyed playing by himself. He has a younger sister whose age is half his ten years. For his first five years, Johnny was really an only child in an adult world, accustomed to creating his own world within his home without the help of brothers or sisters. As you think about his growing years, you realize that there have been times during nursery school and elementary school when Johnny *has* joined his classmates in play and in projects. But he was highly selective and picked only those activities that he particularly enjoyed. His interest in art and painting led him into the groups that were making posters or painting Christmas pictures for the school. He would join groups of three or four classmates in art projects. In fact, as you remember clearly, Johnny actually assumed leadership in Sunday School to organize some of the other youngsters to paint a large wall hanging for the Easter service. During these times Johnny got along well with other children, laughing, working together, seeming to enjoy their company. But when faced with activities that he did not enjoy, he would beg off and remain alone, satisfying himself with books, games, and so on, instead. During these periods when he preferred doing things by himself, Johnny seemed quite contented and fulfilled. He never complained, nor did he mope around the house as if he were lonely or felt left out of the childhood world.

What can you learn from Johnny's behavior that will help you to deal with his preference to be a loner when you feel he should be joining the other children? There are key signals in his actions that unlock Johnny's personality and allow you to react intelligently as parents.

First, Johnny has become accustomed to being alone a good bit of the time. As an only child for the first five years, he discovered how to find his child's world by himself within an adult world during the hours when he could not be in the company of other children. He has learned that he can function by himself. Secondly, Johnny can join other groups of children and he can enjoy and profit from the experience. Though he teams up with them only infrequently and on special occasions, he does so with ease and without embarrassment or fear. Last, and most significantly, Johnny is content and happy during his solitary moments. He is not looking out of the window yearning to be in the neighbor's yard playing with the other children.

Essentially Johnny is neither shy nor withdrawn. Excessive concern about him is not justified. He is a solitary child, who is highly selective in joining peer groups. Should this behavior be changed? The perceptive parent knows that we live in a "group" world. There are many jobs and activities that will throw Johnny into groups as he matures into adulthood. Therefore more group activities will profit him immeasurably in his ability to handle that future adult world.

How can the parent encourage Johnny, who seems so content being alone, to become a "joiner"? The answer lies in discovering more of the selective group activities Johnny enjoys doing with other children, such as his interest in art, and program such activities into Johnny's world. It is highly likely that from pleasurable encounters with other children will come invitations and spontaneous moves on Johnny's part. The expansion of his group experiences may be slow and only minimal, but each will be a major leap in the direction of group adjustment for this basically normal, happy boy.

Now look at Robert, who also stays away from the other children. While Johnny sits quietly and reads contentedly, Robert roams miserably about the house stealing longing glances at the children romping in the next-door yard. Remembering his earlier days, you can learn a great deal about the signals Robert is sending. As a preschooler, Robert was often afraid of his peers. Frequently his playmates were several years younger because he felt more comfortable with them. When he entered kindergarten, he kept to himself and played alone even when the teacher encouraged him to participate in classroom games and projects. He would back away from the friendly overtures of his classmates. Only when a gentle, loving child approached Robert and offered him friendship over an extended period of time could Robert accept the other child's company. It took Robert time to become comfortable with other children. When he was able to make a connection with another child, he was excited and extremely happy. He attached himself to the other child almost constantly and coveted the relationship, often "smothering" his friend by preventing the other child from associating with the rest of the class. When the inevitable end of the closeness between the two friends occurred, Robert would retreat once more into his unhappy world alone.

In Robert's case, the clues add up to a truly "shy" child who wants and needs friendships and group relationships. He is unhappy without them, but shyness and lack of self-confidence prevent him from achieving them.

The reasons behind Robert's shyness could be many. They must be understood if his parents are going to be able to relieve his unhappiness. Could Robert be shy because he feels inferior? Does he sense that he is not up to his peers in the important areas of sports and socializing? If this is the case, then the parents should help Robert discover what he does do well and build upon his successes in a positive manner. Every child can do something, often many things, well. Too often such strengths are overlooked by both the parents and the child in the preoccupation with weaknesses. Faced with a shy child, who has a low sense of self-esteem, parents and child must search cooperatively for the *positive* aspects of the child's potential. This will give him the self-confidence that can help to eliminate the shyness.

Could a youngster be shy because of the pressures and rivalry of an older sibling? Of course! If an older brother or sister does everything well and lets it be known, the younger child can be very intimidated. A bullying sibling can beat the self-confidence out of a shy child. Parents must intervene before the normal sibling rivalry escalates to such serious, destructive levels. Giving each child in the family deserved praise will help to control the first problem. Eliminating the physical as well as the emotional domination of the older child over the younger will stop the destruction of the shy child's self-confidence.

Robert does not need professional help at this stage in his life. What he needs are parents who have received and properly interpreted the signal of his "loner" behavior. After dealing with the causes, his parents must provide possible solutions. Robert cannot be forced into being a group person. He cannot be coerced into losing his shyness. His parents should embark on a slow, calculated, and intelligent course to reintroduce Robert into his peer society. Inviting a single friend for the weekend may be a beginning. Encouraging Robert to accept the invitation to have dinner at another friend's home is another. Easing him into rewarding single relationships will encourage him to continue experimenting with his friends. Robert must not be shoved into large group activities on a "sink or swim" basis or he will surely sink deeper into his aloneness as a result. He must choose, be willing to venture into the birthday party, the football game, or the dating experience of his own free will. Robert's ability to enter into group activity can only be the result of thoughtful parenting and careful planning.

Timmy also refuses to play with other children his own age. But he has problems far more serious than either Johnny or Robert. Let us look at him carefully so we can determine the important difference. Timmy is curled up on the windowseat, head bent, knees drawn up next to his chest. Although the sounds of the children's laughter pass over his head, he simply does not hear the call of companionship outside the window. Often he does not respond when his parents call out to him, remaining fixed in his isolated position. Timmy seems to be living in his own world.

As you travel back over Timmy's past, you realize that this isolation pattern has been growing slowly, almost imperceptively, over the years until it can no longer be ignored. In his first four years, Timmy played fairly well with the very young children in the neighborhood. But gradually he began to sulk and pull away from their games. Soon he was going out of the house less and less. He occupied himself in the house initially with toys and games, talking to himself, and following his mother closely. Then she noticed he was no longer by her heels—he was sitting and staring blankly into space. Occasionally Timmy would be crying for no apparent reason. The child was now visibly unhappy and detached from the world around him. The signal in Timmy's case is frighteningly clear. He is a withdrawn child.

How different Timmy is from either Johnny or Robert, and how easy it seems to make that distinction. But the signals are not always as clear and progressive. The problems often appear to creep up on parents, who then treat the situation as if it had exploded overnight. Therefore, reconstructing the life history of a problem will help the parent bring the total problem into clearer focus.

Timmy needs professional help. He has withdrawn sufficiently from the world he lives in to be signalling that he is very emotionally upset. So many things can tip the scales for a youngster. The death of a parent; divorce; flawed parent-child relationships; serious problems in learning, socializing, communicating; physical or sensory handicaps—these are but a few of the possible underlying causes for the emotional problems to which withdrawing is a key signal. In order to work through these serious situations, Timmy and his parents should ask their pediatrician or family doctor for a good mental health counsellor in the vicinity. The sooner the professional help, the more likely Timmy will work through his problems and become an involved and communicating member of society. Therefore, as parents, we must catch the signals as early as possible. So often we get the picture, we hear the clarion call for help, we see the signals; yet we deny or overlook them, rejecting the possibility that help is needed. Why? Because it is very painful to admit we have a disturbed child. It is hurtful to think we may have played a role. These thoughts must be erased. We must not feel embarrassed, guilty, or angry at either our child or ourselves. Instead we must catch the signal as if it were a football and run with it toward the goal of a healthy child. (For further help with the problems of the emotionally disturbed child, see Chapter 25.)

The Johnnys in this world far outnumber the Roberts and the Timmys. Fortunately, Timmy is in the minority. Too often the parents of the "loner" dread that they have a Timmy and delay looking seriously at the overall picture for fear of what their observation will reveal. In reality, most parents will find that their shy child is a well-adjusted, self-contained, solitary child, like Johnny, who needs only the slightest, sensitive parental encouragement. Even Robert's parents will find that they can lead him away from his shyness without a professional guide. It is the ability to read the signals as they appear and to interpret them intelligently and honestly that will make these parents capable of acting as frontline professionals in their "loner" child's life.

10

Running Away from Home

Lee stood with her tiny fists jammed into her hips. Her face was screwed up to look fierce, but she only succeeded in resembling a wrinkled elf. "I'm running away from home," she announced, her eyes brimming with tears. Her father raised his eyebrows ever so slightly, trying desperately not to smile. Her mother turned her face away, the laughter bubbling up in her throat. "Why?" her father asked, as calmly as he could. Lee stared at him in an exaggerated look of amazement. "You know!" she squeaked, trying to sound as angry as possible. "Because you were punished for not coming home when your mother called you?" her father asked innocently. Lee stamped her foot. "Yes. That's why," she said, making a face. "I'm running away from home and I'm never coming back again!"

Despite the fact that the situation was inherently funny to Lee's parents, Lee at four years old was sending out a very definite signal. She wanted to be seen and heard. What were her messages that needed some immediate attention?

Lee was going to run away from home because she was angry. Running away from home was her way of punishing her parents in return for their disciplining her. So one of Lee's signals was clearly punitive toward her mother and father.

Another message transmitted by the petite four-year-old was the announcement that she didn't believe the punishment fit the crime. After all, she was having a splendid time playing dodge ball with the older children down the street. She could eat dinner with her parents any night, but the older boys and girls had never let her into their game before. Didn't her parents understand? If she ran away from home, they would be forced to reassess what they had asked of her and realize that they were wrong. If running away was successful, then she might be able to stay out as late as she wanted the next time the other children invited her to play.

Another message woven through her signal was that she was about to abandon her parents and home. Lee wanted her parents to realize that she was a PERSON too. She had her rights; she had her wishes. And she had to have her freedom. She was capable of leaving them behind as she marched out into the world without them. How common it is for a four-year-old to realize that she is no longer an appendage of her parents, that she is a singular, independent human being. Sometimes this realization can be frightening. But, at that moment, Lee was tasting her glorious independence and threatening to prove her total individuality.

Lee then had three important messages in the signal, "I'm running away from home": punishing her parents; demanding that the rules be reassessed; and announcing her independence. How do parents deal with these messages in the face of an incident that well might cause them to break into gales of laughter? Laughter was not appropriate at that moment. If Lee felt strongly enough about threatening to run away from home, then the signal could not be ignored or treated lightly.

Let us consider what her parents did. Her father asked, "Are you certain you want to run away from home?" Lee nodded determinedly. "Because you punished me for staying out," she replied, staring at him. He nodded and spoke quietly. "Then perhaps you had better do it, because Mother and I will have to punish you again if you do not come in when we call." The little girl continued to stare at him, her hands now open but still firmly pressed into her sides. Lee's father left the room for a minute and returned with a small overnight bag. "Let me help you pack," he said seriously, taking her arm and gently guiding her into her bedroom. As she stood watching him in amazement, he threw a few items of clothing into the bag. Finally he picked up her Teddy Bear. "Is he going with you?" he questioned. The girl nodded, silently. The beloved bear was stuffed into the bag, which was then zipped up and placed on the floor. "Can you carry it?" Lee's father asked, only his twinkling eyes demonstrating his inner amusement. The little girl nodded. "Yes," she said softly, and picked up the bag. Her father bent down and kissed her on the cheek. "We will miss you, sweetheart." The little girl's eyes began to fill with tears. But she resolutely marched past her father, hugged her mother, and paraded to the front door. Opening the door, she confronted the very dark night. She took one tentative step forward, then looked back at her parents. "It's dark out there." Her father nodded. "Yes it is," her mother said softly. Lee turned around and walked back into the house, unzipped the bag, pulled out her Teddy Bear, and looked at both parents with a wry look of concession. "Maybe I'll go tomorrow." That was the last time Lee threatened to run away from home. Her parents had heard her signal, interpreted the messages, and responded to each so that Lee learned the meaning of love and obedience at the same time.

Skippy was another kind of problem. "Skippy keeps running away from home," his mother reported. "Why?" She shook her head quizzically. "I don't know. But about once a week he is gone. And we have to spend all night searching for him." "Where do you find him?" was the next important probe into Skippy's signal. Mrs. Glass frowned. "Well. He's usually at one of his boyfriend's homes. We're never sure which one." "But you usually know that if you look at one of his friend's homes, you will find him?" she was asked. She paused and finally nodded. "Yes." The questions continued. "You said you searched for him all night. How long is he usually gone?" She took a deep breath before answering, "Actually about an hour or less." She stopped, and then added quickly, "But by that time I'm so upset that it seems like all night."

There is a great deal to be learned about the messages behind the signal in seven-year-old Skippy's running away from home. First, there does not appear to be a specific action that immediately precedes the disappearance. Second, Skippy makes quite certain that he will be quickly found. Third, his mother becomes thoroughly unnerved by the experience, focusing on the youngster for an entire evening.

A few more pieces of the puzzle need to be put together. Mrs. Glass fidgeted in her chair. "Has anything been happening around the house lately?" was the next question. She shook her head. "No," she said emphatically. There was a brief pause. She thought a bit. Finally she frowned and said, "Yes. Yes, there has been. Skippy's oldest sister is getting married in a few weeks." The final question hit the target: "Skippy is your youngest. Do you think he feels left out of what's going on?" Mrs. Glass opened her eyes very wide. The signal was coming into focus for her. Skippy was using his running away from home to gain attention, particularly hers, during a period when the hours which she had willingly and happily spent with him had been seriously cut down by other family needs. Skippy was trying to tell his mother to pay more attention to him—to return to him what he felt was justly his—her affection and her attention. Running away from home can be a dramatic attention-getting signal that expresses the child's feelings of being left out.

Once Mrs. Glass realized what caused Skippy's flights from home, she was able to correct the problem sensibly. She began to include her youngest son in preparations for the wedding, working side by side with him as she addressed envelopes and he pasted stamps, made out guest lists, and shopped for special gifts. Mr. Glass also helped to start the healthy transfer of some of Skippy's dependence from his mother to his father. There was no need for Skippy to run away from home again. His parents' unintentional neglect had been recognized and changed to actions of caring and including. Now they had interpreted the message and acted wisely to rectify the situation. Skippy wasn't really "running away from home." He was announcing that home had somehow run away from *him*.

Eleven-year-old Vicki Sue fled from home the evening her mother announced that she was bringing her date home to dinner. When her mother was questioned as to why the girl might have run away, she stated, "I think it was because Dan was coming over for dinner. Vicki Sue had never met him before and probably was afraid to see him." But there had to be more to the signal this previously stable young girl was giving her mother. "What did you actually say to her?" her mother was asked. "Well, I told her Dan was coming for dinner and I wanted them to like each other because I thought he and I might be getting married in the near future." When Vicki Sue was asked why she left home, she replied bitterly, "She told me this man was coming to our house and she was going to marry him. I didn't even know him. I was being told —not asked—to change my whole life. How could she do that to me?"

The young girl had signalled that she would not accept this announcement. She was manipulating her mother and her mother's potential fiancé by fleeing the house, disrupting the planned dinner, and clearly indicating that any such marriage was against her wishes. There were two very explicit messages in Vicki Sue's signal. One was her attempt to control a marriage that she did not want to occur. The second was the declaration of her disapproval of the way the announcement was handled, an understandable anger.

Vicki Sue's mother had made several mistakes. She should have introduced Dan to her daughter long before the precipitous announcement. She should have allowed time to bring the two strangers together. Including her daughter more fully in her current life and allowing her some say about the future of the family would have prevented the episode. Finally, making the announcement of possible marriage before the introduction of the future stepfather created fear and anger in the young girl. All of these feelings were predictable. Even the running-away signal could have been prophesied if Vicki Sue's mother had only stopped and thought. What could her mother do now that she had received the signal? She had to act wisely, because her future and that of her daughter depended upon her intelligent response to the girl's running away.

This mother had to start all over. She had to introduce her male friend gradually, postpone any wedding plans, and allow the young girl to adjust properly. Vicki Sue deserved the privilege of being able to accept and even encourage her mother to remarry. This often takes time and effort. If the signal had been ignored, Vicki Sue probably would have returned home, perhaps only briefly, to a house torn by bitterness and resentment.

A key issue that parents must investigate when a child runs away from home is whether the signal is one of shame and concern over something the child has done and wants to hide. The parents must be wary. It is far too easy openly to accuse your youngster when he returns home: "What did you do that made you run away?" Instead of opening up a healing communication between parent and child, this type of accusatory behavior only slams doors. "What is bothering you?" is reasonable for openers. "Can I help you?" is a natural followthrough. "Whatever is troubling you can be worked out by the three of of us" will help a mother and father reach the child who has tried to escape from possible shame and embarrassment. Failing in school, being caught stealing at the local store, hurting a neighborhood child in a fight, being picked up by the truant officer at the movie house—these are some of the relatively common episodes that youngsters blow up into problems which they feel will bring down parental wrath. The message, in this case, is the fear of being found out and having to live through the consequences. Many children would rather run than "face the music" in their homes.

Parents who must cope with the childhood signal of running away are obligated to ask themselves the vital question: Why was he so afraid to come to me and discuss the problem? What did he think we would do? Was he right? *Was he right?* Children can be extremely perceptive in their predictions of how their parents will react. If your child flees your home rather than confess and live with your reactions to a minor misdemeanor, then it becomes your responsibility to reevaluate the degree and flexibility of both your attitudes and your punishments. How correct was the child in feeling the need to run away? Was he right? From this signal, both child and parent can learn a great deal. Hopefully the child can discover, after returning home, the real depth of his parents' love and trust. Possibly the parents can develop their own ability to understand, accept, and help their child through a painful situation caused because he has done something wrong. These are major signals about problems that often prove minor when revealed by the runaway child. It is not the problems that stand out ultimately but the past punishments, which are remembered by the runaway.

When Bart was returned home after eight hours away, his grandfather asked him why he had left. The fifteen-year-old boy became tearful and stammered, "Because he hates me." "Who?" his grandfather asked. "My father," the boy replied sadly. The old man put his arms around his grandson and held him silently for several minutes, then spoke softly, "Bart, what makes you think your father hates you? I happen to know he loves you very much." The boy sighed, turned his tear-streaked face toward his grandfather, and said bitterly, "Well, he sure has a dumb way of showing it. He picks on me all of the time and puts me down every chance he gets." He remained still for a minute, then shook his head vigorously. "No. I don't believe it. You might think so . . . that he loves me. But I know he hates me!"

It is fairly common during the early teenage years, when rebellion and dissatisfaction with the adult world play such a major part in kids' lives, that a child can honestly believe he is unloved, even disliked, by one or both parents. Somewhere during his early adolescent years, a derailment of the relationship with his parents has occurred. He has detoured his life around and away from them and may gradually build up feelings of such intense alienation from one or both that he feels he must "get out." The signal that Bart is transmitting is one of incompatibility with the parent(s) to a degree that makes living under the same roof unbearable. Who is at "fault"? Probably both the parents and the child. Each plays a significant role in the daily living that continues through the turbulent, often painful adolescent years. Frequently one blames the other totally, without realistically evaluating the part that each has played in the unhappy relationship.

What can be done after the teenager makes the grandstand play of running away from home? He or she has indicated that something must happen to the parent-child relationship which will remove the stress, the anger, the mounting schism. There is probably little question that the parents feel exactly the same way. Who must take the first step of reconciliation after the signal has been realized?

It is very painful for a parent to learn that his child feels the parent "hates" him. Denial is not the answer; neither is anger. The solution lies with the parent, who must be willing to sit down with the young person and hear his complaints, assess them honestly and realistically, recognize parenting errors that were probably unintentional, discuss viewpoints and feelings, and, especially, *listen* to the teenager as he talks about himself. The "cooling-off period" can begin, and the healing process start, with parents and teenager attempting to meet each other halfway. Parents must remember that if a child runs away from home because of a tense and angry parent-child relationship, the child is seldom totally wrong. Somewhere along the way the parents have not been looking, listening, or understanding. Basically this is what running away is all about. The young person wants to compel people to pay attention to his problems. This is his loud and desperate signal— and the best therapists in this situation can be the parents themselves.

Some adolescents run away from home and never return, creating a major social problem in the country—teenage runaways— with its consequent problems of sexual exploitation, unemployment, drug abuse, and mental illness. These teenage runaways are

vulnerable children, children who will often do *anything* to obtain acceptance or affection—or actions that pass for these emo-
tions. They are seeking to replace their parents with overideal-
ized, impossible expectations, and they will search fruitlessly for
parental substitutes.

How do children and their parents find themselves in such
predicaments, beset by unreasonable angers, hatreds, and expectations? How can families exist so filled with anxiety and hostility
that the youngest, the most susceptible, has to "blow up"—to run
away from home?

Somewhere during the early adolescent years, normal misund-
erstandings have intensified into total blocks of communication
because neither parent nor child understood the values, morals,
lifestyles, or needs of the other. The parents could neither perceive nor accept the natural tendencies of the adolescent to seek
friends within his own peers and conform to the questionable
standards of the modern adolescent. Teenagers, on the other
hand, bolstered by their friends, upheld by exploitative movies,
TV shows, and pronouncements of popular cult heroes, perceive
themselves as wronged by hopelessly old-fashioned parents who
impose upon them an irrational and outdated code of conduct.
The generation clash becomes pathological, then malignant, and
the teenager disappears, only to become an ever-increasing but
little known statistic—a fatality of the modern warfare between
the generations.

Who is lost, parent or child?

The reality is that not only are both lost, but each has lost the
other, severing the most important relationship in a family's life,
the relationship between parent and child.

Why?

Because the parents have failed to perceive and act on earlier
signals. A major disruption of the home is usually preceded by such
signals: a trial runaway like Bart's, prolonged periods of misunder-
standing and unhappiness, increasing actions of independence
from parents, more and more secrecy about the child's activities
outside the home, the acquisition of friends not known to the

parents, constant behavior calculated to annoy or anger parents, frequent statements of hatred and of perceived rejection. Like Bart, the child will signal that living under the same roof with parents is unbearable. He or she must escape.

If your child is a serious runaway, your first task is to have him or her found and returned—immediately. Any young person is too vulnerable to be left to the "human" wolves that inhabit the fringes of civilization, awaiting the vulnerable child as victim. In this instance your local public or private law enforcement agencies should be contacted for help.

Often, however, getting your child back may be the least painful part of the process of restoring the family. The signal of running away implies the need for a total readjustment of the relationship between parent and child—a change in attitude, expectations, and understanding. That change will probably require psychotherapy both for the parents *and* the child. All must be helped—actually taught how to listen to each other. All three must finally be willing to sit with the other, to hear complaints, to assess one another honestly and realistically, to recognize unintentional parenting errors, discuss viewpoints and feelings, and, generally "cool off" the anger toward each other. Each must meet the others halfway, a process that probably has not occurred in many years, if at all. That is why the family will have need of a professional counsellor. Once they realize the problems and understand their errors, the family members will gain insight and then relief from the guilt that has inevitably been felt. Only then can parents hope to bring together the nucleus of a once happy family shattered by the electric forces of distrust and lack of communication.

Don't let your child's messages slip by unheeded. These signals may never come again, and you will have lost a valuable moment of contact. In fact, you may have lost your child.

11

Refusal to Eat

We are an extremely food-conscious people. Many persons of all ages in our society are overweight. Dieting has become a nation-wide fad, yet we continue to overeat ourselves into serious physical and emotional problems. Because food is so important in our homes, is it any wonder that the child who refuses to eat creates panic? Somewhere, through the last few generations, we have adopted the myth that the fat child is the healthy child. Indeed, the more chubby the child, the better the parents feel the child represents their care of him. The child is often *taught* to overeat. He is given sweets as rewards, and becomes "addicted" to them, moving, in their absence, to other foods. The baby's face smiling at you from the can of baby food has the full face of childhood obesity. A full stomach becomes our standard. We accept this standard and overeat ourselves into old age. When we see a child refusing to eat, we immediately seek help and advice. Something must be terribly wrong, we suspect.

Parents have little difficulty in picking up the signal of refusal to eat; it stares at them from the dinner plate in no uncertain terms. But the messages behind why a child will not eat are many and varied, ranging from the innocent and natural to the severe and worrisome. Being able to separate the signals into the proper messages may help most parents ease up on the forced feedings and allow dinnertime to become fun again. Other messages will have more significance and may cover up more complex and hidden problems.

The eighteen-month-old girl sat on her mother's lap, her chubby, rosy cheeks looking like early summer apples on a round, full face. The child was the picture of exuberant good health. Her physical examination had been completely normal. But her mother seemed a little tense. When she was asked if she was having any problems with the little girl, she nodded. "She's stopped eating. I'm worried sick. She isn't eating half of what she used to. Tell me; what's wrong? What can we do?"

This mother was interpreting her young daughter's dramatic cutback in appetite as a serious signal of a health problem. Our examination found that the child had not stopped eating; she had only reduced her intake considerably over what she had eaten during her first year of life.

The healthy little girl was sending off a perfectly normal signal. She didn't need as many calories as she did before because she wasn't growing as fast nor were the tissues in her body building as rapidly. Almost all children reduce their food intake after the first eighteen months or so. This sharp reduction often alarms parents. However, if the mother and father will observe the child rather than the amount of food consumed, they will readily see that the youngster continues to gain at a slower, but normal rate, and remains healthy. This signal in a child's life has a technical medical term, "physiological anorexia." In everyday terms, this means that the loss of appetite has a normal basis in the child's body systems and should rarely be a cause for alarm. The exception occurs when the young child may become too selective and, for example, tries to live on milk and cookies only. Because nutrition must be balanced and not all foods contain the necessary proteins, fats, and iron, the parents must make certain that the smaller meals are balanced ones. Actually being prepared for this signal makes it much easier to understand and accept. Doctors tell mothers whose babies were good eaters: "That's fine for now. But when she gets to be a year and a half or older, she won't need as much food. Her appetite will diminish. That's normal. When it happens, don't be alarmed." Words such as these can create a proper perspective for the mother.

Some children will consistently refuse to eat certain foods, such as green vegetables or meats. This signal may mean that the child does not like the taste of certain foods and therefore rejects them. It is possible to give in to these taste signals as long as other foods, containing equal amounts of needed nutrients, are substituted. Milk is not a replacement for meat. Custards are not a replacement for vegetables. A parent should experiment with foods to discover items that the child will find acceptable. Then these can be served periodically. Parents must remember, however, that when the young child tells them, "I hate that food," what he really can be saying is that he prefers to eat something else. The "hated" foods may cover a wide range of necessary nutrients. Therefore, at times, parents may have to urge their youngster to eat some of the food he prefers and also sufficient amounts of special types of foods that he "hates."

The refusal to eat a certain food may also be a medical signal. For example, some children cannot break down the sugar of regular milk in their intestinal tract. Milk gives them cramps, gas, and loose bowel movements. Children may also have allergies to certain foods or food additives and have problems with digestion, skin rashes, or breathing. Some foods or food additives may even precipitate chronic physical or neurological problems. Children often learn to reject these foods. Before force-feeding any rejected food, the parent should look at the consequences of the food on the child. This is the rational and thoughtful way a parent can respond to the signal of food refusal. When the signal tells the parent that a particular food does not agree with the child's body system, pay heed to it—and consult the child's doctor.

"I simply don't understand her. She will not eat at the dinner table. She shakes her head and says 'No.' But about an hour later, I catch her sneaking to the refrigerator and eating the leftovers." Cindy's mother was reflecting on the unusual eating habits of her four-year-old daughter. As doctor and mother talked, Mrs. Pierce expanded on some of the other changes in Cindy's actions around the house. "She's getting a mind of her own," the mother remarked. "Every other word is 'no.'" As she paused to consider her remarks, we asked her, "How do you manage it when she refuses to do these other things?" Mrs. Pierce smiled. "Well, she's my third child, so I've lived through this independent period before. I push when it's important and I don't when it's not." Mrs. Pierce had just uncovered the secret behind Cindy's signal of refusing to eat and had voiced the correct prescription for dealing with it. She simply had not put Cindy's refusal to eat and later sneak food into the same category. And that was clearly where it belonged. Cindy's signal was another of her messages: "I want independence." Now the question remained: "Is the eating important enough to do something about—to push, as you say?" Mrs. Pierce thought for a minute and then answered, "Yes." We agreed, but added, "Maybe 'push' is too strong a word." What was agreed upon was that Cindy had the privilege of eating at the table if she so desired. The food was in front of her. No coercion was to be used. BUT she was not to be allowed to go to the refrigerator to take her needed nutrition later in the evening. Mealtime was the time to eat.

Mrs. Pierce put the plan into operation. She saw the connection between Cindy's signal of not eating and all of the other independence signals. However, she also understood the need to maintain the family structure around mealtimes. For several days Cindy continued to refuse to eat, but the refrigerator remained off limits for her. Finally her own body solved the problem. Cindy became very hungry and her refusal to eat at the table was over. She remained an independent little girl, but she also became a reasonably well-nourished one.

Karen sat at the dinner table after her younger brother and older sister had finished their dinners and had been excused. She moved the meat around in circles. The peas lay untouched. Her father got up from the table exasperated. "I can't sit here all night," he stormed as he walked out of the dining room. Karen's mother pleaded, "Eat your peas, dear." Karen picked up her fork, speared a single pea, and very slowly brought it to her mouth. She chewed for several minutes until her mother exploded, "How long does it take to eat one pea?" She frowned at her four-year-old. Twenty minutes, four peas, and one thin sliver of meat later, Karen's mother grabbed the plate and dumped the remaining food in the garbage can. Karen smiled sweetly and slipped out of her chair to run outside and play.

The parents met in the living room and decided to talk seriously about Karen's refusal to eat. They carefully analyzed all of the possible reasons. The little girl did not seem to give them very much trouble in any other way. But as they talked, they realized that she had blended in with her brother and sister to the point that they could not be sure about what she did as a special individual. Her mother noted that Karen was their middle child and did not seem to demand as much of her time as the other two. So she had not reached out to offer extra time to the little girl. Slowly, Karen's parents began to realize what Karen was signalling by her dawdling and refusal to eat at the dinner table. "Do you realize that you probably spend as much as an hour a day with her just sitting alone at the table begging her to eat?" Father asked Mother. Karen's mother thought for a minute and agreed. "Could this be her way of getting my attention?" Then, almost in unison, they both nodded.

These parents were able to act quickly on the problem. Realizing that this middle child needed more attention than she was getting because of the competition from her demanding older sister and her infant brother, her mother set aside the afternoon to spend alone with Karen. Her father read to her for twenty minutes before bedtime. Gradually the mealtime ordeals were fewer. Karen never became a hearty eater, but she downed adequate amounts of food during meals. The signal was no longer necessary.

In families where eating is an important part of family life, the youngster becomes aware that food can represent a means to punish the parent. When the child becomes angry at the parents and wants a mechanism to express that anger, refusal to eat usually works quite well. The message here is the expression of anger and, to a degree, punishment of parents. Often the child has been a good eater prior to the sudden loss of appetite. The parents can usually document the incident and the discipline that precipitated the refusal to eat. Rarely is the signal subtle. The refusal to eat has the tone of rebellion; the food is pushed aside with a calculated vengeance. If the parent reacts in a hysterical or even an overly worried manner, the signal will have received the right interpretation but the wrong response. A calm acceptance of the refusal to eat by the parents and the clear demonstration that it is the child's stomach that is empty, not the parents', will often take the sting out of the child's signal. "I know you are angry at us. And you can be if you wish. But not eating hurts you far more than it does us," can be the spoken or conveyed message from the parent. When the desired effect on the parent is not seen by the child, the youngster will usually give up the hunger strike. By that time, the reasons behind the anger at the parents often have long since been forgotten. But the child has learned a valuable lesson in the process. Punishing others can cause the punisher to suffer more than those being punished.

When Harry came into the doctor's office for his camp physical, it was observed that the twelve-year-old had lost a good deal of weight during the preceding six months. He was a tall, thin young man who could not afford much more weight loss. Being concerned, we tried to discover whether his weight loss was due to a medical or emotional reason. He told us frankly, "I haven't been eating very well lately." "Any reason?" we asked. He was reluctant to answer and finally just mumbled, "I haven't been very hungry." Harry kept his shoulders hunched and his forehead slightly wrinkled at all times. He appeared to be a perpetually worried youngster. "Is anything bothering you that might have taken away your appetite?" we asked. He stared at his hands and said nothing. However, his intense silence was a clue. Harry was not eating because something was worrying him. After much gentle probing, Harry finally blurted out, "I think my brother is going to die." His eyes filled with tears and he rubbed them with his fists. "What makes you think so?" we asked the miserable young man. "Well, he's been having to go to this new doctor every week. My folks talk about it in whispers. And he doesn't look too good." He stopped and moistened his dry lips. "Have you questioned your parents about it?" He shook his head. "No. They've looked so out of it lately. Like something is going wrong. I was afraid to ask." He lapsed into silence. Harry was obviously starving himself in his worry about his brother. We asked if we could inquire what was going on from his family. He hesitated, then agreed.

A telephone call cleared up the mystery. Harry's brother had had several infections of the kidneys and had just completed a thorough work-up to make certain that everything was structurally normal. He had been given a clean bill of health by the specialist. When Harry learned the good news, at first he could not believe it. He had lived with his fantasy worry for such a long time. "Now go home and eat," was our parting advice. When we saw him two months later after camp, Harry had gained back all of the lost weight plus several pounds and looked healthy, happy, and relaxed.

Harry's signal of refusal to eat was based on worry. So many older children lose their appetite when something troubles them. In some cases, the worry is real; in Harry's case, fortunately, it was not. However, the question must be asked: Where were Harry's parents during the six months when he stopped eating and was visibly losing weight? True, they were preoccupied with the medical illness of their other son. They had sensed the signal of medical distress, but had overlooked Harry's signal, which was equally important. The first signal of a worried or depressed older child may be the gradual or sudden failure to eat. Sensing that signal and finding out the trouble must be done before the emotional balance and nutritional health of the child collapse simultaneously.

Another reason for the signal of refusal or failure to eat centers on the atmosphere at the dinner table. When dinnertime becomes a period of interrogation or discipline, appetites are lost. Family arguments during meals also cause the food to lose its attraction. A tense dinner table will precipitate the childhood signal of refusal to eat. Often such children will eat quite well with neighbors, relatives, or friends, but push food away at home when faced with the continuous strain and stresses of family meals. If your youngster stops eating only at your table, is he telling you that the tension in the home is more than he can tolerate? This is his signal and you, his parent, must correct the condition within your own house.

Teenagers, particularly girls, may refuse to eat to a point that gradually escalates into a problem of extreme medical seriousness. Girls may lose weight while "dieting" to the degree that they become emaciated. Their menstrual periods cease. Their whole body goes out of balance. They are literally starving themselves to death. The term for this very serious syndrome is "anorexia nervosa." It appears to be on the increase among teenagers, particularly girls. Medical and psychiatric help are a must in these cases. Young people have been known to die from this syndrome. The problem is insidious; the signal can be missed or misinterpreted as dieting or finicky eating. These girls will lie about how much they have eaten and how much weight they have lost. What the parent must observe is the signal that the teenager has not been eating properly over a period of time, and is losing weight at an alarming rate. The other key signal is that the young person appears to be satisfied, even to enjoy this body-wasting process. Every parent of a teenager must be on the alert for such signals. Here is where a strong reaction to the child's refusal to eat signal is absolutely justified!

*   *   *

"Eat a little something" is a favorite phrase attributed to the Supermothers of our time. Too many of us eat a "big something." That too can be a signal. But the failure to eat even a "little something" must be carefully explored by parents. The common minor signals can be interpreted and dealt with by the families themselves. The rarer, serious signals, once recognized, should mobilize the parents into immediate action, asking for the expert help of others.

12

Sleeplessness

Lynn's parents were becoming increasingly worried . . . and exhausted. Their three-year-old was calling out every night about midnight, acting frightened and upset. One or both of her parents would go into her room, sit by her bed, read, talk, and tell stories until Lynn fell asleep again. During the day, the little girl played normally with all the spirit and excitement of a happy youngster. But the nights were another story. At first her parents did not know how to handle the signal. It worried them so that they both suspected the worst possible message. Was she ill? Was she worried and upset about something they didn't understand? As the sleepless nights continued, Lynn's parents' anxiety level rose to the point that they were about to take her to the family doctor.

The day before the visit, Lynn's father commented to his wife, "You know, it seems funny that she calms down just as soon as one of us sticks his head inside the door." His wife agreed. "She sounds like she's crying but I never see any tears on her face when I go in." They both looked at each other and the same idea crossed their minds. The message was coming through.

That night, Lynn's father stayed up and waited in the hallway outside the little girl's room until the usual hour approached. As anticipated, the calling out and crying began. Without turning on the light, he peered around the edge of the doorjamb. Lynn was sitting up in bed, her face an absolute mask of calm and determination, her mouth open, crying loudly without tears or apparent fright. Lynn was giving an Academy Award performance of a sleep-terrified little girl. She obviously enjoyed the late night assignations with her parents, the storytelling, the songs, the warmth of their presence. And she had found the signal to get them to her bedside.

We know this story first hand because it occurred with one of our own children. And it took over a month for us to interpret the signal properly. No matter how wise we think we are in the ways of children, we always have so much more to learn about the subtle and clever signals they send toward us.

Sleeplessness or waking up during the night can be a manipulative signal that has very positive rewards for the young child. In trying to interpret why your little one refuses to go to sleep without the endless stories, or awakens and goes to your bed, or asks to hear your weary songs at midnight, you must try to determine whether the rewards are not the total message, as it was in Lynn's case. After that night of discovery, Lynn got her stories and songs at bedtime and was strongly advised that if she awakened during the night, she should turn on her light and look at her books by herself. The midnight signals with the family storytelling sessions were at an end.

How many of you find it very difficult to go to sleep when you have had an exciting and stimulating day? Your mind races with the recollection of the incidents, conversations, confrontations, the successes and failures of the daylight hours. You toss and turn, begging sleep to overtake and replace these memories of the past day. But often sleep will not come. Children may be doing the very same thing. Repeated sleeplessness on the part of a young child may carry the message that the preceding day was too full of excitement; going to sleep is almost an impossibility. This is particularly true with youngsters when the stimulation occurs during the hours just before bedtime. If you are faced with a small child who is having sleep problems, you must carefully think through the activities that occurred just before bedtime. These should be "coming down," relaxing evening activities so that your child will be emotionally ready to drift off into an easy sleep.

Children need less sleep as they grow older. The hours that were programmed for sleep for the two-year-old are not necessary for the five-year-old. Yet families stick to the prescribed schedules forgetting that their older youngsters need fewer hours of night rest. Putting a five- or six-year-old to bed at too early an hour—eight o'clock, even nine in some cases—may cause initial sleeplessness in the child. As the tossing and turning continue, the child becomes more and more agitated and the eventual sleep may be delayed well beyond the normal time because the youngster has become angry and upset. The message in this sleeplessness signal is relatively obvious. The older the child, the later the bedtime. It must also be mentioned that as children pass through the ten-year-old period and beyond, they begin to require different amounts of sleep each night. Some older children need ten hours sleep while some can thrive quite well on eight. You must observe and know your own child, because there is no single model for a typical child any more than there is for an adult. Parents must respond to each child on an individual basis.

A school nurse was consulted by the first-grade teacher about a child who was falling asleep in class. The little girl arrived at school with circles under her eyes, looking very tired. By mid-morning, the small blond head was down on the desk and the little girl was often sound asleep. The teacher was concerned that the youngster was ill.

Before referring the girl to the school doctor, the nurse wisely asked the child herself why she was falling asleep in class. The youngster answered apologetically, "I can't sleep so good at night." "Why?" the nurse asked. "The noise" was all the little girl replied. The nurse continued her probing. "What noise?" The little girl sighed. "My older sister's room is right next to mine. And she plays her records loud every night." The nurse understood the message behind the child's school fatigue. But she wanted one more bit of information. "Why don't you call out to her or tell your parents?" The blond head shook negatively for a second, then she answered, "I do. But nobody hears me. My parents are downstairs watching the television. That's pretty loud, too. And if I come out of my room and say something, my sister gets very mad at me. So I don't."

A noisy home can keep a young child from getting the proper sleep. Parents are not necessarily thoughtless when this happens to their young child. They simply do not realize that the noise level would keep a young child awake. Often they have learned to sleep through the pulsating beat of The Grateful Dead rather than cause a teenage revolt. Happy that their teenagers are home and engaged in normal, healthy activity, the parents learn to live through the loud music. But the young child has more difficulty adjusting and needs longer hours of sleep. Parents must assess the signal of the tired child who is not sleeping well to determine if the message might be that the level of noise and excitement through which the youngster is expected to sleep is simply too great.

Adults have insomnia because of worry and tension. So do children. Bobby was not doing well in school. His grades were poor and, although he was trying, he could not seem to improve his school performance. He studied harder. He got help from his parents. But when it came time to take the tests, he made mistakes and could not finish at the same time as the other children. Soon he began to lose sleep, lying awake for long hours at night. He would arrive at school very sleepy and foggy, which only worsened his school performance. The vicious cycle of sleeplessness and poor performance escalated until Bobby was brought into our office.

Bobby was a healthy eight-year-old, but his face was sagging and his eyes were dull from lack of proper rest. We asked to talk with him alone. "Why aren't you sleeping, Bobby?" we asked. "I just can't," he replied. This was the repeated answer he had been giving his concerned parents. "Bobby, we want to help. Tell us what you are thinking about when you cannot sleep." This can be a crucial question in uncovering the message behind the sleeplessness if the child is willing to answer openly. Bobby was hesitant at first. He remained silent, his head lowered. We asked softly, "Please tell us. We want to understand so we can help you." Finally he looked up and whispered, "I think about how dumb I am. How my parents are ashamed of me 'cause I'm so dumb in school. And I worry about the tests the next day. I know I'll do bad and I think about how to stop from being so stupid." He sighed as if a heavy load had been lifted from his shoulders. The message was clear. The signal was sleeplessness—the message was worry and shame. But there were layers beneath that message that were far more complex and needed investigation before both signal and message could be cured.

Bobby was asked if we could share this with his parents. Reluctantly he agreed. His parents were not completely surprised at Bobby's worries; they had the same ones, and they needed to act upon these concerns. A complete medical and psychological work-up was scheduled to determine why Bobby was having school problems that led to his sleeplessness. The results showed that Bobby had a significant problem in visual-motor learning, known as a specific learning disability. Bobby was placed in special learning environments within the school for two hours every day. He was assigned a special Resource Teacher. His parents were given specific tasks and lessons to work on with Bobby at home. Gradually his school performance improved. But just knowing that he was not "dumb" and his parents were not "ashamed" but willing to help him improve was all that was needed to get rid of his sleeplessness. Bobby's failure to sleep was an important signal of his underlying worry and fear that had to be recognized and understood. The message and the source were very important to his future life.

Tension and concern can be the triggering message behind the sleeplessness signal. Parents must be willing to accept the fact that their child might have such worries, try to encourage the youngster to communicate these concerns, and then act upon what they hear and find.

When we asked ten-year-old Monica about her refusal to go to sleep, she stated openly, "I'm afraid to go to sleep." "Why?" we asked. "Something might happen," was all she would reply. After an hour's consultation with her parents, the key issue finally surfaced. Monica's mother broached the subject cautiously: "You keep asking if there are problems. There is one problem. Howard keeps threatening that he is going to leave me." She turned toward her husband almost apologetically as if she had broken the rules. Howard Rafferty blushed and nodded. We asked, "Has Monica heard this?" Her mother bit her lip and replied, "I don't see how she can help hearing. The fights are so loud. Almost every night." We told Monica's mother and father that the little girl was afraid to go to sleep because she feared something would happen while she slept. Now everyone in the room understood what it was Monica thought might occur—her father walking out of the house. The Raffertys were advised to seek marital counselling, to keep their arguments muted behind their bedroom door so Monica could not hear, and to try to maintain as stable a home as possible until the final marriage decisions had been made. Then, if separation was inevitable, Monica should be helped to understand and cope with the reality rather than the repeated threats.

Unusual occurrences during a child's sleep such as sleepwalking or night terrors deserve mention. Both of these sleep phenomena are usually based upon deeply embedded emotional concerns that surface during sleep. Night terrors and nightmares can bring about the sudden awakening of the child in wide-eyed fear. Often he or she cannot explain the dream or the feeling that brought about the sense of dread and terror. At these times, the youngster needs the warm, soothing arms of a parent to hold, rock, and reassure. Only if the nightmares recur frequently need the parents seek the help of the family doctor and the mental health professionals. The same is true of sleepwalking. Guiding the child back to bed and comforting the groggy youngster is all that is usually necessary. However, repeated episodes of sleepwalking deserve investigation. The message for one episode is: "I was frightened." The message for recurring ones is: "I am very upset. I need help to find out why."

A sometimes more subtle, rare, and equally disturbing sleep problem is oversleeping. In some children, this symptom may signal childhood depression. The child literally wants to "shut out" the world that gives him so much pain, and his body cooperates through sleep—lots of sleep. In rare instances, oversleeping can signal a medical problem. And in some situations the child who oversleeps may be either bored, overly scheduled, or understimulated. The family doctor is the person who quickly can tell you if your child is oversleeping and help uncover why he is sleeping too much or reassure you if he is merely following the erratic sleep patterns of a normal growing child.

As with so many other signals, repeated sleeplessness in the adolescent can be a serious signal. The message may not be easy to uncover or interpret. But the sense of the problem often is that the teenager is deeply disturbed and needs more than just parental understanding. The adolescent who recurrently has serious sleeping problems needs professional attention. This signal must not be overlooked. The reasons for the sleeping difficulty may be emotional and they could be severe.

Very often a child's signal is expressed by a youngster doing something out of the ordinary. Sleeplessness, on the contrary, emanates from the fact that the child is NOT doing something we expect. These signals must become the basis for thorough detective work by the parents.

13

Sibling Rivalry

Parents frequently watch with mounting concern as their children tease, harass, and fight with each other. The dream of having children who care deeply for each other is being shattered. These parents ultimately may come to feel that "my children seem to hate each other." So often this is the way it appears on the surface while, in reality, the youngsters are indulging in the normal family dynamics of sibling rivalry. How can a parent distinguish whether the fighting among children is within the acceptable limits or there is a signal of underlying problems?

A normal degree of competition exists between all brothers and sisters. The closer the children are in age, the greater the competition. Each child is an individual; living together under one roof will naturally cause a clash of different personalities. This occurs with adults; it certainly is the pattern with children, who are more spontaneous and less well defended. Disagreements escalate to harsh words and arguments; taking over another's territory results in physical fighting. The larger the family, the more frequently noisy battles may occur. One mother of six remarked in an exasperated voice: "There doesn't seem to be a moment's peace in our house. Just as soon as one fight is over, another one begins. I'm not a mother, I'm a referee."

What is it that prompts children in the same family to become rivals erupting into loud, abusive, physical reactions to each other?

This normal signal of sibling rivalry can be attributed to many natural factors:

1. Vying for parental attention.
2. Competing for their own physical or emotional "space" in the home.
3. Establishing their individuality.
4. Indicating that they are old enough to take care of themselves and not be bossed by an older sibling.
5. Protecting their personal possessions.
6. Coveting their own friends.
7. Forcing their ideas and opinions to be listened to and regarded.
8. Living close together for prolonged periods of time in play and family activities.

These are some of the reasons for many of the arguments that take place between siblings. They are behaviors and attitudes that require the child to be assertive, to declare himself, to defend his ideas and his "turf." Despite the fact that the parent finds this constant battlefield a tiresome and annoying place in which to live, the signal is normal and, to a degree, necessary. Beneath the surface of outward animosity and anger among children lies a deep well of caring, devotion, and respect. These attitudes will surface periodically, sometimes too seldom to satisfy the parent. But the mother and father must realize that the siblings must work through these eight points of negotiation *before* the positive qualities of sibling relationships can be seen.

When does the signal of sibling rivalry exceed the norm? When should parents begin to look carefully at the constant battles between their children and analyze, in depth, the underlying messages? It is not always a question of *frequency* that should prompt this analysis. Nor is the *intensity* of the interactions always a valuable clue. Children are volatile and physical beings; the slightest reason can lead to the loudest and most aggressive response. Sibling rivalry should be analyzed at frequent intervals by all parents to make certain that the message indicates normal sibling interaction and not something of more consequence. What could the parents detect from such an analysis that might indicate concern and the need for action?

Willis and Alvin were constantly at each other's throats. They fought verbally and physically from the moment they woke up until they fell asleep in the same room. The Craigs tried being patient with this noisy, disruptive behavior; but by the time the boys were ten and eleven years of age respectively, the parents were at the end of their rope. They simply had had enough of the continual battling. Even separating the boys into different bedrooms did not alleviate the problem. One night, the father turned to his wife and asked angrily, "What in the hell is going on here? Those boys are getting on my nerves. Why do they fight so much?" His wife shrugged. "I don't know. They seem to be competing for everything," she answered quietly. Mr. Craig lit his pipe and took several puffs. "Why, for God's sake?" Mrs. Craig smiled quickly, then assumed a neutral look. "The boys seem to feel that they are expected to compete. Don't you think so?" Her husband thought for a minute. "Is it something we're doing?" he asked finally.

Mrs. Craig knew the message. It had occurred to her during the past weeks when she had tried to think through the problem. Now was the time to help her husband understand. "I think it's something you're doing, Bill," she said softly. "Me?" He looked up sharply. "You seem to encourage the boys to compete for your attention. One has to yell louder than the other for you to hear. When you play ball with them, you talk about who played better. You compare their report cards. I know you do this to keep them on their toes, but I think it has caused them to fight to be the 'top dog.' Mr. Craig thought about his wife's observations. "I believe you're right," he said finally. The message was in front of the Craigs; the father had created an environment of such intense competition within the home that the boys carried this into every aspect of their lives.

The insidious overcompetition of intense sibling rivalry can creep up on families. Parents do not intend to foster the "oneup-manship" that leads to fighting between their children. But by means of the daily manner in which they respond to their children, they suggest that each is being compared to the other. This forces the youngsters to fight for the top position. The answer is for the parents to diminish this highly competitive attitude *in themselves* as well as in their children. The sibling fighting will then naturally decrease.

Another family faced the same problem; their thirteen-year-old son was constantly striking the eleven-year-old. This had become a real and frequent dilemma within the previous year. The boys' mother finally set her older son down and asked, "Roger, why must you always hit your brother?" The older boy tightened his lips and refused to answer. His mother continued investigating: "There doesn't seem to be any cause. You suddenly hit him for no reason." Still there was silence. "Please tell me why," she said, laying her hands over his. Finally the cracking voice of her thirteen-year-old echoed throughout the kitchen: "I feel like I just have to hit somebody. He makes me so mad. And I can't hit *him.*" Roger's mother lifted her eyebrows. "Who?" suspecting what the answer might be. "Daddy," was the telling reply.

In this case the sibling rivalry carried the message of displaced anger. Youngsters often store up their intense anger at an adult, parent, teacher, or coach. After a time, they feel they have to "handle" it. They feel that they *must* physically release, or "act out," their feelings. Often the person who receives the brunt of this displaced fury is the younger brother or sister. Sometimes the child has been harassed or teased on the playground by other children his own age but is unable to fight back. He will enter the house, bottled up with frustration and anger, and immediately let these feelings out on a younger sibling. Interpreting the message of displaced rage is very important for the parent. The youngster then can be permitted to ventilate his feelings verbally if the recipient is one of the parents. He can be shown how to circumvent the harassment if the adult is the teacher or another person outside the home. If he is being goaded by his peers, he can be taught to deal effectively with this situation after the reasons behind the teasing have been discussed. In addition, creative ways of allowing Roger to use his anger can be found. Boxing lessons, gymnastics, physical and artistic endeavors such as carpentry, sculpture, or painting will often diffuse and use the bottled-up feelings in the most positive manner. But only when the message —displaced feelings—is correctly interpreted as the reason behind the signal of Roger's sibling rivalry can the parents act in this perceptive and effective way.

Large families often experience a heightened degree of sibling rivalry. The parents of these multiple child families must ask themselves the important question: Have we permitted *each* of our children to establish his own place in the family, to be his own person? If not, then the children may be battling each other to try to create their own places. It becomes all too easy for parents who are confronted by many growing, active, demanding children to think of the children as a conglomerate body, treat them all the same, mete out the same discipline, listen to the group rather than an individual child, and instinctively regard the youngsters as "our children" rather than each one as "our child." When this occurs, the children will fight among themselves, each trying to carve out his own special piece of the family territory. The healthy large family is structured as a group of individual people. The large family with intense sibling rivalry may be structured as an indistinguishable body of "Smith children." The message in this form of sibling rivalry is the child's call to the parents: "I need my own space. I want to be known as my own person."

"They only fight around me. It's strange. When they play outside, they're fine. But when they come into the house and I'm there, the fighting begins immediately." The message in the sibling rivalry is being clearly stated in their mother's comments. She is being drawn into the children's lives by their fighting. They are creating a disturbance in order to attract her attention, to force her to notice them. The busy parent may not realize the small amount of time he or she is giving to the children, but the children are acutely aware of this. They will search for ways to bring the parent's focus back to them whenever they can. Children express themselves physically far better than they can verbally about such subtle issues as this one. Thus this mother's boys captured her undivided attention away from her housework or her caring for the younger children by creating a disturbance directly under her nose—they made very certain that they could not be overlooked. If in thinking through the signal of your children's fighting, the message is: "I need your attention," your answer can be direct and obvious—make more room for each one of them in your life.

As parents, we often carry the myth of the "perfect child" in our subconscious. At times, one of our children tries to live up to that impossible stereotype and almost fulfills our dreams. Without realizing it, we frequently cherish that child and hold the youngster up as an example before his brothers and sisters. Teachers also unthinkingly do this—with a "Teacher's pet." Watch out! That child is very likely to be the recipient of a great deal of sibling hostility, which is expressed by fighting, teasing, and occasionally, destructive reactions. You keep asking yourself, "Why do the other children always pick on Tommy?" Look at Tommy. What does he represent to your other children? Have you made him into the "model" child? Your other children are not fighting Tommy. They are battling the example that you are unknowingly forcing them to copy. As Tommy's parent, search your true feelings and analyze your behavior. Only when you stop "playing favorites" and expecting the impossible "perfect child" will the sibling rivalry in your house assume normal proportions.

Fighting and arguing is a part of normal play behavior. It appears to add some necessary spice to young relationships. Children argue, fight, and within minutes, make up and start all over again. When a youngster has a large enough circle of friends with whom to play, these normal, brief fights will be dispersed among a number of children, causing little concern to any one of them. But if your kids do not have sufficient friends, if their play outlets are limited or they must play together a good deal of the day, you can anticipate a rising level of battling noise as the day progresses.

Brothers and sisters will fight if they are forced to play together
as friends too frequently. The message in this form of sibling rivalry is the inaccessibility of other children with whom to play and
fight in normal childhood battles.

Can sibling rivalry be a serious problem? It can be when the
fighting, anger, and destructive behavior have a bad effect upon
either children or parents. The negative results of sibling rivalry
can be seen in the emotional collapse of parent or child in the face
of constant battling. Physical harm can occasionally result from
intense, precipitous, uncontrolled rivalry. When one child hurts a
brother or sister seriously in this way, the physical and emotional
scars may be long-lasting. A friend who comes from a large family
that lacked the structure of individuality among the children can
remember a car trip during which the youngsters fought and
battled constantly for parental attention. At the end of the trip, as
the car eased to a stop, the father laid his hand on the steering
wheel and cried. This is serious sibling rivalry, resulting in emotional harm to a parent. It is the degree of the rivalry, the intensity
of the battles, and the effect upon both parents and children that
escalates sibling rivalry into a serious problem. The signal is the
same. The message may be the same; but the intensity could be
destructive.

Most sibling rivalry is the normal and healthy competition between brothers and sisters, which fades but may not totally disappear in time. As our children told one of us who was red-faced and
furious at the noisy fighting going on between his children, "What
are you so excited about? This is the way we play. We're having
a good time. Why aren't you?"

Children are different kinds of people. Often we forget what it
was like to be that different as we grow older. Sometimes we have
to turn back the clock to understand why we are upset when they
are "having a good time." Are they really having a good time, or
is the sibling rivalry expressing a different message?

14

Immature Behavior

You take a good look at your child. You remember the messy rooms. The merciless teasing between your child and his brother keeps ringing in your ears. You face once again the unexpected crying over small hurts and denials. You sigh, and say to yourself, "Will he *ever* grow up?"

What do you mean when you ask that question? Do you wonder if the magic of time will help your child "outgrow" his immature behavior? Will maturity, that wonderful and mythical process, cure those bad habits? You search for the formula used by other parents to speed your child through the normal process of growing up.

Behind these concerns, however, may lurk deeper fears, nagging doubts, and feelings of foreboding. It may take a long time for a parent to admit that there is a reason for alarm. "What if my child never grows up?" "What if he remains this way, acting so much younger than he should?" "Will my child always be *immature?*"

If you as a parent suspect that your child is sending signals of immaturity, there are two immediate questions that must be answered before the situation can be dealt with. The first: "Is my child really immature, or is he just not doing what *I* expect of him?" And the second: "Why?"

How can you tell if your child is immature? You compare him

with playmates his own age. Watch him in a play group, classroom recess period, or neighborhood game. Is your child markedly different or does he seem to act the same as other children his age? You should observe him when he's with other children. Is he accepted or rejected by the other youngsters? How do the parents of other children react to your child? These adult actions often can serve as a barometer of behavior level. Put your child to a comparison test. Do *not* depend only on your own family's expectations on which to base your decision. A comparison with an older brother or sister may be unfair, since that other child may have matured more rapidly. Compare your child to his own peers. Then you will be able to judge if your child is truly immature.

Bear in mind during this comparison search that there is almost no correlation between a child's intelligence and his level of maturity. If your child is immature, he is not necessarily intellectually slow. He may be socially awkward, physically uncoordinated, or emotionally infantile, but can still be highly intelligent. You do your child a great disservice if you lower your expectations of what he or she *can* do because of his immature behavior.

Remember, also, that children mature at different rates. You cannot consider your child to be immature if you measure or compare him only one time. You must make repeated comparisons; then, if there is any doubt, consult an expert in child development or one of the many books on the subject. Give your child the benefit of usual, natural, and normal differences in rates of growth. Only when you are sure that he or she is chronically behind his or her peers should you plan decisive action.

Once you have verified the signal that your child is immature, ask yourself WHY? What messages is your immature child sending you? Is the child one who has matured slower than his peers during his entire life? Is there anything in your child's environment or his upbringing that might have caused him to mature more slowly than other kids?

If your child seems to have stopped at a level of immaturity that has lasted far too long—years—then the question becomes more complex. This signal of immaturity may be carrying several messages.

One of the messages may be a need for overdependency. This message tells you that you may not be permitting your child to grow up. And your child may be delighted to keep the home situation just the way it is.

Tad was a child in an overdependent family situation that resulted in his immaturity.

Tad was small for his age, often being taken for an eight-year-old even though he was eleven. His stature, however, was not the only reason why Tad's age was misjudged. He *acted* like an eight-year-old. He could not sleep at night without an open door. He was afraid of being left with babysitters. He cried easily if his mother did not buy him what he wanted at the drugstore. He was an extremely finicky eater; his parents often shopped for hours to find the foods that he would eat. All of Tad's friends were eight- and nine-year-olds, even though his neighborhood was full of children of all ages.

Tad's parents had two other children, both older. His older brother and sister had not acted like Tad when they were his age. Tad's parents did not see any of the other eleven-year-olds in the neighborhood acting like Tad. They kept hoping that he would outgrow his immature behavior; but as the months passed, it became obvious he was not improving.

They finally sought help, but only after an embarrassing dinner party at a neighbor's where Tad had drawn so much attention to himself by complaining about the food that he had to be physically removed and carried to the car, crying loudly. The noisy scene had ruined the evening for everyone. Tad's parents knew that they would never be invited again to the neighbor's home if it meant including their immature, foul-tempered youngster.

"What can we do?" they asked in desperation. "We give him everything he needs plus all our love. And he loves us, too. He tells us so all the time. Why can't he be as wonderful to everyone else as he is to us?"

"What do you mean when you say that Tad is 'wonderful' to you?" the parents were asked. Their answer was one of classic overdependency. Tad was, indeed, seen as "wonderful" by his parents. He was openly affectionate with them, spending many hours each evening on their laps, talking to them and having them read stories to him.

"On your laps?" they were asked.

"Well, he got used to it. He was very ill when he was five years old and was in the hospital for three months. I guess it just became a habit since then to hold him and rock him," his mother answered.

"Whose habit?" was the next question. They looked quizzically at each other.

Finally, Tad's father answered, "Ours, I guess."

Tad had not matured because he did not need to grow up. Indeed, he was being encouraged *not* to grow up. He was the youngest child and he was a delicate child. If, and when, he grew up and left his parents, he would be leaving two adults without the main focus upon which they had invested all their time and energy. They would be forced to turn to each other. Possibly this frightened them. Both parents and child wanted Tad to stay young forever—and Tad was trying very hard to meet this subliminal desire. The three of them were caught in an overdependency triangle.

It took many counselling sessions with Tad's parents to show them how their needs for a perpetual "little boy" were helping to keep Tad immature. Once they had agreed to try to break their overdependency activities, it took them—and Tad—many more sessions to change Tad's behavior. He slowly had to substitute responsibility for dependency and reasonable behavior for impulsivity. Tad's parents led the way and, gradually, Tad followed them into maturity. They all worked hard, and today Tad is an independent college student studying engineering at a school several hundred miles from home.

Another signal of immaturity carries a one-way message that comes from one or both parents. It is not a message of dependency; it is really a subtle sign from parent to child that the parent can deal better with a younger child. Whatever the underlying reasons, the message received by the youngster is: "Life is easier for me if you remain young and immature." This parental message is usually neither overt nor obvious. Rarely is the message even realized by parents who, if confronted, will deny vehemently that they have signalled their need for an immature child.

A friend of the authors grew up in this type of home. He has talked often about what can happen when the parents want their children to remain young.

Our friend's father was a creative lawyer who worked very long hours and left much of the child-rearing to his wife, a caring and loving mother, but a woman with a personality peculiarly suited to creating immaturity in her five children. She was the most highly acclaimed kindergarten teacher in the state. Her personality developed in line with that distinction.

When our friend's mother taught, there was no limit to her ingenuity and creativity with five-year-old children. She was often given the most bizarre types of children and family situations in the entire school system, and she invariably succeeded in helping these children begin to reach self-satisfaction and a successful level of achievement. Frequently, it was her stimulation and guidance that dramatically influenced their whole lives.

To accomplish these miracles, however, this woman thought, acted, and lived like a five-year-old. She seemed to need to absorb that lifestyle in order to be such a sensitive and superb teacher. Because she related to all children, no matter what their ages, in the same way as she did to her kindergarteners, she held back the emotional growth of her own five children.

Most of them remained immature far into their pre-teen years.

In talking with our friend, we found that he could recall the terrible anxieties of realizing his own immaturities as he approached adolescence—the lack of preparation for sexual maturity; the inability to understand, and then defend against, being hurt by other children; the realization that a rainbow could never be touched; the painful discovery that the events in the world often did *not* have happy endings. Mature children shunned him and his brothers and sisters because of their unrealistic viewpoints. Their creativity went unnoticed by others. Each of the children went through periods of great loneliness as he or she finally realized that they were going to have to mature without the help of a parent. They clung together, but as children they were still vulnerable to the outside adult world. They finally matured—but not without scars.

Parents who consciously try to keep their children young are rare. Often the message to stay young is given only to the youngest child. But whenever it is given, the message signifies that the parent has not faced the inevitable—children must grow up and eventually grow away. If a child continues the pattern of immaturity, a parent must ask whether he or she is contributing to that state. Is there "something in it for me," something the parent is gaining emotionally by the child's immaturity? The parent may be unconsciously feeding the youngster's immature behavior by becoming overly concerned or involved with his or her child. In reality, the parent is fulfilling his own needs. Once the parent recognizes this, it becomes his responsibility to correct his or her child-rearing practices and guide the child into meeting the normal standards of each age group.

An ironic and paradoxical fact about immaturity in youngsters is that it also can be fostered by a situation in which a parent is trying desperately to accelerate his child's maturity. This is the situation where the child uses the signal of immaturity to send a message to the overzealous parent.

Several friends of the authors, believing that cultural exposure was beneficial for children, coaxed their children to attend many cultural events with them such as opera, theater, dance, and art museums when the children were quite young. These parents spent large sums of money to enrich and expand their children's cultural horizons. The performances and exhibits often were not explained beforehand to the children, who therefore became bored and resentful. How could the children tell their parents that they could not understand, or even tolerate, these unfamiliar events? Immature behavior was the obvious answer. They pouted about having to go. They became petulant and moody at the concerts. They became easily distractible and giggled during the performances. When the young children were forced to remain in their seats, they even threw temper tantrums. Finally, realizing the failure of their efforts, the parents sadly discontinued their cultural expeditions. They asked us what had gone wrong and why their children behaved in such an immature way.

The answer to this signal of immaturity lay not in the effort but in the preparation. Time and energy should have been expended in preparing the children for the cultural events, which should also have been held down to a reasonable number. If this had been done, the children might have been truly stimulated and enriched. Because of poor planning, however, they were forced into an action—and a signal—of immaturity. Through their immature behavior, these children controlled their parents' actions. They paced and limited the cultural exposure. Immaturity was the exact opposite of what the parents were striving for in their children. In this instance, and in many similar situations where children are pushed beyond their physical or emotional limits, immaturity becomes an *almost* conscious way of signalling and controlling the problem. Immature behavior by the child becomes a weapon in the parent-child struggles for dominance in specific areas where there is disagreement about lifestyles. When parents recognize this signal, they must seek the message and correct the situation in which they are being "controlled." Parents must listen to the hidden words in the immature behavior pattern. Then they can discuss the basic situation with their child and act upon the *real* problem, which is not, in this case, immaturity. The immature behavior is only the signal. The message is far more subtle.

Sometimes the message behind immaturity is that the child has had no opportunities and no experiences with which to grow. A child with a chronic illness who has been confined to his bed or been in a hospital for a long period of time is prone to develop this signal. The child who has no playmates of her own age is also susceptible. These children may be deprived of the experiences and role models necessary for their normal progress into mature behavior.

When the child is signalling this message, the parents should seek peer models. Neighborhood play groups, a religious school, youth groups, playgrounds, even children's books can provide the stimulus for a child to mature. Children may have to be firmly pushed into these group situations, but pushed they must be! Adjustment as a mature adult depends upon the success of such experiences.

Parents are often alarmed at immaturity which suddenly appears after the child has demonstrated a normal level of mature behavior. This is called "regression" and can be defined as immature behavior that reappears after the child has grown out of it.

A small degree of regressive immaturity can be expected of any child and may be viewed as relatively normal. Almost every parent of a new baby knows that the older child probably will exhibit immaturity when the new baby is brought into the home. The older child may start bedwetting again, sucking his thumb, or having temper tantrums. The wise parent knows that the child is merely trying to compete with the baby for parental attention. The child feels the need to signal that he still requires the attention he was getting before the new baby arrived. Parents should help the child to substitute mature behavior, which earns acceptance and praise, such as helping to care for the lawn or prepare the meals. Signals of regressive immaturity can be just fleeting problems if the parents anticipate and understand the older child's reaction. Acting in a positive way to reward the child's *mature* behavior is the key to silencing this signal.

Immaturity of a regressive type becomes more of a problem to parents, however, when it is a signal from a child who has retreated from a situation with which he or she cannot cope. If a death occurs in the immediate family, a situation most children have not previously faced, a temporary immaturity may suddenly emerge. If a child continually faces a hostile environment, such as an overbearing or punitive teacher in school, or abusive playmates, he or she may slip into immature behavior. The child may be signalling that he is retreating to a period in his life when he felt more comfortable and safer and did not have to cope with these threatening situations. Also he may be signalling his parents for help. He needs an ally, someone to explain or intervene. So the signal is his cry for the parent's comforting hand.

Regressive immaturity is often found in adolescents, who are continually faced with the need to solve problems of increasing complexity and with greater personal consequences. When these problems seem to become too difficult to solve, the adolescent may react in an immature manner—so immature that the parents are astounded. These adolescents are sending the message: "Please help me; I can't cope with this problem by myself!"

Melanie Singer knew that she was much slower than her other friends in maturing physically. At thirteen, she was just beginning to notice the budding of her breasts. Because she was later in starting the typical adolescent growth spurt, Melanie was also smaller and more boyish in her overall appearance. Her parents began to notice that the phone was ringing much less often than it had during previous years, when Melanie was chattering constantly with the other girls. Now she rarely received a phone call or made one to the other girls. One day, Melanie's eleven-year-old sister stormed into the house and confronted her mother in the kitchen. "Mother, you're going to have to talk to Melanie. She's horning in on all our games." Mrs. Singer looked puzzled. "I don't understand," she said. Her youngest daughter stood with her hands pushed against her hips, her feet widely spread apart, and bellowed, "She won't let me have any of my own friends. Lately all she wants to do is play with us. It's not fair, Mother! She's older. And she always wins. Besides, I don't want her there. They're *my* friends." The Singers talked after dinner. They had not noticed the immature regression of their older daughter. Suddenly the past few months came into focus; the lack of phone calls, the weekends without girlfriends sleeping over, Melanie's refusal to stay after school for extracurricular clubs. "You know," Ben Singer remarked to his wife, "now that I think about it, Melanie seems almost younger than Beth at times."

Gloria Singer sat down with Melanie the next evening and said tactfully, "I haven't seen any of the girls around here lately." Melanie looked down at the floor, her face blushing. "Is anything the matter?" her mother asked softly. Melanie nodded, her face averted. "Do you want to tell me about it?" Melanie looked up, her face a canvas of misery. "They don't want to play with me," she said plaintively. "Why?" her mother asked. "Because I look like such a baby. You know . . ." Melanie's voice trailed off as her hand lightly brushed against her small breasts. "Did they say so?" the mother asked. Melanie shrugged. "No," she sighed. "Then how do you know?" her mother probed. "Well," the young girl grumbled, "they look at me in gym class kinda funny. And they're always talking about bras and periods and things I can't talk about." Her mother nodded seriously. "So you just figured that they wouldn't want to have you around. Because you couldn't tell them about those things?" Melanie nodded sadly.

Gloria Singer had picked up the signal but not the message. It had to be pointed out to her by her younger daughter. But once the signal was received, she wisely investigated through sensitive questioning for the underlying message. Melanie was waiting for help to be extended to her. The young girl simply could not be the one to call attention to her problem in the ordinary way. So she used the signal of immature behavior. Gloria Singer was able to tell her daughter about her own feelings when she was in her early teens. She reassured Melanie that time would cure her delayed sexual maturation. In looking at Melanie's reaction to her slowly developing body, both mother and daughter were able to discover that most of the concern about friendships was of Melanie's own making and the alienation from her friends was more imaginary than real. Melanie tested her friends' responses to her and, to her surprise, the other girls were quite pleased that she was coming back into contact with them. "We wondered what was bugging you, Mel," her best friend told her. "We just figured you were getting snobby." Life returned to its normal chaotic teen pace for Melanie; and within months she had the same things to talk about and compare as her friends. The Singers had responded to Melanie's signal of immature behavior in time. One wonders what would have happened to the young girl's self-esteem and friendships if the parents had failed to interpret and act upon the signal with tact and speed.

Are regressive immaturities unrealistic? Yes, as Melanie's case demonstrates. Unexpected? No. Dangerous? Only if they continue for long periods or seem to remove the child so far from parents or friends that his social abilities become impaired and he drifts away from his social world. If an immature adolescent loses friends and retreats into himself unexpectedly and for a prolonged period, parents must seek professional help. Together the professional and the parents can look for the situation that is frightening the child into serious immaturity. They must seek methods of helping the adolescent solve his major problems. Both parents and adolescents, caught in a serious situation of sudden adolescent immaturity, may need the help of a counsellor or psychotherapist.

Parents tend to think of maturation as a steady path of progress throughout the life of a child. In fact the path of maturity is far from smooth and easy for any child. There are starts and stops, giant steps forward and baby steps backwards. At one age, the child exhibits one type of action; at a later age, those actions are given up for more adult-like behavior. Any suspected immaturity is a signal to watch—and wait. We expect our children to move forward through life and grow into mature adulthood. If your child is standing still, marching in place, the time to deal with the signal is *now*. Every moment lost may never be regained.

15

School Phobia

Children can signal their fear of going to school in many different ways. One youngster may balk at leaving the house to get on the school bus. Another may express constant imaginary fears about what will happen to him in school. At times, fantasy tales about school incidents are used by the child in an attempt to avoid going to school. Many children will feign illness to stay home on a school day. Others play "hookey," preferring the truancy risk. Some children actually go to school but retreat from the situation while they are there, drifting into daydreaming or "forgetting" to go to class when the change bell rings. The signal of school phobia can be obvious, loud and physical, or it may be subtle and cloaked in many disguises. But no matter what the cover, the primary message is: "I don't want to go to or be in school."

A child's education is one of the most important parts of his or her life. The question that must be faced in each case of school phobia is "What is the message behind the signal?" What is your child telling you that makes him or her different from the other children on the block who skip off to school every day without a whimper or a complaint? What is happening at school that the child fears, can't face, won't accept?

Mrs. Thornton brought four-and-a-half-year-old Rodney into the office for his preschool physical early in the summer. As she entered the room, her son was clinging to her skirt, hiding his face in its folds. Rodney, her fourth child, had arrived somewhat late in her life, almost six years after his next oldest brother. It was not easy separating the young boy from his mother; but after much gentle persuasion, he allowed himself to be examined. Rodney was a physically healthy young boy. But he was giving a warning of trouble to come—over-attachment. Mrs. Thornton was relieved to learn that her son was in good physical health. As she rose to leave, she was stopped by the following question: "Do you expect problems with Rodney when he starts school in the fall?" She sat down again, her expression one of welcome recognition. "Yes. I do." "Why?" Mrs. Thornton looked quickly at her son, pressed up against her side, and answered, "Rodney never seems to let me out of his sight. I can't go anywhere without him. I don't know how he'll leave me to go to school." She paused and waited for a reply. "What do you do to encourage him to be apart from you?" was the next question. She looked down at her hands. "Not too much. All of the other children are gone most of the day. So Rodney and I do most everything together. I think he needs me because he's so young and afraid of other children."

Rodney was a clear case of "school phobia" in the making. There was little question that he would be very reluctant to separate from his mother and enter the strange environment of the schoolroom. The message behind the signal was contained in Mrs. Thornton's own description. But the question took on a somewhat different phrasing. In this situation, who needed whom?

One of the most common causes of school fears in the young child is concern over separation from a parent to whom the child has become overly attached. Often the message that lies just beneath the surface of the parent-child relationship is simply fear of the unknown—school is an alien planet! "I know you are going to miss me . . . be afraid of being without me . . . want to leave school and come back into the protective cocoon of my arms." Children respond very definitively to these messages. They behave in the way they *think* they are expected to behave. Subconsciously this mother has been communicating her own concern about "losing" her child to the "foreign" school environment, relinquishing her dominant influence in her child's life to some strange person known as "teacher." The child may feel guilty if he or she leaves for school without looking back longingly at the parent who unwittingly has planted the seeds of separation fear in the child. School phobia allows the child to notify the parent that the separation is as painful for him or her as it obviously is for the mother.

Who really has the school phobia in such cases? Who is giving off the signals? The parent often is the first to force dependence on the child and fear of separation. The child returns the signal, having easily deciphered the parent's message. In the child's case, the signal is usually less subtle. A crying, screaming, kicking, retreating reluctance to leave for school clearly expresses the strength and need of the close and continuing parent-child relationship.

How can Mrs. Thornton prevent Rodney from developing school phobia signals? First she must recognize and accept her role in the creation of an overly interdependent relationship with her son. Next, she should begin to encourage the boy to spend more time away from her, indicating that she has her own life, separate from his. She must have the confidence that he can manage without her. To do this, she will have to be willing to do things without her son. In addition, Mrs. Thornton will have to find other children Rodney's age with whom he can play. At first, the youngster will balk, retreat, cry, and attempt to run back to the protective cover of his mother's skirts; but Mrs. Thornton must persist, letting her son know that she wants—and expects—him to play with his peers. Finally, several exploratory visits to the new school, prior to the opening, will help the shy, frightened youngster accept leaving his mother to go to school.

Many parents do not have this opportunity to prevent school phobia as Mrs. Thornton did. A child may suddenly and unexpectedly rebel during the first days of school. The signal may be the same. So may the message: separation fear. Something dramatic must be done. First, get the youngster back in school. The absences will only reinforce the fear; staying home provides the reward of added attention. Accompanying your youngster to school and staying for brief periods *may* help at first, but the ultimate goal is rapid and complete separation of parent and child during the school day. Pushing the fledgling out of the nest is one way to describe what is needed. The child must be made to understand, to *believe* that he can function satisfactorily on his own. Also he must realize that his parents can—and must—manage without him during school hours. This is part of the youngster's necessary emotional growth. A child cannot grow into a self-sufficient adult if he or she is paralyzed by dependency on a parent. Breaking the dependency cycle by correctly interpreting the message behind the signal of school phobia is a major step in the child's successful growing-up process.

Nathan had had no difficulty going to the first grade. He had adjusted well to both teacher and classmates. So it was a surprise when he began crying during class one month in the second grade and begged his teacher to let him go home. She refused, but comforted him and convinced him to finish out the day. Nathan did little work and was falling behind the other children. His teacher finally called his parents to school.

Only Nathan's mother came for the scheduled appointment. The boy's teacher inquired about the father. "Is he working?" Nathan's mother shook her head. "Oh, no. His own father, Nathan's grandfather, is very ill and he has to go to the hospital every day. We're not sure he's going to pull through." Nathan's teacher caught the message and asked, "What does Nathan think about all this?" The boy's mother frowned for a minute before answering, "I don't think he knows. He worships his grandfather. We told Nathan that he was away on a trip." The teacher nodded. "Do you know why I called you to school?" Nathan's mother shook her head. "No, but we've been so preoccupied. . . ." her voice trailed off. The teacher studied her hands for a few seconds. "Nathan has been crying to go home every day. When I make him stay here, he starts daydreaming and doesn't do his work. He seems like such a worried child." "Worried? Nathan? What could he be worried about?" The boy's teacher smiled weakly and answered, "Probably the same thing you and your husband are worried about. His grandfather. I wonder if Nathan suspects but is afraid to ask."

This perceptive teacher had listened to the brief conversation and quickly found the message behind Nathan's sudden school fear. Children who have family illness or turmoil in the home often fear separation from the painful situation and develop school phobia. They feel that something terrible will happen if they are gone from the home; they almost feel that they might be able to prevent bad things from happening if they are present. Nathan was terrified that his grandfather would die when he was away. Fear of death when there has been recent illness or death within a family often triggers real fears in a young child, fears that more terrible events will take place during his or her school absence. Parental fighting, verbal or physical, frequently creates a feeling of dread that one or both will leave or do the other harm while the child is in school. Very often, parents think that they have successfully hidden the tragedy or turmoil from the child. In fact this is extremely hard to do; the home usually reverberates with tension and whispered worries. Few children are so insensitive that they cannot pick up the vibrations of impending family disaster. No wonder that they fight the idea of leaving this time bomb to go to school, not knowing what might happen while they are gone.

Honesty is truly the best and only policy here. Attempting to hide the obvious from the sharp eyes and ears of a youngster is usually futile. Too frequently the youngster focuses on parts of the situation which are magnified out of proportion, or from which the wrong conclusions are drawn. A visit to the hospital for a check-up of a benign breast lump may easily be interpreted by the child as impending physical disaster to the mother; a family argument over monthly bills could lead to a child worrying about divorce. It is far better to level with the child, using common sense, tact, and words the youngster can understand. After an episode of death in the family, the child often needs reassurance that all others in the family are well. If divorce or separation does in fact occur, the youngster should have the parent's firm declaration that no one else will suddenly "move away and out" of the child's life. These are real worries and must be dealt with. When illness occurs, the child can frequently cope with his realistic fears by being permitted to call home or the hospital at reasonable intervals while he is in school. This is a recognition of the basic reasons behind the signal of school phobia and sensitively assists the child in dealing with his honest concerns. Often it is the school phobia which signals that your child knows and is deeply concerned about major family problems. In fact, the fear of remaining in school may be your *only* signal. That is why it becomes vital for each parent to assess the message behind a young child's sudden fear of school carefully and quickly.

Sometimes what is happening at home is neither trauma nor turmoil but the competition that the older child feels about leaving a younger sibling to monopolize parental attention. In this instance, the child is giving the parents two simultaneous signals, school phobia and intense sibling rivalry. The attention paid to solving the rivalry will settle the school phobia at the same time.

The situation at home may not be the real reason for the child's fear of school. If there does not appear to be a rational reason within the home to explain your child's reluctance to be in school, then a careful look at what's happening at school is definitely in order. The problem may rest within the school itself.

It would be comforting to believe that all teachers are warm, understanding, perceptive, and tolerant individuals. Teachers, like other professionals, are human, fallible and varied. If your child fears school, the problem *may* rest squarely on the teacher's shoulders. She or he may be a thorough, caring, and excellent teacher but a person who approaches life very differently from you. The environment of a teacher's classroom may be the opposite of the atmosphere in your home. Usually the child from the very relaxed, permissive home finds the strict, regulated demands of more rigid teachers a difficult situation to live with. Should the teacher be asked to change her or his classroom to fit your child? Hardly. But the teacher can be requested to understand why your child is unhappy—how the two environments differ and how to reduce the fear and discomfort your child is feeling. You, too, must play a role. Reassess the home situation. Are more rules needed to help your child begin to cope with the realities of a structured, demanding outside world? *Together* the parent and teacher can work toward a compatibility of home and school that does not undermine the basic philosophies of either. This will go a long way toward erasing the fear of school in this child.

On the other hand, the teacher may NOT be an individual who can change. She or he may be overly strict and punitive, play favorites, and create an atmosphere that encourages school fear. If you visit the classroom and discover this to be the case, fight like the devil to get your child placed in another room. If this proves impossible, give your child all possible emotional support to remain in the classroom and finish the year successfully. When a child can share the burden of the unfair or inadequate teacher with his or her parents, he has an ally and need no longer give off the signal of school phobia.

Beginning with the third week in the fourth grade, Billy began to refuse to go to school. He concocted all kinds of reasons and finally, out of desperation, began to complain of daily physical ailments. His parents brought him in for a physical check-up to make certain he was not ill. On examination, Billy was found to be healthy, a small and wiry boy. "What's the story with school?" "I just don't want to go," he answered timidly. "Why?" He made a face and pressed his lips together. "Are you worried about anything at home?" he was asked. He shook his head. "Problems in school?" He did not respond, but sat silently, his face turned away, staring out of the window. "Why can't you talk about it, Billy?" He sighed. "Because I don't want my father to know." Billy frowned. "Would he get angry?" we pressed gently. He shook his head. "No. But he would be ashamed." After much coaxing, Billy finally blurted out, "I'm afraid to go. This kid in my class keeps beating up on me at recess. And he's so much bigger than me. I'm scared of him. And my dad always tells me to fight back." He paused, then in a plaintive voice added, "But I can't. He'd beat me up worse."

Billy was afraid of going to school because he was being attacked by the class bully. This can happen in school or on the way to or from school. It was difficult for Billy to share the facts with his parents; he felt embarrassed because he could not defend himself. But the reality was that the other boy was older and bigger and Billy did not stand a chance. This can be the message of a school phobia in a youngster—the physical or verbal abuse (teasing) that he is receiving from another child or group of children in the school. After explaining that his father would accept and understand, Billy allowed us to share this information with his parents. Once they understood the message behind his school fear signal, they acted swiftly and intelligently. They asked the school to pay attention to what was going on, particularly in recess and play periods. In addition, they made a personal visit to the other boy's home, tactfully requesting the help of his parents in solving the problem. Billy's dad also bought boxing gloves for Billy and himself, and together they practiced every Saturday morning. Billy's confidence in his ability to defend himself rose; the attacks in school stopped; the school fear disappeared.

Billy's case illustrates how other children can cause a younger child to send a signal when he is suddenly reluctant or fearful to go to school.

The only child often has a difficult time adjusting to the school experience because an only child is usually not a group person. Friendships with another child can be very close, but intermingling within a peer group may not come easily. Children of large families already have their child "group" built into their lives, but school may be the first such adventure for the only child. As a result the youngster feels shy and awkward and may tend to retreat into dark corners of the classroom or attempt to stay at home to avoid the "sudden mob scene." Parents of only children can prevent this signal from developing by making certain that their youngster has frequent and diverse contacts with other children

during the preschool years. If the only child's social contacts have
been overlooked and the child signals a school fear, then the wise
parent must interpret this message of "aloneness" and begin
working with the child to broaden her or his social skills and
friendships. Inviting a classmate to dinner or for a weekend often
creates a friendship that buffers the only child from awkwardness
in the group situation. After this relationship flowers, adding more
youngsters to the only child's circle of friends is necessary and can
be facilitated through parties, projects, and vacation trips with
friends. The school can help by drawing in the only child during
class group activities, which then might spill over into the recess
yard and soften the child's social rough edges. Only children are
frequently signalling parents about very special concerns. This is
one of them. If yours is an only child, *prevent* this signal from
happening. If it occurs, act upon the signal with wisdom to help
your child solve his or her problem.

Ellie was a happy and radiant kindergarten child. Mrs. Foster
was repeatedly told by the classroom teacher that she wished all
her youngsters were as well adjusted as Ellie. But something serious began to happen in the first grade. At first, Ellie began to
grumble about going to school; she refused to talk about her day
when she came home. Her parents were concerned. Just a year
before, she had exploded with delight after each school day, bubbling up with excitement. Now they were facing sullen silence.
Possibly a "phase," Ellie's father consoled himself. "Let's not get
too excited. We'll wait and see," he reassured his wife as they
talked each night, worrying about the problem. Ellie's report card
was brought home, accompanied by a flood of tears. The grades
were less than Ellie's parents had expected; Ellie herself was embarrassed and frustrated. "Should we go to the school?" Ellie's
mother asked the first grader. Ellie stamped her foot and cried,
"No." Fearful of upsetting her more, the parents stayed away.
Finally the year was over. Miraculously Ellie's mood swung to one
of elation and contentment. All through the summer, the Fosters
thought their daughter had returned from a very negative phase

in her life and were quietly thankful. But, as school approached, the sullenness recurred. By the first day of school, Ellie had become uncommunicative; she hid her head under the pillow when her mother went in to get her out of bed on that opening school morning. She pulled at the covers and refused to get out of bed. Her sobs awoke every member of the family. The Fosters let Ellie stay home from school that day. Instead, they went themselves.

In talking with her first-grade teacher, Ellie's parents received a severe shock. The kindly woman tried to tell them as tactfully as possible that Ellie wasn't as bright as the other children. "She tested below the others. She can't seem to grasp the work. Ellie never finishes her papers." These words were devastating to the Fosters. All they could say was, "But we think she's a very bright little girl." The teacher smiled tolerantly and shook her head. "I know she must be frustrated in school. All of the other children are moving so far ahead of her."

Ellie's parents now had the message behind their daughter's signal of school phobia. She did not want to face the humiliation of classroom failure day after day. They could have accepted the teacher's off-hand diagnosis and allowed Ellie to end eventually in a class for slow learners where she would have languished, hating school more every day. But they could not believe that this was all there was to her signal and the message given them by the teacher. The Fosters requested meetings with the school psychologist, who tested their daughter. After hearing his report, they consulted a private psychologist who confirmed the first opinion. Ellie was, indeed, a bright youngster; but she had a serious visual-motor perceptual problem requiring her to take longer than her classmates to put the pieces of written information together. She could learn the same and possibly more, but she needed special help. The Fosters saw to it that Ellie got this help.

The next step was to convince Ellie that she was not as "dumb" as she thought. Her parents worked with her to share positively in her successes and to stimulate her gently to try again after her failures. Gradually Ellie began to take hope that she could succeed in school. This discovery changed her hatred of school to a feeling of challenge and expectation.

As in Ellie's case, school phobia may be the first sign of a specific learning disorder where the competent child is unable to work successfully at the same level of performance as the other children. Frustration with daily inadequacies builds up hostility and antipathy toward school until the child finally rebels, gives up, and refuses to return to the site of failure one more time. Ellie's parents could have stopped short of fully realizing what Ellie was signalling by her refusal to go to school. If they had not followed through on her message, Ellie might have been relegated to a future of potential educational oblivion.

Every child loves a day or two of vacation from the rigors and regimentation of school. Warm, balmy days encourage wistful thoughts; snow-covered streets invite longings for sleds and laughter. But when the child rejects the total concept of attending school, he is sending off a signal that cannot be ignored.

16

Failing in School

Children become paralyzed by failure—they begin to doubt their ability to deal with everyday situations. Embarrassment and shame overtake them; and they react in many unusual ways, by acting out, denial, or depression. The young boy suddenly becomes the old man, beset by worries, body sagging, face drawn, voice low and soft, vitality and energy ebbed. The mirror reflects back an image that has very little value, a nobody, a cipher, a failure. Few things in life can sap the flowing enthusiasm of youth as dramatically as school failure. A potential "somebody" slides into a defeated nobody, gives up, and sinks into a life of self-hate and withdrawal as failure piles upon failure.

The same despair often overtakes parents as they stare at the report card that announces their child's school failure. Suddenly he or she loses their esteem. Maybe he isn't as smart as we thought, flashes across their minds. Subconsciously they begin treating him differently, remembering the weaknesses on the piece of paper rather than recalling his many strong points. The child senses this subtle change, which only reinforces her or his own lack of self-worth. He or she drifts further and further away from parents until they are beyond shouting distance. But words should not be necessary at this time; the signal has been flashed. *The time for action is now.* Your child has failed. You cannot accept this failure as an indictment, a final statement of your child's abilities or worth. This is not the end but the beginning: the school failure is the signal to start work. Both parents and child must energize and activate every bit of their strength and investigative ability in order to decode the serious messages behind this failure.

Jeremy was unable to keep up with his classmates in the first grade. The teacher called his parents in for a consultation and advised them to allow him to repeat the first grade. Mrs. Britton sat stunned. "You mean Jeremy is going to fail the first grade?" she whispered in disbelief. Mr. Britton began to lower his eyelids, preparing to fight this decision. Jeremy's teacher smiled gently and commented, "I don't think we ought to look at this as a failure." Mr. Britton shook his head sharply. "What is it then? Holding him back is the same thing as failing. Only your fancy educational words for the same thing." The teacher nodded her head easily. "I understand how you feel. But Jeremy cannot keep up with the other children." Jeremy's mother frowned. "Are you trying to tell us that Jeremy is stupid?" The teacher looked up in surprise. "Oh, no, not at all. I'm sorry if I gave you that impression. Actually I think Jeremy is at least average if not far brighter than that." She waited. The teacher wanted the parents to read the signal and uncover the message with her so that they could work together during the following year. Mr. Britton leaned forward. "Then what is the problem?" he asked, relieved but curious. The teacher thought for a moment. "Jeremy seems younger than the other children," she said simply. "But he is," Mrs. Britton exploded. "He was a November baby. Most of the other children are months older than Jeremy." The teacher smiled. "Well, that might explain it. Do you think that could be the problem?"

The Brittons sat quietly for a few minutes. Finally Jeremy's mother returned the teacher's smile. "Of course. Now that I think about it, Jeremy plays with younger children. I guess he just wasn't ready for the first grade." Jeremy's teacher sighed. "I agree. Next year he probably will be. And isn't it better for him to feel like he is succeeding rather than always falling behind the others?" Mrs. Britton nodded. "But he'll be losing a whole year," Mr. Britton made a final stab at rebuttal. The teacher said quietly, "I guess we have to decide which is more important to Jeremy. Waiting a year or moving ahead to certain frustration next year. And maybe all of the years ahead." The Brittons thought for several minutes. Finally Mr. Britton, glancing at his wife, replied, "We want you to keep him back. It's the best thing for him. But let us know how to help you next year." The teacher assured them that she would. Jeremy's parents left the school understanding the message in Jeremy's failure. They were prepared to accept, observe, and help their son because of the sensitive manner in which Jeremy's teacher had worked with them. Alas, not all teachers are as patient, perceptive, and cooperative as Jeremy's.

If your young child is doing poorly in the early grades, it may be necessary for you, as the parent, to interpret the message behind his inadequate performance. The first question that you must ask yourself is: Was he ready for school? Was she too young for the pace of the other children? Would repeating an early grade allow him to develop the educational and emotional maturity to taste the success of learning? *You* know your child better than anyone else. You observe the level of her activities, the age of her friends, the comparison between him and other children. There is no one better prepared to make that decision than you. But honesty and clear vision are needed to admit that your child entered the school situation prematurely and needs the "catching-up time" so that he or she can avoid failure in the future. The signal of failure may be frightening, but the message and the action may simply be one of delay, patience, and better home preparation for what is expected in school.

Gail did well in the first grade. She loved school and her report cards reflected her enthusiasm. But her first report card in the second grade indicated that she was failing. She had been rather quiet about her school experience during the fall months that year, and her parents had assumed that she was doing reasonably well. They became distraught when she timidly handed them the poor report card. "What's going on?" her father bellowed. Gail began to cry and ran into her room. "Take it easy, John," her mother said calmly. "Let's try to find out what's happening. Something is very wrong and we don't know what it is." The irate man frowned and settled back into the dining room chair, trying to ease his anger. Gail's mother called her into the dining room again. The girl entered very slowly, glancing apprehensively toward her father. He moistened his lips and spoke to her in a quiet voice: "Gail, we know you can do better than this. What is the problem in school?" The little girl looked down at the carpet and mumbled, "She hates me." "Who?" her father asked. Gail looked up into her father's face, her eyes seeking his understanding. "The teacher," she said in a low voice. As they began to talk, Gail poured out her feelings of anger and frustration at her new teacher. It became obvious to her parents that the teacher and their daughter were not getting along. "She punishes me for everything. Even when I talk," Gail said bitterly. The parents learned that Gail was spending a good deal of time in the hall outside of class because she chatted frequently with her neighbors; and when she was allowed to return, the teacher often ignored her for long periods of time. Gail admitted that "I just don't want to do anything for that woman." Gail had given her parents the definitive message behind her school failure. She disliked her teacher and had been punishing the woman by refusing to try to learn in her class.

Conflicts with the teacher can be a very real cause of school failure in the young child. Even the older child may react negatively to a teacher to the point of doing poorly in class. Gail's parents went to school and met the teacher. She was a strict disciplinarian, who would not tolerate the ebullient, spontaneous behavior of their daughter. The teacher agreed that Gail might do better work in the other second-grade class. She made this recommendation to the principal, who shifted Gail to another classroom. But Gail's teacher warned the parents that Gail would have to learn some self-control if she was to get along in any other teacher's classroom. She told them she was suggesting the shift only because she felt that the tensions between Gail and herself might take longer to correct than was advisable considering Gail's loss of several weeks' work. Gail's parents discussed with their daughter the changes that she had to make to prevent the same thing from happening in the new classroom. Gail grudgingly agreed. The next report card was considerably better; these parents had followed through on Gail's signal and after working through the uncovered message with the school, had been able to reverse the trend of possible failure.

Changing classes is ideal—but not always possible. Adaptation to the unchangeable is a second choice that offers its own benefits. Then the parents *must* help their youngster learn to adapt to the unfamiliar and often unfair atmosphere of that particular teacher's classroom. Is it unreasonable to ask a child to do this, you may ask. Not so. Life is a series of encounters that forces us to adapt to the "unfair" demands and idiosyncrasies of others. It is excellent but painful training for the future if a child can learn this important lesson early.

Some families take a rather casual approach toward education. The parents do not stress the importance of school; rather, the emphasis may fall on other social or family issues. The child may not see much reading going on at home. The television set has become the primary source of family entertainment. Little of intellectual interest is discussed at the dinner table; gossip and complaints over the day's work activities are the main topics of conversation. The bomb falls when the child brings home a report card with very low grades—marks that reflect this home atmosphere. When the parents confront the youngster, he stares up at them, somewhat perplexed, and responds, "I never thought school was that important."

It may be difficult for parents to admit that the lack of home stimulation has prompted their child's poor school performance. Few of us actually sit down and analyze the degree of educational curiosity we are stimulating in our children. But when faced with a failing child who demonstrates an obvious disinterest in learning, we, as parents, are forced to question the example we set and the

small, constant signals we are sending, because the signal of a
child's school failure may be an echo of our own signal of intellectual lethargy. Turn off the television set; forget the superficial
table talk; get down to the business of creating a home that invites
the child's mind to enjoy the wonders of learning.

Stacy was a beautiful and gentle child. She played well with the
other children on the block, often seeking out the friends of her
younger brother. Her parents rarely had to discipline her. Stacy
listened as the conversations of her verbal family whirled around
her head. She smiled, laughed, played with her dolls and her
games with delight. During her kindergarten year, she proudly
brought home her drawings, which were tacked up on the kitchen
wall. When her parents looked at her kindergarten evaluation,
which hinted that she was behind the other children, they turned
to their happy, contented little girl and shrugged. "She's quiet.
She'll catch up," they reassured each other. But the following year,
her report card indicated that Stacy was failing. They were requested to come up to school. Stacy's teacher sat across from them
with a thick folder in her lap. "We did a lot of testing of your
daughter, as you know," the teacher began. Stacy's parents nodded. They remembered signing the forms. "We wanted to be
sure." The teacher was having some difficulty coming to the point.
"Sure about what?" her father asked, the sound of the teacher's
concern beginning to alarm him. "Stacy is a 'slow' child," the
teacher said staring into the faces of the shocked parents. "Are you
sure?" her mother finally whispered. The teacher continued in a
soft voice: "The tests were done by two different people. We kept
looking for other reasons. But we could not find any. She tests
lower than the average. She will not be able to keep up with the
other children in a regular class." Stacy's parents sat stunned. No
labels had been placed on their child but the words "mentally
retarded" kept surfacing in each of their minds. Finally they asked
if that was her problem. The teacher frowned. "No, she is not
mentally retarded, just below the 'average' in intellectual ability
—but far enough below that she will always have problems in a

regular class. Stacy needs a special resource class for children with lower learning abilities in addition to her regular class."

It is extremely painful for parents to face the reality that their child may be failing in a regular class because he or she does not have the intellectual ability of his or her classmates. Immediate images of the retarded child cross their minds. Quickly the questions follow: "how much?" and "how far?" in school will be possible for their child. "What will he be able to do when he grows up?" Stacy's parents eventually asked all of these questions. The teacher could not answer the far-reaching predictions they wanted and needed. But she could reassure them that Stacy could learn, though more slowly than other children her age. Her future was by no means hopeless as far as her educational and social life were concerned. The teacher asked if Stacy's parents wanted her tested privately. They nodded. She understood. When the final report confirmed the school's data, she and the principal met with the couple to plan the best possible education for Stacy, indicating that the parents would have to join the school to provide Stacy with an all-around maximum effort at learning without frustration or shame.

In Stacy's case, the signal of school failure was the same as from Jeremy and Gail, discussed before, but the message was much more significant. The child with a lowered intellectual capacity, or even mild mental retardation, often first presents his or her problem to the outside world during the late preschool or early school years. It is a signal that must be noted and investigated so that the child can have the earliest opportunity to start the slower but methodical process of getting a proper education that maximizes his or her potential.

Other children who fail in school during the early years leave the superficial impression that they could also be hampered by slow intellectual development, as with Stacy. Often these children are *not* slow learners. They may have what is known as a "specific learning disability." These children, in fact, may be of normal or better than average intelligence but performing far below their

potential. Why? Because they have difficulty in mentally process-
ing the information they are receiving from their environment.
They must find new ways of learning that detour around their
weaknesses and use, to the maximum, their mental strengths. For
example, a youngster who has problems with the sequencing of
letters and words, suggesting a visual-motor problem, may have
excellent listening skills for learning. A tape recorder with the
lesson on tape can be played back as often as necessary and may
assist this child in overcoming his visual learning problems. But
this is only one of the many routes parents and educators may
uncover in helping the child make his way out of the jungle of
perceptual and learning problems. The important aspect of the
school failure signal is that the underlying cause is often difficult
to uncover and may need an aggressive, unfaltering approach by
the parents. Many professionals, such as school psychologists,
educators, physicians, and teachers may need to work with the
child, and confer, before the definitive area of the learning problem is uncovered. The parents should become the "captains" of
this team, guiding the professionals toward an ultimate diagnosis
and planning for their child's future education. The "slow learner"
is not always a child with limited intelligence. Parents must not
stop at this message if there is *any* doubt in anyone's mind that
underneath the surface of the child's sluggish schoolwork lies a
learning disability.

The Sagners stood facing their nine-year-old son. The boy's
hands were thrust into his pants pockets but his face was set in a
stoic expression of unconcern. In his father's shaking fingers was
a report card, with all "F's" running like an endless stream down
the grade column. "What is this all about?" Charles's father demanded. The boy shrugged and said simply, "I guess I failed."
"Everything!" his mother screamed. "Guess so," Charles said
calmly. His father moved to strike him but his mother caught his
raised hand in mid-air. "Aren't you worried, Charles?" she asked
in an exasperated voice. "No," he said, and smiled. There was
silence in the room as Mr. Sagner's face flushed and his mother bit

her lower lip. Finally the boy asked insolently, "Are you worried?" His father exploded, "Oh, my God!" Charles stood still watching the pained expression on his parents' faces, then said evenly, "May I be excused?"

When the Sagners told us this story in the office, we asked, "Has this ever happened before?" The Sagners indicated that he had been doing well in school until this year. "Does he ever talk about having problems?" The Sagners shook their heads. "No." "Have you noticed anything different at home?" With this question, Mrs. Sagner glanced at her husband. "Yes," Charles's father answered slowly. "He has been much more of a problem this year." "In what way?" was the next question. Mrs. Sagner responded, "We have a strict house . . . Bob makes the kids toe the mark. This year Charles has been challenging his father a lot." There was a brief but significant silence. We asked, "What has happened to him because of this?" Mr. Sagner took a deep breath. "Well, he's not allowed to ride his bike. He's been grounded on more weekends than I can count. Charles spends more time being punished than anyone else in the family." Mrs. Sagner looked at her husband as if she was discovering what she had come to us to interpret. "What does Charles do or say as a result of so much punishment?" we asked. This time Mrs. Sagner replied, "Nothing. He just goes to his room and closes the door. I've been wondering why he never reacts." She was frowning. "Do you think you know now?" we inquired. She nodded. "He's failed in school as a way of punishing us," she said wearily. Mrs. Sagner had already deciphered the rebellious message behind the signal of Charles's school failure.

In families where education is a prized accomplishment, there is no better arena for a child's rebellion than the school, particularly when parents make the school seem to be a threatening environment because they place undue emphasis on academic achievement and hence put the child under unnecessary and often destructive stress. Charles was notifying his parents of his anger and frustration at them by bringing home a failing report card: he knew the response that would occur. It was a predictable and impulsive act of rebellion on his part. Often such a move is calculated; at other times, the youngster may not be aware that he has selected low school grades as a means of retaliation. He only knows that he is very upset with the authority figures at home; he feels he has to tell them, but cannot. So he expresses his message through a vulnerable, socially wounding point for most parents—school grades. If this is the message behind your child's failing signal, you must step back and look at your behavior the past days and weeks. How justifiable is your child's negative reaction? Have your punishments been too severe? Have they fit the crime? Could the strict rules be loosened enough to give your youngster emotional and physical "breathing room"? If the answer is "yes," then the first steps in answering the message are obvious and must begin at home rather than in the school. If the child is overreacting, then the parents must permit him or her openly to express the anger so that it can be discussed, accepted, understood, and diverted away from school performance. "I know you're very angry with me for punishing you and making those rules. And I understand. But failing in school will hurt you more in the long run. The best way to let me know how angry you are is to tell me. I will listen. And I will accept it. Sometimes I cannot change or loosen the rules or the punishment. But we will both be better for knowing how we feel." This is the essence of the initial reaching out that must take place when the parents realize that rebellion is being diverted into areas of serious concern such as school failure—and it must be done calmly.

Occasionally children fail not because they are deficient but because the teaching is so abysmally poor that they cannot find their way through a disorganized maze of information. Even the brightest child can be turned off from learning because of a sterile classroom or a chaotic, jumbled daily lesson plan. These children are not "bored." They are disgusted and frustrated by their inability to comprehend the wanderings of the teacher's poor class preparation or educational techniques. Just ask your failing child what his classroom is like; look at his notebook; check his examinations. Ask for permission to visit his class; demand to see for yourself the kind of teaching he is getting. And if the signal of your child's failure rests with the teaching, then become your child's advocate—take up arms and fight for your child and the others in the classroom by insisting either on more teacher supervision or a change, if possible. You are *paying* for your children's education. Get your money's worth for each child. Don't let them fail because you overlooked the message contained in their signals of classroom failure.

When Howard's mother called his fifth-grade teacher after reading his poor report card during the spring session, the teacher was very pleased to hear from her. "Mrs. Mullan, Howard seems to have given up," she said. "He did his work up until the last report card but then he simply stopped trying in class. He doesn't hand in his work assignments. I couldn't do anything else but give him failing grades this time." Mrs. Mullan listened with concern. "Do you have any idea what might be the problem?" she asked. "Yes," the teacher replied, "but let's talk in person."

The next day, Mrs. Mullan sat in the teachers' lounge drinking coffee with Howard's teacher. "I may be wrong, Mrs. Mullan," the teacher began, "but something happened in class that I think may be important." Mrs. Mullan leaned forward, indicating she wanted the teacher to continue. "Well," the teacher went on hesitantly, "I gave papers back several months ago and Howard had done fairly well but less so than usual. He came up to me after class and begged me to give him a higher mark. When I asked him why, he started to cry." She stopped for a minute and looked at Howard's mother, who was beginning to squirm in her chair. "He said something like this: 'Please give me a better grade. My mother and father will be very angry with me if you don't.' " The teacher stopped and watched the other woman. But Mrs. Mullan remained silent. "When I asked him why you all would be angry at a grade like that, he answered that you expected him to be the best in the class. Is that true, Mrs. Mullan? Do you?"

Mrs. Mullan nodded. "I guess we do. Or at least that's what we must make Howard believe." The teacher made a face. "Mrs. Mullan," she said gently, "Howard is a smart boy. But it isn't likely he'll be the best in this class. This is the top class in his grade. He could never live up to what you expect." Mrs. Mullan put down her coffee cup. "Do you think, then, that *we're* the reason behind Howard's poor marks?" she asked quietly. "Yes. I do. I think Howard stopped trying to do the impossible. He just simply gave up." Mrs. Mullan looked at the teacher searchingly. "What should we do?" The teacher smiled at her encouragingly. "Just let him know that doing his best is good enough, even if he doesn't turn out to be the top in the class."

In Howard's case the teacher had observed the signal and interpreted the message long before the failing report card. Maybe she waited until the failure appeared in order to awaken the family about the serious consequences of their unrealistic, excessive expectations. Certainly she was effective. *The message was driven home!*

Setting standards of performance too high for a child can only lead to frustration and finally despair. Even the brightest child will ultimately give up trying constantly to be the very best. Everyone deserves the freedom to let down a bit occasionally. Each of us needs the prerogative of failing occasionally and then picking ourselves up and succeeding thereafter. The constant pressure for high achievement is an "impossible dream" which quickly turns into a nightmare for the child. The result is frequently school failure, based upon the child's total refusal to play the winning game to please parents. The teacher gave Mrs. Mullan the solution to the message. "Doing his best is good enough" should be every parent's motto.

In the older child and adolescent, several new messages may lie within the signal of school failure. The teenager is influenced tremendously by his or her friends. Often it is "square" to be very good in school. It may not be "cool" to study and work at school when the top priorities of the age are social and sexual. To belong to the crowd is one of the most important motivating factors in the adolescent's life. If failing or doing poorly in school is a direct or indirect result of that need to go along with the peer group, the parents have a difficult battle to wage. The need to present a case for "being one's own person" despite the pressures of the teenage peer group is one of the parents' key tasks. Attempting to do battle with the ideas and ideals of the teenager's friends may result in the parents being shut out of the young person's life completely. They will be forcing a decision at the most vulnerable point in their youngster's life, a time when it is extremely difficult to decide which is more important, the family or the crowd. Forcing the teenager to make this decision is thoughtlessly cruel and basically unhelpful. The phase will usually pass; in time, with proper parental patience and guidance, the adolescent will grow into a more independent, thoughtful adult. But these are years when parents are skating on very thin ice in their relationship with their teenage child. This is the time for parents to give advice, not orders, to listen more than talk, to set examples rather than lay down laws, and to try to treat the feelings behind the message rather than the message itself. If your teenager's grades have slipped because of pressure from the adolescent crowd, it would be far better to focus on the strengths of his or her individual accomplishments and talents and hope that the school marks will improve. The odds are against you if you take up a crusade to improve the grades; rather, try to improve the child through emphasizing what she or he does well or likes to do. A subtle but necessary response to an important signal!

Maggie suddenly stopped caring about school. Her sophomore year in high school had been outstanding. But in her junior year, her parents noticed that she was no longer studying, only moping around the house during evenings and weekends. When they inquired, gently, why, she would turn them off by changing the subject. As they feared, her first report card that year was a disaster. "You'll never get into college with those grades," her father tried, but the message was falling on deaf ears. "Maggie, dear, let's go over the work together," her mother offered; but the young woman stared and mumbled that she had no work. Desperately the parents sought advice from the person closest to their daughter, her best friend. At first, Carrie was very reluctant to talk about her friend. Finally she admitted that she knew something was wrong with Maggie. "Do you know what could be the trouble?" Maggie's parents asked. "I think so." "Then please tell us," the parents begged. "I can't fink on Maggie" was Carrie's immediate response. She thought for a second, then added, "But if you invite me to dinner. . . ." her voice trailed off. Maggie's parents picked up the clue and arranged for dinner the next night. Over the dinner table, Carrie chatted about minor school events with Maggie. There was little vitality in Maggie's replies. Finally Carrie said very off-handedly, "You know, Maggie, just 'cause you didn't make the school play doesn't mean anything. You act like it's the end of the world." Maggie looked up, her face burning. "Sure, *you* can say that," she said bitterly. "You've got one of the leads. All of the important kids were picked, but not me. But I don't care. School is for the birds anyway." Carrie sat quietly finishing her dessert. She had helped her friend deliver the message. She had not betrayed a confidence, but had provoked Maggie into admitting why she had given up on school work and was failing.

Teenagers who feel left out of the group activities frequently will slide into a state of deliberate inertia; the anger and hurt often overtakes their motivation to succeed and do well. A sense of worthlessness often adds to their isolation. Maggie was feeling all of these. The result was school failure. Parents must carefully consider the other aspects of the teenager's life when they are analyzing the messages behind the unexpected signal of poor grades. Boys who are cut from athletic teams often refuse to give of themselves in class work or other school activities. Grades plummet! Young people who are excluded from group activities such as clubs, dances, dating also may retreat from the total school picture. Failure often follows. Exclusion from the teen group for any reason—social, sexual, or otherwise—may be the underlying message behind the listless school performance of a previously bright and achieving teenager.

Parents have to follow Carrie's advice to Maggie. Helping the young person to realize that the exclusion is not "the end of the world" is an important step. Another is gently opening up for the adolescent's inspection all of the possible positive things in her or his life. Focusing on talents or accomplishments will often erase the hurt, the rejection, the loss caused by the "being left out" syndrome. At times, the parents may have to work with the young person to find new avenues through which he or she can reach friends and be accepted. Everyone has the potential to make and keep friends, but the teenager often has this skill in short supply. Sensitive parents can offer their years of experience to help in "coming back" after hurtful relationships, and in finding the strength and social skill to overcome an episode of rejection. Only when the teenager finds a way back into his or her own circle within the school situation will grades rise and failure become an issue of the past.

The messages behind the dramatic signal of school failure in childhood and adolescence are so incredibly varied and complex that parents may well shake their heads collectively, and say, "You have to be a child psychiatrist to work your way through this problem." *That is not the case at all.* The only skills needed by the parent of a failing child are: the awareness to accept the signal of poor grades calmly; the capacity to investigate the underlying message carefully; and the wisdom to act upon their findings with tact, speed, and understanding. A big order? Indeed. But parenting may well be the most important and most difficult job we have in our lifetime. Our maximum response is required when the signals indicate that our children are in trouble.

17

Overreaction

Almost every family has lived through an experience similar to that of the Alexanders.

John Alexander's boss—and friend—died. John was faced with the decision of who in his family to take to the funeral. George was only eight years old and Jeanette six, but John felt that it would be "right" for them to attend the funeral. After all, he thought, they had to learn about death sometime. It might as well be early rather than late.

Many people attended the memorial service. All of Mr. Coventry's friends and employees were there, most without their families. As they filed into the chapel and took their seats near the front, the children recognized many of their father's friends; but they did not smile or nod to them, for they had been told about funerals. They knew that they were supposed to be "solemn" and quiet.

It was not until the eulogies that John, with a sinking heart, realized that the Coventry family had requested an open casket service. He had not remembered to tell the children about this part of a funeral ceremony; he had not prepared them for it. He put out a hand to each child as the usher moved slowly down the aisle to the coffin. With each step, the room seemed to become more silent and tense as the adults prepared themselves to view their friend for the last time. John felt the hands of his children slip out of his and move to their mouths in mingled fear and astonishment.

The lid was raised, and, as the first wave of recognition passed through the congregation, the air split with the sound of childish laughter. John tightened his grip on his children's arms, but to no avail. Both children were trying to control their laughter. Their hands were pushed up against their mouths, but they could not stop. Heads were turning toward John in silent condemnation. In mounting shame and anger, he led his children from the church, while the eyes of the mourners followed him in scorn and disgust.

What had happened in this instance was an example of a signal —overreaction—that carried a clearcut message: anxiety. John had made several mistakes in taking the children to the funeral. First, he should have realized that they were too young to cope with the problems of death in so dramatic a fashion. Since the deceased had not been immediate family, they could have been spared the experience.

Secondly, he had not prepared the children for the opening of the casket, the sudden actual confrontation with death. Consequently, the unexpected and alarming view of a dead man produced in them so much fear that they could not cope with their feelings. They exploded in inappropriate merriment, the opposite emotion experienced by everyone else in the chapel.

Anxiety and tension can create overreactions in children. The setting does not have to be as dramatic as a funeral. Perhaps the family is waiting for an important letter or phone call about the illness of a close relative. A child may be getting ready for his first speaking part in a play. A teenager may face her first important date. Any situation that activates a period of tension in a child or in the family can create an invitation to overreaction.

Such tension may not always be recognized by the parents. Often a child is tense because of events or situations about which the parents are unaware. Overreaction in a child is natural, but often hard to explain. Parents who discover a series of overreactions in their pre-adolescent child should start their search for messages. The first step is a careful determination whether the child has good reason for persistent feelings of anxiety. If so, the overreactions may be the pressure valve for the problem. If parents can help their child talk openly about the anxiety-producing problem, they may be able to alleviate their child's tension.

Although tension and anxiety often trigger overreaction, a parent must search for other messages as well. A different kind of message can also prove to be embarrassing to a parent, as Jennifer's mother found out.

Jennifer was holding her doll, cradled in her arms, and was rocking her to sleep. "Sleepy-time, dolly," she cooed. When four-year-old Jennifer was satisfied that the doll had fallen asleep, she began the careful transfer of the doll to a tiny bed, humming a random lullabye.

All of a sudden, the doll slipped from her arms and fell to the floor, accidentally upsetting a cup of water Jennifer had used at her tea party. The doll became wet, her hair uncurled from the moisture, and, as Jennifer picked her up, the water dripped onto Jennifer's leg.

She screamed and hurled the doll across the room. "You stupid old cow!" she cried. "What did you do that for? Why did you get me all wet? You're a naughty doll—a naughty, naughty doll! Now, you come right here and clean me up. Do you hear me? You come here and wipe off my leg!" Her eyes were narrow and angry, her voice shrill and high-pitched.

Jennifer's parents, sitting at a nearby table, were startled. What an alteration from the sweet child of a minute ago! Jennifer's mother rose quickly, reached Jennifer in a second, and gave the little girl a resounding swat on the bottom. Her voice was very loud as she told Jennifer, "That's *enough*, Jennifer! You pick up that doll, and you pick it up NOW. Do you hear me? I want you OUT OF HERE and into your room IMMEDIATELY! I'll settle with you later, but now, GO!"

She turned to her husband, her voice shaky and surprised.

"What do you suppose that outburst was all about?" she asked him, obviously wanting to talk about it.

"Jennifer's or yours?"

Jennifer's father had put his finger on the problem of Jennifer's overreaction. She was imitating her mother's outbursts. Her mother frequently changed mood quickly and unexpectedly. She overreacted. Why? She had been experiencing a great deal of tension in her daily routine. Long, tiring household tasks, serious budget problems, and concern over a deferred career were among her stresses. She "let off steam" with sudden overreactions, loud outbursts of minor importance and short duration. Jennifer was copying that overreactive style.

When Jennifer's mother and father realized what was happening, they paused and reassessed their own behavior. They realized that Jennifer's mother had to find ways of releasing her tension other than through moody outbursts, perhaps via some activity outside the home: tennis, dance classes, or evening courses. She watched her actions in front of Jennifer. And Jennifer's outbursts soon stopped for lack of a model.

When a child imitates overreactions, the "star" does not necessarily have to be provided by the parents. It can be other children, other relatives, or even television. Have you watched the overreactions of actors on daytime soap operas? Whatever the cause, if your child exhibits many sudden mood swings, first rule out tension. Then, investigate to see if there is an imitative pattern that your child is following. Can this model be changed? Perhaps not, if the model is a teacher, relative, or the TV. In that case, you must point out the model, and inform your child that such actions belong *only* to the other person. You should stress that those outbursts cannot be tolerated in your home.

Most overreactions can be detected and corrected at home. However, occasionally the home environment is the fertile ground where the overreactions begin. It is the family lifestyle to overreact, to be expressive, emotional, verbal, demonstrative. Therefore the youngster's tendency to overreact goes totally unnoticed in this volatile home setting but can cause the child considerable trouble in social situations elsewhere. When accused of overreacting by friends or teachers, such a child stands confused and hurt. Why is it all right for me to be myself at home but not out here in the outside world? Is there something wrong with me —my family—or is the problem with all the rest of them? When a child grows up in an environment where everything is punctuated by exclamation points—where overreactiveness is a rule rather than the exception, where emotional responses are encouraged and considered healthy—this child stands to be hurt in the more placid, controlled world around him.

What is such a home like? Usually the families are fairly large, verbal, close knit, and contain a number of teenagers.

The Castle family fits this pattern. They were a family that you could easily like and admire. The parents, two professional people, had reared their four children to value creativity, intellectual pursuits, and open communication. Their dinner hours were unique. The Castles had events, not dinners. Food took second place to conversation. Each child and adult contributed to the verbal repast. The son might relive his heroics in that day's lacrosse game. His older sister often related the newest gossip of her theater group, and, perhaps, tried out lines from the new play she was auditioning for family opinion. The other teenage girl, eyes downcast and welling with tears, frequently shared the "ups and downs" of her relationships with steady boyfriends. The youngest, a boy, might come to the table furiously, frustration written in every decisive movement, determined to find—and then kill— whoever stole his bicycle. The next night he might dominate part of the dinner by recounting a school problem. Within a single evening, all the children participated in contrasting moods of bravura, tension, sorrow, and anger. These family dinners set a pace and style that communicated to the children, "Look, it is all right to have different moods, to be sensitive to each other, to have rapid swings in feelings, and to express all of these things openly."

This philosophy did not work as well in school as it did at home. Teachers were taken aback when a Castle child switched from compliance to sudden anger in only a few seconds. Classmates were often overwhelmed when one of the Castle children would be a friend at one moment, and after a minor slight, reject them within the hour. Most of the other people in the lives of the Castle youngsters could not understand such radical, fast overreactions. They were, consequently, frightened of those mood changes. Finally, one of the classmates of the older Castle girl confessed to her how upset she was getting over her friend's behavior.

After much discussion at the Castle dinner table, Mr. Castle summed up the resolution of the family: each person is entitled to his own moods, however and wherever he feels them. But we have to remember that everyone also lives in a social group where other people must be considered. Therefore, in the future, all of the Castles will have to concentrate on the expectations of others as well as just their own needs. Overreaction will have to be controlled outside the family. It was decided that the Castle dinnertime would remain a place where all moods and feelings could be shared and where reactions (and overreactions) would be tolerated.

If your family resembles the Castles, then your children may be learning about overreaction within your home. When your kids are having difficulty with overreactions in school or other social situations, then it is wise to check your family behaviors. If you find such a problem, help your youngsters understand how home differs from the outside world. Seek ways of stabilizing the mood swings within the family environment. Most children who are prone to sudden mood swings experience difficulties in attracting and maintaining friends.

With adolescents, however, overreaction is often very prevalent. The life of a modern adolescent is full of crises and traumas. "Will I get asked to the party?" "I got a 'D' on that test." "OUR TEAM WON!" "I don't want to see you *ever again*, Harold." The teenager takes every new emotional crisis very seriously, swinging rapidly from one to the next. Each problem is monumental—and maybe it should be. These teenagers are busy practicing for adulthood.

But parents will, nonetheless, worry about the dramatic overreaction of the typical adolescent. Your daughter may giggle with her girlfriend on the phone for forty-five minutes, then the minute the phone is hung up she bursts into a torrent of tears. Or your son, when he appears to be suffering the biggest disappointment in his life because he missed the lead in the class play, can call a friend and casually joke about girls as if the play had never existed.

A signal of extreme mood swings and intense overreactions may carry a serious message of underlying psychological trouble. This signal is often called, clinically, depression or over-excitation. A child who is doing well at home and school suddenly locks herself in the bedroom for a long weekend. You hear her crying. She will not answer your questions; this person may be severely depressed and need the help of outside professionals.

Or, occasionally, we face the child who becomes constantly excited, and who, for no apparent reason, runs at top speed for several days. This child might become impulsive, overly talkative, and will often sleep only when she or he has finally become totally exhausted. Such over-excitation may be a signal of serious emotional disorder.

These are examples of children whose extreme mood swings and overreaction announce trouble. The interpretations of their messages clearly indicate that psychological help is needed. Soon.

Overreactions are signals that need to be defined by their suddenness and duration, by the age of the child, and by the family environment. The underlying messages can be either benign or potentially serious. The swinging mood causes overreaction. It strikes not only the child but the world around him, causing pain and withdrawal.

18

Friendlessness

"Why don't you go outside, Marilyn? It's a beautiful day, and I can hear the other children playing out on the street."

Marilyn's mother found her voice rising slightly as she tried to sound cheerful and encouraging. It was important to her that Marilyn, her five-year-old, play with the other children—all children should play with friends. But in the past few months, Marilyn had preferred to shut herself inside her bedroom or mope about the kitchen. Getting her to go outside and play with any of the many children who lived on her block had become difficult. Marilyn seemed to do everything possible to avoid it.

When her mother forced her to go outside, Marilyn would often play solitary "jacks" in the empty lot, or sit on the steps with her cat in her lap, watching the other children. She never saw Marilyn laughing happily in group games. During the past few months, Marilyn seemed to avoid any contact with other children. "You could have a lot of fun"; the mother almost choked as she realized the desperate sound of that statement.

Marilyn gave her usual, delaying reply. "Mommy, please let me finish this game. Then I'll probably go outside."

"How long do you think the game will take?"

"Oh, I don't know, Mommy, I've just started it."

Her mother knew that if she pushed Marilyn, she would encounter only more resistance—first excuses, then a firm refusal. By using serious threats, she could make Marilyn go outdoors. But, with an anxious shudder, Marilyn's mother realized that Marilyn would not play with anyone. She appeared to have no friends. She was a loner.

Marilyn was sending a signal: "I have no friends."

What are some of the messages this signal may carry? One question that Marilyn's mother should ask is whether, in her experience, Marilyn had the *ability* to make friends. Has she had friends in the past? Did the friendships last very long? Why was a friendship broken?

This is not asking whether Marilyn wanted to make friends. Rather, we ask whether, if she wanted to make a friend, she has the right social skills to do so? Can she talk well to other children? Can she find common interests with other children?

Parents often presume that all children can make friends if they want to because friendship comes "naturally." But many children lack the skills simply because they lack the experience. An only child, Marilyn, for example, may not have many friends because she has had no experience in interacting with other children. If an only child lives in an apartment building or a neighborhood where there are few children her age, she may not have sufficient opportunity to talk to her peers. This, obviously, seriously limits her chances to find friends. A child in this position can only relate to adults. Throwing this child into the group of her peers, whether it be the first day of school or a visit to a relative's home, will probably terrify her. She will see all those strange creatures, her peers, with whom she cannot relate. Usually she will decide to remain friendless but comfortable in the company of adults.

The message, "I don't know how to make friends," must be taken seriously. It may mean a life of friendlessness if the child is not encouraged and helped to meet other young people and learn the necessary social skills of friendship. The parents of a child who is obviously awkward at making friends because of lack of experience can locate areas where the youngster can be exposed to that experience. Church or other religious groups, municipal recreation programs, boys' or girls' clubs, Scouts, "Y's," preschool programs, neighborhood play groups, hobby and interest clubs—these are the programmed activities during which the "loner" can refine his or her social abilities. Developing a pen pal is a healthy, unthreatening way of exploring some of the skills necessary to make a friend initially, since the pace of a pen pal friendship is slower and the "contract" of friendship less intimate. The child is usually able to talk about this more openly with parents because the letter can be shared and discussed. However, parents must help to extend the successful pen-pal relationship into gradual open contact between their child and his peers.

It is never necessary to expect, nor even to want, your child to have a large number of friends. A few good friends will do. But to develop important friendships, the child must have both experience in making friends and access to children his or her age. As parents, you will want to see that your child has both.

Far too often, however, other messages are being sent when a child is friendless. One of the more serious messages is: "I don't have enough self-confidence to make friends. I don't see what there is about me that people can like. Therefore, I won't try very hard to make friends because I'm sure I won't succeed or, if I do, I'll lose my friends again."

What can cause a child to feel this way? As Nancy was walking toward the kitchen to get a drink of water, she heard her mother talking to a neighbor over coffee. She stopped outside the room and listened:

"I tell you, Madge, I'm really worried about Nancy. Oh, she's a sweet kid, but she just doesn't seem to have as much upstairs as my other kids. Her older brother makes far better grades than she'll ever get. If Nancy gets 'B's' and 'C's' in school, we think we're lucky. There's nothing she does well—and that's so rare in this family. I can't seem to find a thing that turns Nancy on. She has no friends. I ask her to bring children home, but she rarely does. And when she does, I never see the other kids around here a second time. I just don't know what to do."

What Nancy heard were the actual words that described what she knew her mother had been feeling for the past year. Her mother had managed to uncover all of Nancy's faults. The child knew it. Somehow, Nancy's positive qualities had escaped her mother. Nancy had grown to believe she was a social failure—a disappointment to her mother. She kept repeating to herself, "Of course, I don't have any friends. How can I even try, when I'm such a nothing person?" Nancy lacked the confidence and the positive self-image to consider herself worthy of being liked—by anyone.

What a shame that Nancy's mother felt that way! She was missing the joy of watching her Nancy flourish. But this was not only *her* loss. Unfortunately, she also was taking something away from her child—the ability to have normal social relationships. If only the mother could have looked for, and discovered, Nancy's strengths rather than her weaknesses. What positive qualities Nancy's mother could have found if she did not insist that Nancy had to be compared to so many others. Because of the not very subtle signs and words of disappointment Nancy received from her mother, she came to believe the worst about herself and put these negative feelings into action—she retreated from other children and refused to make friends. Nancy's message was: "You've convinced me! I'm not good enough to have friends!"

Unless Nancy's mother can correct her negative attitude toward her daughter, perhaps through counselling, Nancy's social relationships may be damaged for a long time, perhaps for her entire life.

Some children, however, feel that they are not worthy of friends by their *own* judgment. Children who see themselves as fat, homely, handicapped, or in some other way not physically or socially appealing, may need help to discover—and believe—that all people can be beautiful within themselves.

A child who is slow in school often faces the serious problem of continual failure. His or her grades will always be low and, each year, the child will have to worry whether he will pass. Sometimes such a child is singled out by cruel classmates as the "dummy." It is hard to convince the child that the cruelty is not meant to harm, but is an expected part of childhood group behavior. This youngster with school problems often exasperates the teacher. Each day the child trudges to school dawdling on the way, afraid to face the morning routine that once again proves he is not as good as the others. Is it any wonder that he feels no one wants to be his friend?

Some children get their low self-confidence from their immediate environment. The child whose family lives in an apartment building where the other tenants are mostly childless or elderly can suffer the withering glares of adults who think that children should be contained in museum showcases. Children new to a neighborhood may find that all their potential playmates are already organized into tight little groups, or "gangs," that exclude them. Neighborhood groups often reject children of different ethnic, religious, or cultural backgrounds. These children can become the "scapegoats" of the other children on the block.

Whenever children send the message, "I'm not good enough for friends, because my environment tells me so," there *are* some tactics that parents can use.

The best approach is to sit down with the child and talk about self-esteem. It is often helpful for the parents and child to make a list of the child's good qualities as well as those qualities the child has come to see as "bad." This can enlighten the parent as to what their child thinks of himself. Those aspects that pressure a child into seeing herself as worthy or unworthy, such as appearance, weight, school grades, or athletic abilities, should be openly discussed and placed into a framework of importance. A true perspective must be obtained, a perspective which asks such questions as: "Is it really important that the group of kids up the street like you? Look how well you are doing in the school drama club or on the school newspaper." *Every* child has positive qualities. These good points can be discovered, commented upon, and nourished. The child who is not physically attractive may enjoy music and, if given the opportunity, excel in it. The slow child in school may be able to develop an interest in art and contribute to the school by making posters or displays. The child bullied by street groups may have the commitment and talent to make the church choir. Encouragement in pursuing these activities to the point where the child tastes success can compensate for the negative areas of low self-worth. Success may mobilize the child to change his or her whole self-image. The child must like himself, at least a little, in order to take the initiative to make friends. "We must like ourselves before others can like us" is a universal truth and applies especially to children.

There are some children who do not want to make friends of their peers because they prefer the company of adults. This is too often true for an only child, who has been reared in an adult environment where too few other children surrounded him or her during the crucial early years.

This signal can also occur when the parents play "pal" to their child with such intensity and attention that the child considers peer friends totally unnecessary. This is a dangerous message: "I don't need other friends, Daddy (or Mommy), I have you." It is a message that requires the parent to take immediate steps to answer and correct. A child cannot expect a parent to be a buddy at all times. A parent has to be a parent first, particularly where discipline or punishment are needed. The parent must punish an act of disobedience, no matter how the child pleads for a friendship response. "If you punish me, you can't really like me," must be answered in the context of parent, not friend.

The parent, equally, cannot expect the child to be *his* only friend. Adults need adult friends. When the parent entertains his friends, he should not be hampered by the jealous child who feels that other adult friends are threats to the parent-child relationship. If the parent encourages this exclusive friendship with his child, he is depriving the child of both the joy and the necessity of having friends his own age. But these peer friends are vital to the growing child. They are needed to share the discoveries of growing up. Can a young man share with his father all the boyish exuberance and wonder as he discovers the sexual world around him? He needs another boy for this type of foolish fun that is part of growing up. A little girl gets much more pleasure from playing the nonsense games of childhood with another girl than she ever could from her parents. Can a child learn the joy of skateboards and jump ropes with the father or mother? No, the child needs another child for these things—and the child needs a parent for the areas only a parent can handle: support, advice, discipline, setting an example, and comfort. A parent cannot let a child "adopt" him as the only friend.

A mature woman friend of ours, the mother of an only child, was once faced with such a problem when her eight-year-old daughter wrote her a Valentine card. There was a printed greeting on it, but at the end of that greeting was scrawled: "Dearest Mommy—You are my best, my only friend in the whole world. Julie."

The woman read the card, then sat down with her daughter. "Julie, did you send Valentine cards to your other friends?" she asked. The youngster shook her head. "No," she said proudly, "just you."

"I want you to sit down and write Valentine cards to ten other children right now, Julie. Pick the ten who you like best." The mother's voice was firm.

Julie's eyes got misty, and she asked, "Why, Mommy? I was trying to tell you I love you, and you are my friend. . . ."

"Please get the cards, Julie. Write them out. We'll talk about this after you're done." Julie's mother sat quietly by her daughter's side as the child slowly and carefully addressed the ten Valentines.

When Julie's work was finished she looked up, her eyebrows raised in question. She was obviously confused and hurt. Mother put her hand on Julie's shoulder.

"Julie, I do love you, and I really loved getting your card. But I love you more as a parent than as a friend. A parent has certain responsibilities, you see, like helping a daughter understand that she cannot hurt her friends by not sending them a Valentine. A friend doesn't have to worry about those things. If I have a choice, like I just had, I will be your parent first—not your friend first. To find friends, you have to look around for people your own age, just as I find friends among people of my own age. So I'll be your friend sometimes, Julie, but mostly I have to be your parent. And you'll find your very best friends among your playmates. Do you understand?"

Julie nodded, her eyes raised in sudden recognition. "Mommy, can I go out and mail my Valentines?" The message had been perceived, accepted, and answered.

As children move closer to adolescence, friendlessness becomes a more important danger signal. The adolescent youngster who has no friends faces a world of double jeopardy. Not only is such a person lonely and rejected, but also he or she is missing the last chance before adulthood to learn how to make and hold meaningful human relationships. With this in mind, if your adolescent signals "no friends" in one way or another, time is of the essence. You must attend to your child's signal and find the message.

One of the characteristics of adolescents is their patterns of variable growth rates. Some teenagers have almost fully matured sexually by age fourteen while others may not have their voices change or breasts enlarge before they are sixteen years old. Likewise many adolescents, particularly in their early teenage years, may be more psychologically mature—or immature—than others of the same age. When a teenager is much more immature than his or her classmates, rejection may occur either by the child *or* by the classmates.

John, a freshman entering high school, was referred in the middle of the first semester to the school counsellor by his home room teacher because "he was extremely lonely, with no friends." A one-hour visit revealed the reasons. John was restless and inattentive. He would only listen to part of what the counsellor was saying, interrupting her frequently. He would often change the subject in mid-conversation. John told the counsellor about several practical jokes he had played on classmates, pranks which had caused physical or psychological discomfort to the victims. When asked about friends, he changed the subject again. Finally, he admitted that his only friends were those he left in intermediate school the year before. Sadly, John confessed how much he missed them. When the counsellor asked him why, John replied, "Because they like to do the kinds of things I do. They don't always try to act so grown up."

John was an immature adolescent. He knew only one way to

obtain friends, through pranks and mischief. He was unable to adjust to the new, more mature demands of high school. The counsellor scheduled John for several sessions per week for a few months so that together they could explore what high school was all about, and how to make friends in this environment. John was lucky to have these sessions, for he soon saw how alone he was, and how easy it was to make friends if one knew the ground rules. He had learned an important concept: the basic rules of friendly behavior change from one environment to another. Maturity consists of recognizing these new rules and responding to them. He also discovered that new friends were his reward for learning to adapt.

Some adolescents purposefully decide not to seek many friends. These are the youngsters who do not believe in conforming to what they consider unacceptable rules. Seventh Day Adventists may not come to Saturday play rehearsals. Orthodox Jews may not want to eat in the cafeteria or will bring their own food. Unlike their non-Jewish classmates, the boys may wear "caps" on their heads. Certain communal or religious sects may want to wear unusual clothing. The peers of these children often consider them "strange" and avoid them. These youngsters, therefore, have made a difficult decision: they must ignore the basic social rules of the high school in order to live with their beliefs. Such children can only be strengthened in their convictions at home—and by a wise counsellor, if available. They can be encouraged to find young people with similar beliefs, but they should also be encouraged to mix with other children as their beliefs permit. Wise teachers will talk about the normal differences among people of varying races and religions within the context of good classroom teaching. This sets the stage for understanding and acceptance. Parents of children with these special beliefs should work with the school personnel to help the environment become a tolerant one for their children.

A more insidious problem, however, is presented by the child who simply does not want to conform to group norms because he, independently, considers them wrong. This rejection of the teen group lifestyle is often healthy. Many children do not *want* to smoke pot, drink, have early sexual activity, drive fast and recklessly, show disrespect for adults, or rebel continuously. Singly or combined, these traits do characterize many teenagers. When an adolescent rejects such group activities, he or she may find that there is significantly less chance of becoming friends with teenagers who indulge in permissive lifestyles. Such adolescents may be ridiculed, labeled "goody-goodies," and shunned by the "popular" kids in school.

If you, as a parent, receive the message, "I have no friends because I don't do what everyone else does," investigate what this means. What is "everyone else" doing? You may have to conduct this investigation through teachers and counsellors as well as through your child. If you find that this signal represents a healthy rejection, you can help your child find other youngsters who share his more conservative beliefs. These companions often can be found in religious groups, recreational or sports groups, local youth clubs, and other organized activities. You must also help strengthen these convictions! Make your child feel good about his or her resolve. Emphasize the positive end results of his or her convictions. You should assure your youngster that the maturity demonstrated during his or her teens will have long-term dividends. This ability to be "himself" or "herself"— as well as such strength of character—will surely lead to many mature, worthwhile adult friends in later life.

Friends make up the exciting periphery of our lives: they add dimension and perspective. Friends fill out our life's canvas with warm colors. The friendless child is sending a signal of a daily journey through a dark tunnel of loneliness. It is up to you to uncover the message and help your child expand and enrich his or her life.

19

Excessive Attachment

The expression of love between parent and child can result in one of the most rewarding and meaningful relationships possible between two people. In most families, the child matures in a blanket of security that encourages him to trust his parents, knowing that they will provide the necessary nourishment, protection, and counsel. The parent, on the other hand, thrives on playing the role of counsellor and provider, and thrills to the responsibility of guiding a child's mind toward that of a creative, productive, and caring adult. Both parent and child expect, want, and need that relationship.

Sometimes, however, the relationship changes. One of the parents no longer lives with the child. The parents may divorce, or one of the parents may die. As a result, the child may seek an attachment outside the family. Parents should expect and encourage their children to seek external relationships. But until the parents watch their child marry into a new "family," they expect these external relationships to be limited to friendship only. When a child develops an "excessive" attachment to a person outside the immediate family, an attachment that obviously will not result in marriage, the parents have the right to be concerned. They must ask themselves, "What is my child seeking?" After this is honestly answered, the parents' next question must be, "Can we provide whatever our child is seeking within *our* family situation?"

171

The case of Sheila and her son Michael illustrates some of the soul-searching questions that parents must ask themselves when they are trying to determine if their child is developing an excessive attachment to another person.

Sheila had arranged a picnic in the park with Michael and two adult friends, a couple. Now, as she sat back on the grass and watched Michael and Rick play ball, she had a sense of uneasiness mixed with contentment. Sheila smiled at the sounds she heard— the familiar warning calls as the ball was about to be thrown, the high-pitched squeal as the child chased a missed catch, the playful bantering between the older man and the younger boy. They were sounds she had badly missed since her divorce two years before. These were, she realized, the joys she was unable to give Michael: the excited moments that were his heritage, his right.

Gloria, Rick's wife, sat down next to her. Sensitively, she voiced Sheila's thought. "The two of them *do* look good together. You know, it's such a shame we don't get to do this more often. Rick really loves Michael." Sheila remained pensive and still. Gloria turned and looked at her friend's concerned face. She spoke gently, "Sheila, why don't you let Rick and Michael be together more often? Is it because you're afraid Michael will become more attached to Rick than he is to his own father?"

There was a pause. Finally Sheila's eyes met those of her friend, her voice begging for understanding: "I can't let Michael do that."

Gloria smiled. "There can be a great difference between a father and a friend. Right now Michael needs a friend." She reached over and touched Sheila's hand, gently. "Sheila, let it happen."

Sheila's situation is being faced by millions of parents today. One of the parents is missing from the family, and the other knows that the child needs both a male and female model in order to help him or her learn how to live comfortably with various roles and situations. In some families of divorce, the "missing" parent may still be visiting frequently and have great impact on the child. However, the transient parent may not be able to play the necessary role model of relaxed father or mother. The visiting parent is often harassed by the reminders of the broken relationship with the other spouse, worried about money and business, troubled by adjustments to a single life, and desperate to be "all things" to the child. The child needs this parent, but in the context of a stable, long-term relationship, in which the child has time to know his parents and carefully observe the many roles adults play in society.

Not all divorced parents have this problem, since a number of couples today make Herculean efforts to spend more concentrated time and energy on their children, and, in this way, provide them with the proper models. But many children, in actuality, lose one parent through moving or restricted visitation privileges. One adult male or female model is among the "missing in action" in the divorce war. Will, can, the child seek out a substitute father or mother?

Most children try to remain loyal to the parents they remember from their early years. However, when a child reaches six or seven years of age, and begins to explore what being a boy or girl is like, he or she needs—then—to be able to watch and to ask questions of someone whom he trusts. When a parent is not available, the child will try to make friends with a figure of respect such as a teacher, coach, or grandparent; sometimes a child will have to settle for a person of disrespect. Perhaps even an older child in the neighborhood may assume this important place in the child's life.

In Sheila's case, Rick wanted to assume this role; and Michael indicated how much he needed Rick, a male adult. Gloria's words had made an impact on his mother: "Let it happen." Rick had a maturity and judgment that Michael needed to follow. Would Michael love Rick more than his father? No one will ever know— love cannot be measured or categorized. But Michael is capable of loving both Rick *and* his father, each in a different way. In ten years, Michael will remember Rick as "that special person who helped me for a few years when I was a child." Rick probably will be replaced, later, by another male who counsels teenagers, or coaches sports, or teaches history. Men will pass through Michael's life as temporary "models," but Michael will always have a real father to remember and love.

Why not help children find their models? How can you influence their selection and make certain that your child has the best of adult models to emulate?

An intelligent father we know recently separated from his wife. He was concerned about a proper role model for his eleven-year-old son during those early, rough days of anguish. He immediately enrolled his son in a "Y" league football team, knowing of his son's passion for the game. The father was not always able to attend the games. His time did not permit him to go to the practices, but he sought the first chance possible to meet and talk with his son's coach. It was a frank and open discussion. The father told the coach that the separation was occurring. Then he asked the coach about his philosophies of coaching and about the ways he could deal with his son. He was pleased with the answers he got. He soon liked the coach as a person, and felt that the coach would be a good role model for that difficult period in his son's life.

In the following months, the father talked often about football —and the coach. He found that the boy related to the coach with ease; he was learning healthy facts about sportsmanship and male behavior which he could discuss with his father.

At the end of the season, the father and son, together, bought a gift for the coach—a memento of appreciation and also a signal of "goodbye." The coach had helped during a period of need in the child's life and he was about to become history, a helpful, friendly part of the son's past. This father learned that he could help his child find a male or female adult role model and feel comfortable that his son would love him as much as ever. The entire family profited from that lesson.

The situations just described have all been "normal" examples —a child seeks an involvement with an adult to fill needs for models and for adult caring. The solutions to these needs were healthy. Not all such situations have happy endings, however. Some children develop *excessive* attachments to adults—they seek a *substitute* mother or father.

This situation develops all too easily when a child feels a lack of affection, or possibly an actual rejection, from his parents. Excessive attachment is a "one-way" process. The child "gives his all" to the other person. If this attachment is not reciprocated, a painful situation develops for your child—another rejection. If your child signals "excessive attachment," the message that is possibly being sent is that something is lacking in his or her life, some vital adult relationship. You must restore those missing parts of the child's life as your response to the signal of excessive attachment.

But children also need *more* in their lives than just adult figures. They need friends. If the same feelings of rejection or loneliness develop in the area of friendship, the child is ripe to pick the wrong friend and become excessively attached to other children. Zack illustrates this point.

Zack was a child with a rare visual ailment that made him look —and feel—different from his classmates. Due to a muscular problem, his eyelids drooped so much that he continually had to lift his head backwards in order to see in front of him. The children in class often mocked him by tilting their heads backwards when they walked. Even though Zack had better than average intelligence, he had difficulty seeing the blackboard and did mediocre work in school. Sports were a natural disaster for him. Zack had no friends and was extremely shy with his classmates, lessening the chances of ever starting the process of developing friends. The school principal suggested that Zack receive psychological help.

Zack's parents were debating how to pay for his psychological therapy when he mentioned, one night at the dinner table, that he had played marbles that noon with a child named Clancy. Who was Clancy? "Just a new kid in school," Zack told them. The surprised parents dropped the subject of Clancy that night.

But Clancy was brought up the next night, and each night that week. Clancy became a household word in the family. "Clancy and I played cards together," "Clancy and I sat together for lunch." The boys called each other on the phone. They went to movies together. They appeared to be good friends. Zack's parents were excited and pleased. What miracle had caused this to happen to their unattractive, handicapped child?

One day, as Zack's mother was cleaning his room, she accidentally tipped over his change bank. Her hand involuntarily flew out in front of her to catch the change, but only 33 cents dropped into her palm. She knew there should be more. She lifted the bank and shook it, but there was no more money inside.

Puzzled, she questioned Zack that night. At first he denied knowing about the loss. But Zack's parents persisted in their questions. Finally, hesitantly, Zack lowered his head and stated, in a voice so low it had to be repeated, "I lost it."

"Lost it?"

"Clancy won it from me playing games."

Zack's parents looked at each other and then, sadly, at Zack. His lips were trembling. They did not need to tell him. He had only 33 cents worth of friendship left with Clancy.

That night, Zack's father made an appointment with the psychologist.

Zack illustrates the situation of a child who feels—realistically—that something is missing in his life, something very important. Friends. To have a friend, Zack paid dearly. What he bought was only a phoney friendship. Because Zack had no self-confidence and knew the other children thought he was unattractive and "funny," he felt he could not be discriminating in his own choice of friends. Over the months, Zack had only one opportunity for friendship. Although he realized that "the friendship" would terminate when his money ran out, he chose it over loneliness.

Our world is full of people like Zack, children who are beaten down by the rejection of others. They are not only children with obvious physical or mental handicaps, they also may be children who have received little acceptance or love. Rejection can come from many sources. These children crave a friend to erase the reality of the causes behind their low self-image. They need this friend to reassure them that they belong in their world.

As a result, these youngsters respond with excessive attachment to the first person who offers them a relationship on *any* terms. Often this "other person" brings his own problems of loneliness to the relationship. Indiscriminately, these children seek any source of friendship they can find; they hold onto it as long and as tenaciously as possible. These excessive and unrealistic attachments will usually end shortly, and the child will be hurt even more. The cycle begins again. The child seeks yet another lonely creature on which to become excessively attached.

When this situation occurs, the parent must seek professional help: the child's self-image and self-confidence are deteriorating. Counselling will be necessary to help the child explore his or her strengths and potentials. What is the ultimate goal of this therapy? To bring the child to the point of feeling like a person worthy of being someone's friend, often a long-term process.

A problem far greater than excessive attachment is overdependency. Overdependency is a relationship between two persons in which each has an excessive attachment for the other. The inner beings of both "feed" on each other. They act out a need for each other that transcends the usual bond between people. The two cannot envision an existence separate from one another.

Occasionally, the parent-child relationship is carried to an extreme of overdependence. Most of us remember family legends about overly dependent relatives who have been labeled as eccentrics. Their stories are recalled at family reunions, bringing smiles to everyone's faces. Remember the aunt down the block? She walked her son to the bus stop every morning, cried as he boarded, and greeted him there when he returned. She walked him there until the twelfth grade. What sent the family into peals of laughter was the fact that the family lived only one block from the bus stop.

Or the story of Cousin Gertrude! She lived with her widower father from the time his wife died, when she was twenty-three, until her death at sixty. No one ever saw her leave the house for more than an hour, and nobody ever visited them. They existed on and with each other.

Such memories should not cause laughter. They are pathetic, even tragic stories. These "eccentrics" lived in situations of overdependency. The lives of the people involved were shrunken by the problem. The messages in these overdependencies is: "My self-image is dependent upon another person."

What factors create an overdependent relationship? One parent, reacting to the loss of the other parent, may seek a relationship with a child to substitute for the lost one. An overdependent relationship can also begin from a situation of long-term illness, where a child or a parent becomes dependent upon the other for care, finds this relationship rewarding, and continues long after the illness is over.

Occasionally an overdependent relationship will develop between parent and child for complex reasons that require professional help to decipher and cure. If you recognize overdependency between a parent and a child, you must remember that the parent is the only member of the pair who can restore the proper perspective to that relationship. Often it is the parent who *feeds* this overdependency. He or she seeks, in the child, an antidote for his or her own insecurity or loneliness.

The parent, and the parent only, is the person who can actively seek the professional help that is needed to break the overdependent relationship. Without such help, both parent and child will lead the rest of their lives in the shadow of each other. They will have difficulty with any other relationship. Each will miss the rainbow-hued variety of life's experiences, settling instead for a lifetime of monotonous sameness.

All parents want their children to have meaningful relationships with others, but they do not want such relationships to be "hurtful" or excessive. Children, as they grow and experience the changing scenery of friends and acquaintances, will be hurt by some, gratified by others, loved by few. The parent must watch these relationships, sorting out love and affection from excessive or overdependent relationships that can wound or cripple. When the signals of excessive relationships are found, they must be explored and resolved before the attachment becomes fixed in time.

20

Frequent Physical Complaints

Mrs. Karns was embarassed when she brought eight-year-old Eunice into the pediatrician's office for the fifth time in three weeks. The secretary smiled and said innocently, "You're getting to be a regular these days." Then she turned away and did not notice that Mrs. Karns had flinched at her remark. Each of the previous four times, Eunice had mentioned vague but disturbing physical complaints. Each time the doctor had not found anything wrong. And here she was for the fifth time, with a new symptom. But Mrs. Karns was afraid to let it pass, to ignore her child's complaints. Suppose something was really wrong? She waited her turn for about an hour and finally was ushered into the doctor's office. Fifteen minutes later, she heard the same diagnosis all over again. "I can find nothing, Mrs. Karns. Can you think of anything that would cause Eunice to have so many physical complaints?" The mother leaned forward in her chair, faced the child's doctor, and finally mustered enough courage to ask, "What kinds of things, doctor? What should I be looking for?"

Eunice's mother was desperately seeking the messages behind Eunice's signal of recurrent physical symptoms. What should she be thinking of, looking for, observing?

The child who complains frequently of physical symptoms such as vague abdominal pain, headaches, nausea, sore throats, fatigue, back and chest pain, and so on, but is repeatedly found to be healthy, may have many subtle or complex reasons for signalling false illness. A careful scrutiny of past and current events in the child's life can often uncover the inherent messages the child may be sending by these recurrent somatic symptoms.

Let us consider Eunice's situation. The first question the doctor asked was, "How *long* have you been hearing about these complaints?" Mrs. Karns thought for a second, then replied, "About three months. I've been here eight times in that period. More lately." Checking Eunice's record, the doctor noted that she had been a relatively healthy child. She had the usual check-ups and treatments for childhood diseases, but her visits had been widely spaced until quite recently. Mrs. Karns confirmed that fact. "It's just been lately. Never before." Eunice was the third of four children. The other children had also been in good health. "Anyone in the family been ill recently?" the doctor asked. Mrs. Karns shook her head. "No. Everyone is just fine. Except Eunice," she replied ruefully. The doctor paused. Then he inquired, "Has anyone that Eunice knows been ill recently? Or died?" Mrs. Karns looked up, somewhat surprised. "Yes," she said slowly, "Yes, there has been. One of Eunice's friends has been very ill. She had a bone tumor and her leg had to be removed." Quietly the doctor asked, "When was that?" Mrs. Karns nodded her head, and she realized the message behind the signal at that moment. "Three and a half months ago." There was silence in the doctor's office. "That's it, isn't it?" The doctor nodded; that was it.

Because of their general good health and their unfamiliarity with illness, children rarely have any concerns about their own health or life span. But when illness or death strikes near to hand in a member of the family, a neighbor, or a close friend, the reality of their own vulnerability hits very hard. Many children will become concerned about their bodies and imagine symptoms that frighten and alarm them. Their new awareness of serious or sudden illness and death makes them wonder if they could possibly be the next victim. Unless children receive the sensitive reassurance that such serious illness and death strikes the young very infrequently, they will begin to imagine all types of physical problems. Only when they have been reassured by someone they trust, the family doctor or nurse, will they rest comfortably. Often a new symptom, however, will replace the old; the cycle may begin all over again. Parents who receive the signal of repeated physical complaints can often prevent these symptoms from occurring by dealing openly and tenderly with serious illness and death when it appears in their children's world. Reassurance at that crucial time may satisfy children's fears and no signals will emerge.

Eunice needed that encouragement and reassurance. The doctor asked his nurse to work with Eunice and her mother. The nurse explained to Eunice that hardly any children suffer from serious illnesses and emphasized Eunice's own current good health. Her mother reassured her daughter that there was nothing wrong with her, that she had no physical problems of any kind. The nurse suggested that Eunice call if she was worried about her health. Eunice did make one call about three days later. The nurse was comforting and repeated reassuring words over the phone. That was the last phone call and the last office visit for imaginary illness.

Marvin was an only child. Every time he developed a fever or other symptom of expected childhood disease, his parents would become overwrought. He sensed their panic and concern. Marvin watched them frantically conferring in the hallway outside his room; he heard the slightly hysterical phone calls to the doctor and lived through each illness with both parents hovering by his bedside. Not only did his parents become alarmed at every ache and pain, but the boy gradually became frightened that something serious was going to happen to him. The hysteria in the home had made the youngster a hypochondriac. Was it any wonder that when he was eleven years old, his mother complained to her next door neighbor, "Marvin drives me crazy. He complains of a new pain or ache every day. He has me running back and forth to the doctor's office. If I don't take him, he just lays up in his room and worries"? Marvin's signal was so very simple, but his parents had lived so close to the forest that they could not see the trees. They had planted the fear of ill health in the boy's mind at a very early age; now parents and child were reaping the harvest of their mutual excessive concern. Marvin was a chronic worrier about his health and suffered from imaginary illnesses.

Marvin's may be an extreme case, but many children suffer from frequent physical complaints who have received the identical message either through the family's concern about their health or through watching one or both parents constantly fret about their own health problems. Marvin's signal was direct and decisive. The emphasis and hysteria about health must be downplayed. Consultations with the family doctor and nurse should be undertaken to convince the young person that he or she is healthy and very likely to remain so. A child's energies must be channeled away from this preoccupation with the body and toward the outside world of other children. Only then will a child with Marvin's recurrent false health signs manage to dispense with such behavior.

"Sympathy symptoms" fall into a very similar category. The signal again is the recurrent physical complaint, but the complaint is usually the same each time. "He suffers from stomach aches just like his father," one mother told us. Upon questioning, we learned that the ten-year-old boy's father had a chronic ulcer. The entire family's eating habits and social life centered on the father's abdominal pain. The constant focus on his father's physical complaints caused the youngster to simulate the father's physical problems. It was difficult for mother and father to accept the fact that there was nothing wrong with their son, that he was mimicking his father with "sympathy symptoms." Once the message was processed and accepted, the family was able to understand how unnatural it was for a ten-year-old to be surrounded by antiacids, special diets, and interrupted daily plans. Both son and father suffered equally from the father's ulcer. By eliminating the family focus on the father's stomach, the boy was able to gradually dismiss the symptom of stomach aches.

Wilma came home from the third grade, let herself into the house, set the table, and waited for her professional parents to come home. She helped her mother cook dinner and after dinner was sent up to her room to do her homework. When she was finished, she was allowed to watch television. But she did so alone because both parents were busy reading journals or going over the day's work. Weekends were not much different. Saturdays her mother taught a special course, while her father golfed. On Sunday, they went to church together. In the afternoon, Wilma was instructed to play while her parents entertained. Occasionally the family went out to a movie together on Sunday nights. Usually both parents were too tired and went to bed rather early.

During that year, Wilma began to complain of headaches about once a week. Occasionally she told her parent she felt nauseated or dizzy. Each time one of her parents took off time from work to stay home with her. By the next day, Wilma felt better and returned to school. Finally after five weeks of missing many days from work, the parents brought Wilma to the doctor to find out why she was having these recurrent symptoms.

Physically, Wilma was a healthy child and there was no organic basis for her complaints. Her parents were confused. "If she's not sick, then why is she getting these headaches?" her father asked. "It can't be much fun for her," her mother argued. "She has to stay home and rest on the living room sofa." We inquired, "Who stays home with her?" Her parents glanced at each other. "One of us has to. We don't believe in babysitters." Still Wilma's parents were not perceiving the message from Wilma's signal. "What could she gain by staying home?" they were asked. They shook their heads. "Nothing," her father said. "He's right. There's only Wilma and one of us in the house all day," her mother added. We did not respond, but just let the last statement sink in very slowly. These were intelligent people; as the mother's words echoed in the room, the message emerged clearly before them. "She wants our attention," her father stated simply. "I think so," we said. They nodded and left. Wilma's parents were wise enough to use the interpretation of the message in the best parenting manner. Each was able to include Wilma more often in their busy daily and weekend schedules. She saw and communicated with them more. The headaches ended. They were no longer essential in getting the attention from her parents that she so desperately desired.

The signal was the repeated physical complaints; the message was: "I need more attention." So often imaginary illnesses convey this message from the child. If a youngster can't get close enough to busy parents to tell them verbally that she needs more of them, she will find a signal that will do it for her. Wilma's headaches were effective in opening her parents' eyes.

Children can also use physical symptoms to get out of specific situations that are particularly unpleasant or threatening for them. The recurrent stomach aches on Monday morning usually mean that the child is attempting to avoid school. Sunday nausea could signal a reluctance to accompany the family to church. The headache that crops up every time a visit to a relative's home is suggested has its own clear message. It is important not only to interpret the signal and uncover the simple message behind recurrent symptoms, but to take that additional step and ask, "Why?" Why the fear of school? Why is church so upsetting? What happens at the relative's home that the child is trying so hard to avoid. Usually the answers to these questions can be easily discovered, and parents can work on positive remedies to help their children. The recurrent physical symptoms will normally disappear!

Millie began to throw up every Saturday night. This was particularly upsetting to her parents because Millie was seventeen years old and the episodes usually occurred just before she was scheduled to go to parties or movies with friends. The parents had to make constant excuses for her. The message was not difficult for her parents to perceive: Millie wanted "out" of her Saturday night dates. But what was particularly important was why she was so frightened. In Millie's case, it took several serious talks between mother and daughter finally to discover the cause. Millie had found herself moving with a very "fast" crowd. She was unready and unwilling to comply with the crowd's sexual patterns. And yet she was afraid to go against her all-important peer group. So she found what she thought was the easiest way out—throwing up every Saturday night. Millie's mother was able to help her declare her independence from the group's demands and remain "her own person." To Millie's surprise, the group still accepted her, even respected her, and she was able to join them during times when she could feel safe. Millie was not just trying to "get out of something" by the recurrent physical symptom on Saturday nights. She was also attempting to cover up what she thought was something basically wrong with her—her reluctance to become sexually active before she was ready.

The physical symptom signal can also be used to cover up a problem in another area. A poor report card can stimulate stomach cramps. Fear of losing a swimming meet can bring on overly severe muscle pain. Lack of self-confidence about a date can precipitate unusually bad menstrual cramps that cause the date to be broken. Parents must dig deeply under the message to discover the concern over the potential poor performance that creates the need to cover up.

In the adolescent, repeated unexplained vague physical complaints can be an ominous sign. In the unusual case, these frequent headaches or stomach aches are the smokescreen masking a serious teenage depression. Youngsters sometimes go from such recurrent symptoms, which were ignored, to suicide attempts in an effort to get the emotional help they had been signalling for so desperately. The parent of the teenager who has these continual unexplained physical complaints should not ignore such episodes with a cavalier wave of the hand and the "growing pains" excuse. A physician should be consulted. And the parents must stand back and take a hard, realistic look at their teenager to determine if the physical symptoms are covering a deeper emotional unhappiness.

These repeated vague physical complaints, which have no medical findings, are rarely of any consequence to the adolescent's physical well-being. The teenager should be checked by the pediatrician to make certain that nothing abnormal does exist. When the young person is declared healthy, then the work of the parent must begin. Now is the time to search for the reasons behind the signal.

21

Antisocial Behavior

How many parents can remember those acts of mischief that grew into family legends, passed down from generation to generation? Most families have stories about Uncle Hank who was caught stealing chickens on a Saturday night or Cousin Mildred who used her lipstick to write all over the window of a store from which she had been fired. With enough thought, you probably can remember your *own* childhood misdeeds—the soaping of car windows, the toilet-papering of trees, the alteration of road signs, the hiding of classroom material from the teacher. Time blurs these memories when you confront such actions in your own children. It would help if *you* could remember how your own mischievous acts originated, and how it felt to perform an antisocial act.

Usually your mischievous deeds took place with a group of friends. You acted rather spontaneously, without much thought about the consequences. Everyone was laughing; you were an important person for the moment. You were doing something exciting, something unique and daring in the eyes of your companions, and you were pleased by the attention you were getting from your friends. The deed itself was exhilarating—you might still remember the dryness inside your mouth, your pounding heart, and your eyes and ears triggered for any sound of detection. But what you also remember is the way your friends acted. They "egged you on" and made you feel that you were truly one of them. You knew your parents would not like what you were doing, but that just seemed to add an extra thrill. What really mattered was the approval of your friends. That was the reward: punishment was worth the risk. It would be small, compared to the sense of belonging to your own crowd of kids.

Those acts of mischief, vandalism, antisocial behavior, or whatever name we give to them, often are a normal part of growing up. They stem from a child's need to feel independent, rebellious, or part of the group. Indeed, the feelings that prompt these acts of mischief are universal. Every day millions of children and adults read comic strips filled with stories of childhood mischief. They chuckle with recognition, and mentally pardon the childhood caricatures from guilt. "After all, children will be children," parents chuckle as they watch Tatum O'Neal tear across the screen. However, if the child is their own youngster, the laughter may choke into anger.

It is not unusual for children to perform antisocial actions as they grow up, but *not* "just because they are children." Children do not ordinarily *want* to misbehave, to destroy the property of others, or to cause extra work and expense for the people who are the victims of their mischief. In the process of growing up, children seek to find out who they are, both as individuals and as members of a group. On occasion, they want to "get back" at the actions of "unfair" authority figures. The antisocial acts of children may be responses to these needs.

Alex illustrates a case of "normal" antisocial behavior.

One day, unexpectedly, Mr. and Mrs. Morris marched Alex into our office and demanded an appointment. It was obvious to the receptionist that something was terribly wrong. His face streaked with tears, Alex was being literally dragged in. His father, his massive hands around Alex's thin arms, was squeezing the boy's elbow with such force that Alex was grimacing in pain. His mother hung back from her husband and son, her eyes downcast and furtive, almost trying to avoid being identified as part of the family. While the three of them waited for the first available time, they did not speak to each other. They looked as if they could not trust their voices, or even their thoughts.

When they entered the inner office, Mr. Morris pushed Alex in front of him into a chair. "What can we do with a child who destroys things and ruins the happiness of others?" he demanded loudly. "How do you teach a child gratitude for what you've provided for him? All we get is disrespect!" He glared at Alex, while Mrs. Morris took out a handkerchief to wipe her eyes.

It was obvious to us that the parents expected a "trial" for the boy, with one of the authors the judge and the other the jury, a situation not helpful for either parent or professional. In order to begin clearing up the problems, we immediately asked that the boy be excused while we talked with the parents.

Alex had ruined his sister's wedding.

Considered one of the major events in the life of the Morris family, Cindy's wedding ceremony and reception had taken months of planning. Almost every day, Cindy and her mother and father met with the myriads of people required to execute the lavish celebration successfully. Alex had not made a fuss about having to remain in the background during this hectic period. His parents had felt that there was not much a ten-year-old could offer in this adult operation; a wedding was for grown-ups.

The wedding ceremony went well. The reception, however, was another matter. Some of the guests felt that the substitution of salt for sugar when serving coffee was mildly amusing. Mrs. Morris tried to remain calm, her smile frozen, as she brought new sugar bowls to the table. But when a screaming guest found Herman, Alex's pet frog, sitting in the punch bowl, and the harassed bride and groom found four flat tires on the honeymoon car, the actions of the now-discovered Alex were no longer considered funny—or even tolerable. Alex was condemned by the family as destructive, antisocial, and completely out of control. The Morrises angrily wanted to know what they should do about punishment. "Why?" his mother repeated wearily.

The message was fairly obvious. What the Morrises had overlooked was Alex's need to feel involved and important *before* the wedding. Alex had been almost totally ignored during the planning. As the big day approached, he felt increasingly unimportant and, even worse, unwelcome. Alex had wanted to do something that would bring attention to himself in order to regain his parents' interest. He resented his sister for dominating the spotlight for so long, so he decided that he would draw attention to himself by disrupting the reception. Alex wanted to announce his anger by his mischief. He did not realize the seriousness of his pranks. He thought that while everyone was laughing, his family's attention would shift back to him. The youngster was surprised, then horrified, when he realized how much damage he had done. The effect of his pranks was sharply, strongly, and painfully relayed to him by his irate parents and his sobbing sister. By then it was too late. He had signalled *too* loud and *too* hard—he had hurt the people he loved.

Alex had suffered enough from the reaction to his pranks. He did not need more punishment. Rather, he needed an opportunity to explain and apologize. His parents were helped to understand that Alex had signalled, in his clumsy way, his need for the attention and involvement he had been denied. Future acts of mischief could be avoided by involving Alex more fully in the planning of family activities. Alex was encouraged to call his sister and apologize. He asked if he could "earn money so I can get them something so they'll know I love them." His parents permitted him to do this. Alex was atoning for his mischief—and learning in the process.

Alex's story illustrates a *temporary* series of antisocial acts and shows the kinds of motivation that may cause a child to engage in antisocial behavior, whether temporary or long term. When a child feels the need for more attention and love, he or she may not think too clearly about the "proper" way to obtain it, and may do anything possible to get that attention "now."

Likewise, a child who feels he or she has no friends may engage in antisocial activity in order to obtain a fleeting moment of acceptance. Children who have grown up in family situations in which they don't feel "worth very much" may do anything asked by their peer group in order to gain that small moment of "belonging." The need for peer acceptance can be the motivation for serious antisocial behavior, especially in adolescence, when group acceptance becomes particularly important.

Jan was an only child, a thirteen-year-old who lived in a high-rise apartment in the middle of a large city. There were few children his own age in the neighborhood; consequently, his only friends were children from school. Both of his parents worked, and were often tired in the evening—so tired that they rarely asked to meet Jan's friends. They believed, without investigating, that Jan was accepted by his peers in school and that his friendships were healthy. It was comfortable and convenient to make that assumption.

Therefore his parents were bewildered and anguished when they received a telephone call from the police. Jan and his group of friends had written their names in black spray paint on parked buses. "How could he do this to us?" was their initial, confused cry.

Jan was not doing anything *to* them. He was performing an antisocial act *for himself;* he was gaining acceptance from his peer group. Jan was spontaneously acting the way the group wanted him to act without regard to his parents' wishes. His parents loved him; he was not sure that the group did.

This common form of adolescent behavior is difficult to control, for it means that you must present an almost impossible choice to the teenager: either to act against the wishes of his friends or to change that group of friends. Neither choice is easy for most adolescents. Open communication between parents and teenager can, however, help a youth make changes in his or her peer group situation. Parents who frequently invite their child's friends into the home can be aware of their adolescent's immediate world, his weaknesses and his strengths. Meeting and getting to know your teenager's circle of friends allows you to anticipate future problems. You are also meeting the other young people to whom your youngster may be turning for guidance. Sharing this role of adviser is essential for the parents of a teenager. Parents who make an effort to talk, but not lecture, to their teenage children about values, actions, and adolescent morals will learn as well as teach. It is during such calm, two-way discussions that parents can suggest the teenager could retain his values despite group pressure.

Jan's parents had to punish him for the antisocial behavior. But the basic actions that Jan's parents—and you—can take to combat antisocial behavior that is motivated by the need for peer acceptance are actions of *prevention*. When your adolescent becomes involved in serious antisocial behavior and you are unaware of his or her teenage world, you must look elsewhere for help and guidance. Sometimes the high-school guidance counsellor, a teacher, a coach, or a school club leader can be of help. Another friend who has a child in the same school or the same crowd may shed some light. Antisocial behavior that is motivated by peer pressure is a signal with a message that requires two immediate responses— punishment, followed by a prevention program.

The motivation behind antisocial acts can also be rebellion against the parents. The traditional adolescent-parent impasse, where neither child nor parents can communicate, is a common social phenomenon. Each finds himself in an impossible position. Something has to give. An explosion occurs—rebellion by the teenager—a breaking of tradition, values, or morals. This rebellion often takes the form of an antisocial act and signals, in the boldest terms, that communication *must* be established, at whatever cost. An antisocial act requires some type of response from the parent, even if the response is a punishing one. To a teenager who cannot communicate with his or her parents, a negative communication often may seem better than a frustrating silence. There is never a "Rebel Without a Cause"; the cause is often the need to express desperate feelings.

One of the differences between the signals from antisocial acts of young children and those of adolescents can be found in the person to whom these signals are being sent. In young children, an antisocial act is usually related to a problem between parent and child. These problems can often be helped by the parents. In adolescents, the problems that motivate antisocial acts are more likely to be related to persons outside the family, and they are likely to be acts accompanied by frustration and anger. The adolescent who is continually harassed by people at school will rebel against the school. Perhaps the problem with authority is created by the teenager's boss at work. The adolescent feels backed up against the wall; he cannot talk to the authority figure. The young person sees a dead end as far as possible change goes. So he vents his feelings by antisocial behavior. "This one's for you!" the young person silently tells the unfair teacher, as he hurls a brick through the gymnasium window. His actions are his unspoken words.

A parent may sense, or actually know, that an external authority such as the teacher or boss is having a continuous conflict with the adolescent. He may suspect that this disturbed relationship is the reason behind the young person's antisocial behavior. The signal says "frustration"; the message says: "Help me find a way out of this impossible situation." The parent should talk directly and immediately to the outsider who appears to be causing the youngster's pent-up anger. A compromise on the future relationship between child and authority figure *must* be reached. Sometimes it may be necessary to sever the relationship. Perhaps a class needs to be dropped or a job changed. Whatever the solution, if the problem has caused antisocial behavior, the message to the parent is loud and clear: Do something NOW to rescue your child!

As Gary's parents did.

Both of Gary's older brothers had been varsity swimmers. Their high-school letters were displayed proudly in the den. Gary knew that his father wanted him to live up to the family tradition. He practiced long hours at the "Y" pool. Soon Gary was feeling good about his backstroke, concentrating on that style because it was different from his brothers' prize-winning crawl stroke. The year he went out for the varsity squad was the year that the old coach retired and a young man took over the team. The new coach seemed unimpressed with the Wilkins name. In fact, Gary sensed that the new coach resented the fables about the Wilkins boys. From the first day, the new coach pressed Gary, riding him severely, demanding more from him than from the others. Gary's swimming time began to lengthen as he felt his muscles tense in the water. The harder he tried, the tougher the coach's reactions. Soon Gary was spending all his spare time at the pool trying to better his swimming time. His studies suffered, and his grades fell. One week before the first swimming meet, the coach announced in front of the entire team that Gary Wilkins had been cut from the squad. That night Gary sneaked three large bags of garbage into the school and dumped the refuse into the clean pool. Within minutes the guard caught Gary running from the building. The next day, Gary's embarrassed parents sat facing the school principal. Gary crouched in the corner of the office, his face turned toward the wall.

"Why, Gary?" the principal asked. Gary refused to answer. "Please answer, son," his mother pleaded. But the boy remained silent. The principal tapped on his desk. "If you don't tell me what made you do that terrible thing, young man, I will be forced to expel you." The threat fell upon deaf ears. Gary merely turned his body around so that no one else in the room could see his tears. Mr. Wilkins watched his mute son and thought of all the possibilities that could have caused his son to act so irresponsibly. Slowly the message within his son's taut, unhappy body came to him. "Were you cut from the team, Gary?" his father asked directly. His son nodded his head slowly, his face still averted. His father took a deep breath. He knew that there had to be more. "Well, the coach told me you weren't swimming so well," Mr. Wilkins commented casually. Gary merely shrugged. There was a momentary silence. "He also mentioned that he thought you were a troublemaker on the team." Mr. Wilkins threw this remark softly across the room. Gary bolted out of his chair, his face distorted with rage. He poured out his anger at the new coach, yelling and crying at the same time. Finally his father rose, walked over to Gary, and put his arms around his son's shoulders. Mr. Wilkins then turned to the principal and said very quietly, "I know my son. And I believe him. I think you and I have some investigating to do."

Without the sensitivity and insight to probe deeply enough to find the message behind Gary's signal of vandalism, Gary's father might have watched his son's school record ruined. A meeting between the father, the principal, and the new coach brought about a clearer picture of what had created the fire behind Gary's impulsive act. Gary refused to swim for that coach again. His father understood, but encouraged his son to try out for another swimming team. Gary became a medal winner in a different league. His signal had not paralyzed his family into shameful inertia—it had forced them to help the boy deal with an impossible and destructive situation.

Occasionally a parent will rear a child with as much communication as is possible, give as much love and attention as is feasible, and provide the youngster with flexible but rational values, only to have that child continuously engage in antisocial behavior. Such behavior may be that of the sociopathic child—the child who *always* has, and *always* will have, trouble distinguishing between right and wrong. This is a rare child, but a child who can be born into any family. Chronically antisocial, such a child does not seem to learn from punishments; he or she has no conceivable motivation for the antisocial acts, and seems free from obvious mental illness. If this is the case, you must get help from a professional person without delay. You will have to unravel the threads of your child's experience to see what reasons lay behind such damaging social behavior.

You may find that your child is *not* sociopathic. Perhaps there is a disturbance of logic or learning about which you were not aware. It has been found, for instance, that many children with serious learning disabilities appear sociopathic in adolescence because of the complex interactions between their learning problem and their school and home environment. These children move from failure in school to failure in society. Only a trained professional can guide you and help your child through the process of interpreting his or her chronic, serious antisocial behavior.

If your child begins to act in an antisocial manner, he or she is sending you a special signal which may say, "Give me more attention" or, "I am punishing you." When this happens, you, as parents, can act upon the signal and the underlying message and work with your child to reverse the negative way inner feelings are being expressed.

The signal could also be flashing "I hate school!", or "I don't have any friends." If this is the message, then you, as parents, must intervene and help your child build healthy friendships or sever unhealthy relationships. To do this successfully, you may need professional help.

Finally your child may be saying, "I can't help myself. I don't know how to be different." This signal also requires immediate professional help.

No child wants to live forever on the fringes of society as a chronically antisocial person. Children want to co-exist safely with peers, family, and adults who live by normal social values, and they need the freedom of acceptable self-expression. An antisocial youngster is painfully uncomfortable, recklessly smashing through life, desperately signalling for your help.

22

Male Effeminate and Female Masculine Behaviors

So many incorrect concepts of effeminacy in males creep into the thinking of adults that a discussion of the term and an explicit description of what we are talking about is absolutely necessary. Not only will the signal have a more precise meaning, but an understanding of the term will relieve a number of young males of a horrendous burden—an unnecessary label.

Effeminate behavior in the male is an ACTION description. The effeminate male is one who has adapted the overt physical mannerisms of the opposite sex. In other words, an effeminate young man is one who walks and talks more like the opposite sex than his own. The swishing gait with rolling hips, the limp wrist, the sibilant, high-pitched speech, the frequent tossing of the head—when these are predominant behavior patterns—constitute visible effeminacy in the male.

Our society has incorrectly equated the term "effeminate" with the *interests* of the young man. If a boy shows a proclivity toward the artistic, such as piano, dance, or drama, he is often inaccurately labeled effeminate. A young man who enjoys cooking or working in the garden or sewing tears in his clothes is stupidly and cruelly viewed as being effeminate. This is carried to the extreme in the very young boy who is prohibited from playing with dolls. All of these myths, held by adults, are based on the misconception that there is something that can be clearly defined as "masculine"

196

behavior. Because this fantasy has been passed from generation to generation, boys, and later men, spend their lives repressing many of the pleasures they might otherwise experience and attempt to cultivate instead the "macho" image of masculinity. The athletic, unemotional, nonaesthetic, male, strong and silent, is the nation's false stereotype of the "masculine" male. Many young men try desperately to attain that image and fail. This inability to find the distorted masculine stereotype can create grave doubts within a young man about himself and lead to serious emotional problems.

If we are allowed to mature with all of our interests emerging and flowering, we discover that every man has a blend, a balance of the so-called masculine and feminine traits within his personality. Some have fewer feminine interests, others more. *In no way does this make the latter effeminate.* We can only feel fortunate that the male with aesthetic qualities exists in our society, or we would have been deprived of many of our great artists, pianists, actors, chefs, authors, architects, and dancers. However, many young men with the potential to excell in such areas are turned off because they fear that they will be considered "sissies" if they pursue these natural talents and interests. For the mental health of the young men in our society, we MUST get rid of the destructive stereotype of the "masculine" male as the ultimate achievement for our growing boys.

There are times when a parent looks at his son and detects the emergence of the outward physical characteristics of feminine actions. Correctly, he (it is usually the father) interprets this signal as effeminate behavior. And immediately terror strikes as he projects the total sexual collapse of his son. This need not be the case at all. The effeminate behavior is a signal that must be analyzed by the parent to determine what message is being sent by swaying hips or girlish laughter.

Oscar Stern had been divorced from his wife for five years, but he had kept in close contact with his four children. He had two older daughters, a son, and his youngest was a girl. When his son was fourteen years old, Oscar began to detect the signs of outward effeminate behavior in the boy. He became increasingly alarmed. He tried discussing this with his ex-wife but she could see nothing wrong with Robbie. Oscar talked with his older daughter. "Robbie's OK," she said casually. "He just acts that way because he's around all of us so much. Remember, Dad, there's no other man in our house." Oscar's oldest daughter had put her finger on the message behind the emerging effeminacy of his son. As Oscar Stern thought through the problem, he realized the truth. When he visited, he rarely took Robbie out by himself. He had had little individual contact with the boy. Almost everything was done with several of the children together. Robbie had a few male friends, but, not being particularly athletic, he preferred to concentrate on his talent for carpentry. Working alone in the basement, he created satisfying pieces of furniture. Oscar Stern realized that it had been a natural development for Robbie *unconsciously* to copy the physical mannerisms of the women who surrounded him. He had few male contacts to emulate. Oscar restructured his visits. Every other visit, he and Robbie did things together, things that Robbie wanted to do. Oscar was surprised to learn that his son liked baseball. Together they began going to the games. They visited furniture shows together, went to films, and often just went to Oscar's apartment to eat and talk. Robbie became attached to his father in a more positive way than ever before and Oscar Stern became a real model and presence in Robbie's life. The effeminate behavior gradually disappeared.

Being in a predominantly female environment can subtly move a young man to adopt some feminine mannerisms. Every young man should have male role models to copy. If his father is not around due to death or divorce, or is living in the house as a passive, uninvolved observer, the youngster will need to find other male figures with whom to relate. It would be ideal to motivate the passive father, but often this is impossible—and sometimes undesirable since the father's passivity and disinterest can be more damaging than helpful to the boy's image development. Male teachers of music, art, drama, literature, athletics, or religion, Boy

Scout leaders—even a Big Brother—may provide the solution to the problem of effeminate behavior in the young male within a household of women. The signal is the effeminacy; the message is the lack of male role models. The action is to correct the message, providing an environment with more males.

The mother of the boy with effeminate behavior has a real responsibility in looking for the message behind the signal of her son's effeminacy. This responsibility carries the difficult task of being totally honest and candid in first a self-analysis and then an analysis of her relationship with her son. Effeminacy in a young man may be the indirect result of the son's over-identification with the mother. In some instances this is caused by an overly strong bond between the mother and son, who are too dependent on each other for emotional nourishment. Here the shift must occur from the mother to a male figure in the young man's life, be it his father, grandfather, another male relative, or friend. It takes a "well-put-together" mother to give up the emotional rewards she is receiving from her son and offer some of these to the male person. But the ultimate reward will be the loss of the boy's effeminate behavior and, as a result, a better adjustment to society. If the mother cannot do this for her son with ease, she should receive counselling to help her find the replacements to fill the void that will be created when she loses the close relationship with her son. Then the shift will not be so painful to the mother that she cannot bring herself to act.

Another reason for a son's over-identification with his mother might be the mother's role in the family. Often the woman literally rules and runs the house. The male child mistakenly identifies with this dominant figure, assuming some of her outward mannerisms as he also assimilates her inner strengths and resources. However, it is the feminine affectations that the world observes in her son and mocks. Such a mother must reassess her role in the family and realize that she is providing the wrong role model, "masculine" behavior. It is not uncommon for a father to be present in such a wife-dominated household. But unless the mother is capable of transferring some of the family leadership to the father, and unless he is willing to accept this responsibility, the young boy will continue to see the mother as the pivotal force in the family and the emulation will continue. A dramatic breakthrough must occur. Family counselling may help. In the meantime, the search for other male role models for the young man should begin, if his father is available but unwilling. The message behind this boy's signal of effeminacy is: "Mother is the male. I should copy her." Reverse family sex roles may work for the parents but they can play havoc with the sexual identification of the children.

Fourteen-year-old Mike was tall, willowy, awkward, and had relatively poor muscular coordination. Though he tried, he could not play sports and become a valuable member of any team. As a result, he was repeatedly rejected by the other boys in school and around his athletically oriented neighborhood. He tried watching but was constantly told he was "in the way." Yet Mike desperately wanted male friends. He enjoyed movies and acting very much. He would invite other boys to go to films with him, but they would refuse because they had a game that night. He tried joining a dramatic class, but his awkwardness and shyness worked against him, and he was shunned by the other boys in that group. Finally, Mike found a friend in a neighborhood girl who had a heavy, ungainly body and had been made an outcast by the other children. Together they built a deep and meaningful friendship. But within weeks, Mike was adopting many of the girl's physical mannerisms. He was becoming overtly effeminate.

Mike demonstrated the message of male rejection as the basic cause of his effeminate behavior. Had he been able to associate with the other young men, it is highly unlikely that he would have shifted toward the female gestures. Often parents are not aware of this painful process occurring in their son's life. Only if they stop and look at his daily schedule will they realize that their son has too few male friends. Mike was ashamed to discuss his problems openly with his father. This was his own personal failure, and he suspected that there was something wrong with him as a male. His dad had to observe the patterns developing in Mike's life carefully and approach his son with gentle concern before the boy could unburden his frustration. Wisely, Mike's father made no attempt to destroy the warm friendship Mike had with his female friend. He merely tried to add a balance in Mike's life. He and Mike went to the YMCA together, enrolled in the swimming club, and practiced together, enjoying each other's company while Mike improved his swimming skills. Mike's father encouraged his son to join one of the boys' clubs in the YMCA on other nights. Slowly Mike realized that he could be accepted by other males, first and most importantly, by his father, and next, by his own male peer group. His image of himself as a male improved and the effeminate behavior disappeared almost completely. Mike's father had seen his son's signal, had encouraged Mike to help him interpret the message, and then, thoughtfully and appropriately, joined his son in an effort to solve the underlying problems.

Effeminate behavior also may be a subtle, frequently subconscious way that a young boy can rebel against his father; often this will occur in the early teens. Alan told us: "I hate my father," quite openly when the family relationships were explored. His mother had brought him into our office because she was becoming increasingly concerned about his signalling effeminacy. "Why?" we asked. He was so full of anger that it was difficult for him to speak. "What does he do that makes you so angry?" Alan literally spat out his reply: "He's so sure of himself. He thinks he's always right. He controls my mother and my sister. He also tries to control me. Everything about me has to be tough. If I cry, he calls me a 'sissy.' If I want to help Mom with the cooking, he makes fun of me. The worst thing is he keeps telling me I throw a baseball like a girl. Being a he-man is the most important thing in his life. Much more important than me!" Alan resented the unrealistic, macho, overly masculine attitude of his father. It represented and personified his father's unfair and unreasonable actions. He wanted to deny this man, to reject him and everything he stood for. His effeminate behavior was the most effective way of striking at his father's most vulnerable area.

The solution to the message behind Alan's signal lay within the ability of his father to see himself as Alan had. The father had to change his attitude and approach toward his son. This is not always possible. In the case of Alan's father, it was not. He refused to give up his distorted views of a "man's" role in the home and in society. Alan's father could not and would not change. Recommendations that he seek help fell on deaf ears. Alan's mother was advised to seek out other male role models for her son, other men who would appreciate the positive qualities in the young man and reward him for these attributes. Fortunately her brother was more than willing to assume that role. Very carefully, so that the father would not feel overly threatened, Alan's uncle began having dinners with Alan, getting involved in Alan's interests, and opening some of his own hobbies for the boy's appraisal. An important "other male" relationship had begun in Alan's life and his effeminate behavior was no longer necessary. What a pity that the male figure could not have been Alan's father.

Parents may sometimes misinterpret the "dressing up" of young boys in girl's clothing as signals of effeminacy. Many youngsters under the age of puberty will go through periods of curiosity about the dress of the opposite sex. For very brief periods of time, often just once, they will put on their mother's or older sister's clothing and stare at themselves in the mirror. There is a sense of "What would I look like if . . ." about this exploration. It has no deepseated meaning other than the transient curiosity of the very young. At times, an older sister will dress up a younger brother in female clothing as part of their play. Again, this should not be viewed with undue alarm by parents, creating shame or worry on the part of either child. If these are brief episodes, they have little consequence in the child's life. Parents should not worry if their seven-year-old son dressed up like a witch on Halloween. It is for one night only and a "funny" costume. The brief episode of dressing up as the opposite sex has no greater meaning than that. Only when the dressing in female clothing continues as the young boy grows should the parents become concerned. In this event, the signal is different, but the messages may be the same as those we have elaborated for effeminate behavior.

Bennett was sixteen years old when he came to see us, at his parents' request, about his effeminate behavior. Bennett was chubby and short. His body form had more the appearance of a young girl's than that of a male; the wide hips, slightly full fatty breasts, and poor muscular development set him apart from the other boys his age. It was apparent that his parents' concerns were real. Bennett was decidedly effeminate. Tactfully we told Bennett about his effeminate behavior. "I know," he said sadly. "Is there anything we can do to help?" we asked. He shook his head. "No," he said in a low voice. "I guess I'm just queer. So I act like I am." There was a brief silence as the words, the message, sounded throughout the office. "Why do you think you're queer, Bennett?" He shrugged. "Well, look at me. I look like a girl. And the kids treat me like I am. The guys all call me 'fag.' I'm sure *they* must know." He stopped and began twisting his hands in his lap. "How about you, Bennett? Do you think you're homosexual?" The word exploded in the boy's face. He looked up, startled. "I don't know. That's what worries me. I must be if they all think I am." The interviewer shook his head. "Absolutely not, Bennett. What other people think you are is not what you are. You are what is in your own head. Now let's talk about what Bennett is thinking, not anybody else."

With this introduction, the conversation moved into the exploration of Bennett's sexual drives and confusions. What emerged was the fact that Bennett was *concerned* about his sexual identity rather than certain about it. He had allowed the opinions of others to convince him that he was "queer" and his effeminacy was the result. Many young men have very real doubts about themselves as sexual beings during the adolescent years. When these concerns escalate into a belief, whether real or false, that they have homosexual tendencies, young males will ease into the effeminate behavior they presume to be part of their problem. Parents must be alert for these signals because it is at this stage of the male adolescent's sexual growth that help can be very useful in assisting the young man to sort out his feelings accurately. The message in Bennett's signal of effeminacy was his own concern and doubt about his sexuality.

One of the major myths of our time is that male effeminate behavior means homosexuality and that all homosexuals are effeminate. Neither is true. Many men exhibiting physical actions that are effeminate are active, well-adjusted heterosexuals. The vast majority of male homosexuals are not effeminate and cannot be distinguished from their heterosexual peers. Parents must deal with effeminate behavior as an outward physical signal, not necessarily as a sign of inner sexual tendencies.

*   *   *

Today fewer parents appear to be concerned when their daughters are demonstrating masculine behavior. This is a sign of our times. For years, the young girl has always been allowed to climb trees, play football with the boys, and wear pants rather than dresses. Her parents would merely shrug and wait for the "tomboy" phase to pass. Rarely would they worry. With the advent of the "blue jean" teenage society, the young girl can grow into adolescence without shedding much of her tomboy behavior. Feminist movements have liberated most young women to compete with their male friends in school, business, and athletic activities. Even the traditionally "masculine"-oriented church leadership is beginning to admit that women are truly equal.

Occasionally, however, a girl can push the masculine image to extremes, denying her femaleness openly and almost rebelliously. This could be a signal that warrants the attention of parents to decipher the message behind the behavior.

As with the effeminate male in the all-female environment, the young girl reared in a predominantly male household may copy the lifestyle and mannerisms of the men around her. She, too, needs the correct sex models. Introducing the young girl to the appropriate adult female will open her eyes to the positive aspects of being a woman. The decision will be hers ultimately; but as a parent, you have provided her with opportunities that will help her "enjoy being a girl," as a popular song proclaims.

Like the young boy, the young girl will dress up in boy's clothes, stride around with shoulders thrown back, speak in a false, deep voice, and audition for the role of male. This is again a normal exploratory phase in the young girl's life and only becomes a signalling problem when the sex reversal in clothes becomes too extreme or too prolonged, suggesting that it has become an essential part of the young girl's lifestyle.

Beth was a source of constant embarrassment to her mother. By the age of twelve, she persisted in wearing boy's clothes and refused to put on anything feminine. Beth's greatest concern was whether the neighborhood boys would allow her to play stick ball with them in the evenings. When girls from school called, Beth was short and terse with them, always turning down invitations to slumber parties and weekends. She had a sister two years older who was feminine and popular with her girlfriends and who dated frequently. When Mrs. Wilson asked her daughter to explain her behavior, the girl laughed and replied, "I'm me. That's the way I am." This in no way satisfied her mother. Finally, Mr. Wilson was brought into the picture. His wife begged him to have a talk with their daughter. "After all, she's closer to you anyway. She'll probably tell you what she won't tell me." There was a tinge of resentment in Mrs. Wilson's voice.

Mr. Wilson took Beth aside one evening and asked, "Honey, why don't you wear dresses?" The girl grimaced. "I don't like them," she replied. "Why?" her father persisted. "Would you wear dresses?" the girl challenged. "But," the father replied, perplexed, "I'm a man. Men don't wear dresses." Beth nodded and said nothing. Finally her father pleaded. "It would make me very happy if you would dress more like a girl, sweetheart." The girl wrinkled her forehead. Then, "That sounds funny coming from you," she said abruptly. "Why?" "Because . . ." Beth stopped for a very long minute, "I always thought you'd like me more if I were like a boy." Mr. Wilson swallowed hard. Beth had slammed her message home very distinctly and hit the mark.

Mr. Wilson had wanted a boy very badly when Beth was born. He played rough games with her as a child, taught her football, and substituted his daughter for the wished-for son. The little girl grew to love and respect her father, picked up the not-so-subtle signals he was sending, and responded accordingly. She was trying desperately to be the son he had wanted but had not had.

The Wilsons now understood the message behind Beth's signal of excessive masculine behavior. Female role models were already in the home—mother and sister. What the mother needed was to know how to get closer to her daughter. To do this, Mr. Wilson had to step aside carefully but without rejecting Beth in the process. He had to indicate that he was pleased and delighted with his daughter *as a girl* and support her growth into a woman.

Some girls will develop masculine physical mannerisms because they perceive that, in life, men "get all the breaks." The aggressive, ambitious young woman may develop certain masculine characteristics in order to prepare herself to cope and fight in the "tough world of men." This is no longer as necessary as it was two decades ago, when a woman in the fields of medicine, business, or journalism had to be as masculine as her male peers to be accepted. Today, in most professions, women can succeed by being themselves and allowing their talent and femininity rather than pseudo-masculinity to prove their worth. Occasionally a girl has not received that message and assumes the masculine stance early in life to compete with boys in sports, classwork, school politics, and such extracurricular activities as the newspaper or the debating society. Parent and teacher must be prepared to detect that signal and the underlying message. They have to answer that message by telling the girl that in today's world such excessive masculine behavior is not necessary to succeed. Therapy may be needed to help drive the message home. It becomes extremely important that girls NOT be allowed to attribute any failures or losses to their femininity, but be urged honestly to assess the real underlying reasons for failure. Otherwise any advice will go unheeded and the excessive masculine mannerisms will continue.

An adolescent female who finds herself wanting to avoid involvement with her crowd in the sexual-social area may use male mannerisms to "turn off" the other kids. Sometimes the message is that the "crowd" is too preoccupied with sex for the young girl; at other times, the young girl has a poor self-concept and protects herself from rejection by assuming an unacceptable masculine stance. This is not an uncommon protective smokescreen thrown up by the homely or obese teenager. Parents must remain aware of this possibility because the underlying message is fraught with pain and confusion. The girl does not want to lose her feminine behavior; she gives it up reluctantly to protect herself from further emotional harm. The reassurance and understanding of the parent will go a long way in assisting such a young girl to shed this uncomfortable male mantle. Once she can look at her problems realistically, the girl, with her parents' help, can begin to deal with her other problem. Knowing that it is normal for her to wait for sexual activity will ease her dilemma. Finding positive qualities that overshadow poor looks or excessive weight will also go a long way toward healing the second series of wounds.

*   *   *

Although this chapter is dedicated to debunking the myth that the child who exhibits actions characteristic of the opposite sex is homosexual, parents will sometimes find that the stereotype *is* confirmed. The adolescent may be homosexual. Or parents may be reading this chapter because they suspect that their child is homosexual and are seeking guidance. Whatever the case, such parents need advice.

In *Sex and the American Teenager** Dr. Kappelman offers this counsel to parents in a chapter entitled "Homosexuality, Bisexuality, and the Teenager":

---

*New York: Reader's Digest Press, 1977. Reprinted with permission.

What can you do if your teenager announces or if you discover that he or she is homosexual? I do not mean that you find out about a single episode, but that the young person firmly states that his sexual predilection is homosexual.

First, and most important, hold back the immediate shock reaction, the instantaneous horror or anger or shame. It took courage for the young person to make the announcement; it will take equal courage for him to admit the truth if he is confronted with valid evidence. Do not destroy this courage by reacting badly from the beginning. Restrain yourself from quickly condemning the young person and announcing your complete disillusionment. Both you and your teenager will need courage to discuss this difficult issue, reach a mutual ground of understanding, and agree on the behaviors and actions that are to ensue.

Next, attempt to get from the youngster an accurate interpretation of his definition of his homosexuality. Is it based on a single encounter? Is it firmly rooted in numerous homosexual episodes with persistent same-sex fantasies and erotic dreams? These are two entirely different states. The former may well be a misinterpretation by the teenager of a minor sexual encounter; the latter may be an honest admission of exclusive homosexuality in the teenage period. Without embarrassment or judgment, help your teenager discuss his sexual preferences and the basis for his announcement of his homosexuality. Do not ask him the erotic or lurid details of his sex life. Give your teenager that important rope of dignity as a support. Delve, but not too deeply or intimately.

If the issue appears to be a misconception on the adolescent's part, attempt to help him understand that there are many alternate experimental experiences lying ahead. If the panic or fear about the homosexuality is so tense that he seems fixed on the issue, seek professional help if the youngster is willing.

Ask the pediatrician or family physician for the name of a psychiatrist or clinical psychologist who deals perceptively with the issue of homosexuality. Certain religious agencies in your area such as Catholic Charities or Associated Jewish Charities may have specific adolescent counseling services usually manned by well-trained social workers and psychologists. Hospital clinics (pediatric, adolescent, or psychiatric) may provide long-range counseling. The medical director of the local university or community hospital may be another good source for advice. If your adolescent needs and wants help, do not stop until you help him find the right source.

* * *

It must be noted that not all homosexual teenagers are in need of psychotherapy. A majority appear reasonably adjusted to their sexual pattern and have no desire to "change." The switch to a heterosexual orientation would be doomed to failure in these cases. As the parents of a young homosexual who does not want an alteration in his sexual preferences, you must learn to see your child not as a "homosexual" but as a growing young man or woman who has an alternative sex style. Your child is a total human being. His only singular difference from what you want him to be may be in the area of his sexual preferences. Do not banish him from your love and concern on that singular basis only. He will always be your child.

Finally, remember that your child's sexuality is but one small part of the total person. And bear in mind that many successful, well-adjusted individuals in all walks of life (including the professional fields, artistic areas, and the police force and armed services) are homosexual or bisexual, adjust and adapt well, and offer a valuable and important contribution to our society. Despite Anita Bryant's inferences, we must make it quite clear that very few homosexuals are child molesters; and, as noted by the recent decision of the American Psychiatric Association, the majority of homosexuals are NOT sick persons. There is nothing "sinful," "immoral," or "sick" in being homosexual as long as the young person is adjusted and adapted to the society around him or her. In addition, the society that nurtures the young person, particularly the youngster's parents, can add to the potential of the young homosexual-bisexual's adjustment by a gentle and supportive acceptance of the sexual fact—if acceptance and understanding is basically what the young person is seeking. Look at your total child— not merely the alternative and different sexual road he or she may be taking. We cannot change the feelings of the general society.

The homosexual youngster will be hurt and scorned. But the strength to weather these painful personal insults will come from the consistent, loving, and understanding support of accepting parents: the knowledge that whatever is thrown at the youngster in disdain is directed at a person who has the capacity to know and like himself or herself.

We do not advocate homosexuality as a sexual style. We accept it. This should be the parents' attitude as well. There is so much beauty in your child. Never allow the cloud of alternative sexual preference to darken the sunlight of his or her life and accomplishments.

23

Suicide Threats

As strange as it may seem, childhood suicide is not an uncommon tragedy. The danger of the child wanting to destroy her or his own life increases dramatically as she or he approaches and enters adolescence. During the first two years of Maryland's suicide prevention program, for example, sixty-five youngsters were identified who had attempted suicide. This was in only *one* hospital in one large urban city. The median age of the youngsters was sixteen years, 75 percent were girls, and 18 percent had made a previous suicide attempt. Obviously, in about one-fifth of the cases, the important signal of suicide had gone unheeded.

There are two vital points of differentiation that the parent—as calmly as possible—must make in interpreting suicide in childhood. The first is the difference between a threat and an overt action. The action speaks for itself. It is an actual attempt on the child's part to *do* something. The threat may have several messages. The child may only be talking about the possibility, without having attempted anything. Or the child may be quite serious. Parents and/or professional counsellors must differentiate the intent of a potential suicide. Is the action only a call for help or is it an actual desire to cut short a young life? The threat may be either manipulative or innocent; or it may be the first sign that action is about to occur. The parent is faced with a complex set of possibilities, which must be sorted out as quickly, carefully, and as calmly as possible. To help parents who may have to cope with this frightening signal, various underlying messages will be discussed here in an effort to shed some light on what the child is really telling the parent and the outside world when she or he threatens or attempts suicide.

Occasionally a young child will say, "I wish I were dead!" How serious is that signal? Often the youngster is merely verbalizing an extreme sense of frustration at a situation or event he or she feels helpless to conquer or solve. Rather than immediately jumping to the conclusion that this child is emotionally ill or potentially suicidal, the parent should gently probe for the significance of the message behind these ominous words. Sitting down with the youngster in the quiet of his or her room and asking simply, "Why?" will frequently uncover the worries and concerns over what the child sees as an unsolvable problem. Being left out of the school play, being cut from the baseball team, failing in school, or losing a cherished friendship, all can lead a young person to make the dramatic overstatement of wanting to die. In reality, the child is NOT considering suicide, but voicing the feeling that the problem is so serious it warrants the most extreme expression of despair. After learning what the reasons are behind the signal, interpreting the message, the parent can then reach out to the child by asking, "Is there anything I can do to help?" This provides the desperate youngster with an ally, someone to whom they can look for support and guidance in solving the problem. And it is very important because so often it is the sense of isolation and inability to cope with the problem that causes a young person to express the wish to be dead.

Sometimes the parent is directly involved in the reasons behind the child's abject sense of despair. Fear of parental reaction to a school failure or concern over parental disappointment at failure to make an athletic team may be key factors in the child's "giving-up" philosophy. When this is the case, the child may initially be too upset to accept or acknowledge his or her parents' help. But parents must keep searching for ways to make the youngster understand that they *can* accept his problem, *can* live with it, and are *willing* to help to solve the problem. It is extremely important for parents to give the child the distinct impression that something CAN be done to work through such a frustrating and seemingly hopeless problem. Once the child understands and accepts this fact, the abject despair that precipitated the signal "I wish I were dead!" will be defused. He or she will have found parents—friends —to help him or her through the difficult situation.

What lies behind the child's message may need very careful scrutiny on the part of the parents. "Why is she so upset about an apparently isolated situation?" should be a question. "Are we playing a role in creating such overreaction? Is someone else?" "Are there other areas in which she has been signalling us that she has a very poor opinion of herself?" The first three questions will require investigation of causes. Why is she failing in school? What can be done to help her either make the athletic team or find another way of proving herself to her friends? How can parents take the heat off failures? These are examples of important questions that must be asked and answered by the parents when faced with a young child who dramatically declares that she has run up against a brick wall in her life. When the answer is "yes" to the last question, that of self-image, this answer should precipitate a more serious and concerned approach to the signal. The family doctor and mental health professionals should quickly be brought into the picture. Any child who has poor self-esteem needs help from both parents and experts outside the home. He or she could be on the road to emotional illness and suicide.

Danny was only a fair student in school. He enjoyed sports and excelled in both baseball and football, winning school letters which he wore proudly on his sweater. But he had to force himself to study to pass through the eleventh and twelfth grades. Danny's father was a dentist; his mother a teacher. His older brother was highly motivated, bright, doing very well at an Ivy League graduate school. His example was frequently used to try to stimulate Danny to better academic achievements in high school. During the twelfth grade, the subject of college naturally arose in a family discussion. For many weeks, Danny avoided talking about where he wanted to apply. Finally his father confronted him with a large list of colleges and said firmly, "Pick several and we will start applying." Danny paused, then asked timidly, "What would you think if I took a year off and worked, Dad?" His father stared at him in disbelief. His mouth tightened. "I wouldn't accept that at all." Danny's message was not being heard. Reluctantly, Danny wrote for the applications, chosen finally by his father. As the forms began to arrive in the mail, Danny's anxiety mounted. He stuffed the application forms in his top bureau drawer and tried to forget them, but his father asked, repeatedly, if they had been mailed. "Not yet. Tomorrow," was Danny's anxious reply.

In January of his senior year, Danny was suddenly called into his father's study. "Your mother found these crumpled papers in your bureau. You have not applied to college, and that's completely unacceptable to us! Sit down right this minute and fill them out," his father commanded. Danny's hands trembled as he took his pen and started to write on the forms. After about fifteen hesitant minutes Danny looked at his father's stern face and said in a small, pleading voice, "Don't make me go to college, Dad. Not now. *Please.*" The father banged his fist on his desk. "Fill out those goddamn forms. You've got to grow up sometime. Now is as good a time as any. NOW!" Danny started to sob. Finally he stood up and shouted in a choked voice, "If you make me go to college, I'll kill myself!" But again the message was blocked by Danny's father's personal aspirations for his son. "Stop being such a damn fool. You'll do no such thing. You can take these forms with you. Be sure they're in the mail by this weekend."

That Saturday night Danny stayed at home, an unusual action for the popular young man. His parents did not question him. They dressed and left for the neighborhood dinner party. When they returned, they found Danny lying on the living room floor, asleep. A bottle of sleeping pills was by his hand and several pills lay on the floor around his body. The bottle was empty.

Danny was rushed to the nearest hospital, his stomach was pumped, and he was observed for several hours. He awakened quickly, since he had taken only three of the sleeping pills. He had flushed the rest down the toilet. As he lay in his hospital bed, his father walked wearily into the room and sat down by the bed, his face a study in guilt. "You really meant it," was all he could say. Danny nodded. "Please, Dad, please let up on me. And listen." The older man nodded. Quietly, Danny began to explain himself. He talked. His father listened finally—and heard. For the first time in their lives, true communication had begun between them.

Because he had failed to "hear" his son on the several occasions that preceded the suicide gesture, Danny's father had forced the boy into trying a desperate signal. Danny had no intention of killing himself. He merely had to show his father the impossible situation into which he felt he was being pushed; the signal was the suicide *gesture*. The message was manipulation of his family so that someone would pay attention. The deeper meaning was the need for a level of communication between Danny and his parents that would allow him to live his own life. How tragic that it had to be forced by a false attempt at suicide! And yet there are thousands of Dannys who make these dramatic gestures every year. They do not mean to harm themselves, but only to send the signal that they have to be heard. The frighteningly serious aspect of this signal is that occasionally a harmless attempt backfires—the youngster dies.

Contrast Danny's story with Henry's. Henry was also a high-school senior. He was the oldest and highest achieving of six children in a very religious family. Henry was an excellent tennis player; he was captain of the swimming team; he had the lead in the senior play; and he made the honor roll every term. His family thrived on the achievements of their oldest son. And Henry realized this. There was only one problem in Henry's life. During his senior year, he came to the realization that he was homosexual.

At first he tried desperately to deny his feelings. He threw himself more avidly into schoolwork and athletic activities. He dated girls more and more frequently. But the reality of his sexual orientation kept recurring to him whenever he paused long enough to have a private moment by himself. Cautiously he raised the subject with his parents in an oblique way one evening after dinner. "You want to hear something interesting?" he started his conversation. "One of the guys on the swimming team told me he was gay." "Gay?" his father asked. "Yes," Henry gulped. "Homosexual." He sat back and waited for his parents' response. "How sickening," his mother said. "You be sure to keep away from him!" Henry turned away from her and looked hopefully toward his father. His father frowned. "His father should beat it out of him. He doesn't have to be!" the older man said firmly. Henry felt his heart pounding. "But he's really a great guy. And he said his family understands." "Understands!" his father exploded. "If he were mine, I'd kick him out of the house before I'd live under the same room with a perverted son." Henry said nothing but excused himself and went into his room, deeply depressed.

Throughout the weeks that followed, Henry's parents began to notice that he was staying in his room a great deal. He had virtually stopped dating, and when his friends called, he would tell his parents to say he was not at home. He unexpectedly quit the swimming team. His grades began to fall. His parents could hardly fail to notice the change. That signal they could understand, but not the message. His father called him to the dinner table before the other children sat down and asked him what was bothering him. "I can't tell you," Henry said in a low, depressed voice. "Why not?" his father demanded. "Because you'll hate me." The boy started to cry. "That's ridiculous," his father responded, touching his son's arm. The boy looked up and said very quietly to the older man, "I was the boy I was telling you about, Dad. I'm the homosexual who was on the swimming team." His father stared at Henry for a minute and then spoke angrily, "Don't ever say that again. Not in this house. Do you hear?" Henry nodded, crept away from the table, and stayed in his room throughout dinner. Before he left, he told his father, "I can't live with you feeling that way." His father turned away.

That night Henry successfully hung himself in his closet.

Henry had verbalized his signal; he had indicated his unwillingness to live any longer while having to face his problem alone, without parental understanding. Not only had they missed his message through their unwillingness to face Henry's personal situation, but they had forced the young man to take desperate action. Is this too stark, too extreme a case history to make the point about the serious suicide threat in the adolescent? Not really. Because most teenage suicides fall close to this pattern: problems denied by parents, signals of threatened suicide ignored, refusal to accept dramatic changes in adolescent behavior as signs of serious depression, and the consequent rejection of life.

An adolescent will commit suicide alone. But he has involved many people in the hours, days, or months that went into making that tragic decision. People who fail to perceive the signals or messages that cause the singular act of self-destruction assist that suicide.

A factor in adolescent suicide that is often overlooked by parents and professionals alike is that there can be *subconscious* attempts at self-destruction, used by teenagers to escape from the stress within their lives. These are the most subtle of signals. The young person who has repeated automobile accidents may NOT be a careless driver. He may be trying, subconsciously, to kill himself. The diabetic girl who repeatedly "forgets" to take her insulin may be signalling to the parent and the physician her desire to die. The young person who persistently experiments with unknown drugs from strangers may have the hidden agenda to take the "final trip." A suicide need not be announced nor the attempts made flagrantly obvious. The adolescent who constantly throws himself or herself into life-threatening situations may be toying with death in a calculated way. This is a signal that must penetrate! Parents must become sensitized to a suicide possibility as they shake their bewildered heads at the fifth auto accident or the third dangerous fall.

Suicide threats and attempts appear to be very explicit—"I want out of life." But that may not be the message at all. "I want help . . . or understanding . . . or acceptance," is more usually closer to the actual message. The young person may be merely acting out or may be seriously ill emotionally. The threat may be innocent or serious. There may be no more complex or serious a signal than suicide threats and actions. It should be very obvious to the reader that the *signals* in Danny's message-giving suicide gesture were very similar to those in Henry's life-ending suicide threat. It may not be easy for the inexperienced parent to tell the *messages* apart; in fact, it may be dangerous for the emotionally upset parent to even try. *The parents must consult the family physician and other mental health experts in every case.* Objectivity and professional analysis are always needed to sift through such signals, their messages, and the underlying problems. Pay attention to this signal—call for help. You may be saving your child's life.

24

Promiscuity

When today's parents were themselves teenagers, the word "promiscuous" had a very definite meaning. In the forties and fifties, it signified someone who indulged in frequent sexual activity, usually with different partners. However, in today's liberated adolescent sexual society, the word has lost some of these connotations to take on a blurred and indistinct meaning. "How often is too often?" "How many partners are too many?" One would project that for every teenager questioned on these points, an equal number of different answers would be forthcoming. Thus for today's adolescent population, "promiscuity" may have a different meaning to each teenager.

However, for most parents, the word still carries the original meaning of frequent sexual experiences. In other words, the youngster who is quite sexually active is often viewed with alarm by his or her parents as being "promiscuous." Because this situation in one's child may create concern in the parent, the problem deserves discussion. But even more important, the adolescent who is sexually active is giving off a signal. The signal is sexual, but the message very often is not. It is therefore important to look carefully at the possible messages—the reasons why a young person may be challenging parental morality by acting out sexually.

Occasionally a parent will overhear a young teenager boasting in whispered conversations about sexual exploits. Before allowing panic to set in, the parent must give the situation a thorough "once-over." One of the commonest ways a young teenager can make himself interesting and important to his friends is to boast about sexual exploits, real or fantasized. In this day of female independence, such action extends to the adolescent female population as well. Most frequently the thirteen- or fourteen-year-old is "talking a good game." The message is that the youngster needs to be a somebody with the other kids—boasting of sexual conquests has come down through the generations as a way of accomplishing status. What can a parent who overhears this signal do? Should it be ignored? Hardly. Even though a confidential conversation was overheard, the message is important enough to break the cover and expose it gently and tactfully, after a short delay. "I've been hearing so much about girls and boys your age trying out sex to see how it feels. Would you like to talk about your feelings about that?" might do for openers.

We used this line with one of our children. The response was instantaneous: laughter and delight. "Did you really believe I would do that? We just like to rap with each other about sex. It's sort of new and exciting. Besides, some of my friends just talk a good game."

Relief? Yes—some. But also concern. It was important for our daughter to understand that her sex life was both private and sacred—not something to be used as idle conversation or boasting. We had learned that the era when a girl's reputation was sacred had long since passed in our children's world. But the importance of a high personal regard for a private sex life was still essential to us. This was the basis of our discussion and our concern about the overheard conversation. If it is a boy who has resorted to the boasting about his sexual conquests, the discussion is equally vital. Teaching a young male teenager that his ability to be a man has nothing to do with the number of his sexual encounters is equally important. Unless he absorbs this point, he may search out his identity from bed to bed for the rest of his life.

Older teenagers rarely boast about *imagined* sexual exploits; they engage in sex but then rarely talk about it. However, there are many ways that parents can discover promiscuous sexual activity in their adolescent. Finding birth control devices in the bureau drawer, walking in unexpectedly on a Saturday night to find the couple on the sofa in the living room, discovering evidence of sexual activity in the back seat of the car—even having the youngster discuss openly with the parents the need for contraception, medication for venereal disease, or intentions to live together at college. What could be the meaning of the promiscuous sexual signal? Once you understand the message behind the sexual activity, what should be done?

It is highly likely that a teenage couple, seventeen years or older, who have established a warm, caring, steady relationship, are engaging in some sexual activity. Parents should anticipate frequent sexual activity after a couple has been together for at least six months. Waiting for sex until marriage is not a common phenomenon among today's teenage population, no matter what the family upbringing and background may have been. For parents to deny the possibility of sexual activity is to hide from the obvious signal. What should the parents do? It would not only be futile to demand that the couple refrain from sexual exploration but would also alienate a child from parents who are perceived as square and old-fashioned. This could cut off all possible routes of communication about many other important issues that will arise in the future. To keep communication lines open with your child is essential. Therefore, the intelligent thing to do when this sexual signal is received from the "steady" adolescents is to accept the situation and offer your son or daughter help in obtaining information about birth control methods. Are you encouraging sexual activity by such accepting behavior? Absolutely not! They do not need your encouragement to be sexually active. What they need is your understanding and, particularly, your advice.

Mary's mother discovered through the unkind remarks of a gossipy neighbor that her daughter was promiscuously active with many of the young men in her teenage crowd. At first her mother was shocked and ashamed, vehemently denying the possibility.

But after sitting over a cup of coffee alone, she came to believe that there probably was truth in what she had been told. Overheard bits of conversations, unexplained absences, late night dates, and overlooked clothing stains all fitted together to confirm her doubts. It took much courage for this mother to confront her daughter about the signal of the girl's random sexual activity. But finally she did so. Mary was quiet at first, then she admitted that the story was true. "Why?" her mother asked. The sixteen-year-old had a great deal of trouble putting her feelings into words. At last she stammered incoherently: "I get lonely." "I don't understand, Mary," her mother said. The girl bit her lip, then tried again. "I don't have many girlfriends. And these boys are fun." Despite her inability to verbalize the message contained in her promiscuous behavior, the girl had helped her mother. "Mary, are you saying that you think having sex with these boys is part of being friends with them?" she offered. Mary nodded; that was the message.

At times, teenage girls confuse encouraging companionship with the opposite sex and having sexual relationships with them. They enjoy the company of boys and are afraid that if they don't "go all the way," the friendship will not satisfy the boy and will therefore end. A distinct difference between friendship and sex has become blurred in the teenage girl's thinking. Mary's mother offered to clear up this confusion. Mary offered to listen. They had negotiated a sensible and honest communication with no strings attached. No promises were made, no anger expressed. There was simply an exchange of ideas. Mary's mother pointed out that sex did not have to underlie every boy-girl friendship. If this was the basic requirement, then the friendship was on very shaky grounds because the girl was giving far more than the young man. She was risking pregnancy. Only when the friendship had moved into the realm of a truly important relationship between the two young people, a relationship that seemed to have lasting value, was the mutual decision to extend the friendship into sexual activity an appropriate move. Mary listened and said little. However, her mother realized by Mary's expression and attitude that what she said was meaningful to her daughter. And she felt more comfortable now that she had given her daughter advice about her responsibility to herself as a person.

Another possible message in the frequent random sexual behavior of a teenage girl may be found in her own image of herself. Too many girls feel that they are homely, ungainly, not bright, or socially inept, and must therefore barter their bodies for the attention of the young men in their crowd. "The only thing they want to take me out for is my body—the sex. I know that. But I don't care. At least they want to take me out," one reasonably attractive young girl told us. She was being treated for venereal disease and was responding to some tactful follow-up questions about her sex life. This youngster's image of herself was totally distorted. She was pleasant to look at, quite bright, played the piano well, and was a charming and articulate adolescent. How had she developed such a poor concept of herself? In her case, the reasons were complex and painful. An absent father, a selfish, negative mother, and a beautiful, successful, favored older sister all combined to destroy her self-confidence. The signal was her random sexual behavior: the message was her poor self-image. The treatment was far less simplistic. Referral for psychiatric counselling for both the teenager and her family was essential.

Randi came from a highly structured family. Both the mother and the father kept very close watch on all four of the children. There could be no deviation. Dating was regulated. The hours when Randi had to return home from school and from dates were set; her friends were not allowed in the house except on Saturday nights, and Randi's mother had to approve both her clothes and her friends. If Randi were seven, this might appear normal though still a bit excessive. But Randi was seventeen. Was it any surprise that Randi's parents dragged her into our office one morning because the girl had belligerently bragged during a family argument that she was known as "an easy lay"? In chatting with Randi privately, we found that she was extremely active sexually. We

asked her if she wanted to talk about it. "I don't care. If you want,"
she said casually. "Then can I know why?" one of us inquired.
"Why not?" the young girl replied. "Sex is the only thing I can do
that they don't have any control over. Besides, they must think I
do anyway. Otherwise why would they be so damned worried
about every move I make?"

Randi had put her finger very specifically on the reasons behind
her promiscuity: the message was rebellion. She was being controlled so tightly by her family that she felt the need to break loose.
Since the parents' actions signified an element of distrust toward
this girl, she rebelled in the most vulnerable area of their concern
—her sex life. These parents needed several sessions of counselling
to perceive their overly tight and punitive handling of all four
children. Gradually, they were able to understand that the more
unrealistically constraining the demands placed on the girl, the
more likely she was to break the rules. It became very important
for Randi's parents to be able to move beyond their dismay and
anger at her sexual promiscuity and look at the reasons why. How
could they heal and correct these family problems? Slowly, Randi's
parents became capable of loosening the reins on the seventeen-
year-old girl and demonstrating that they trusted her. In return,
Randi no longer felt the need to rebel sexually. She was still sexually active, but became more selective and sensible about her sex
life.

Often the sexual activities of the middle teenager are transient
periods of experimentation. The young person is testing herself
sexually, finding out what she is all about as a sexual being. Usually
the sexual activity is far from excessive. Here is where good sexual
education in the home and at school pays major dividends. Knowing about their bodies, the need for birth control, and the prevention of venereal disease can make these forays into the sexual area
free of serious, major complications. Should parents try to limit
this experimentation? They may, but it will usually go unheeded.
The best parental action is prevention: discussions about responsibility toward one's own body and that of the other person. If the

teenager has the knowledge and the background to make responsible and sensible decisions, the parent has done the best job possible. The signal is sexuality; the message is experimentation. The treatment by the parents is proper training and advice *beforehand* and an available ear to listen!

Frequent sexual activity is not limited to the female. But somehow society still does not view promiscuity with as much alarm when it occurs in the male. Not only is this a sexist and chauvinistic outlook; it is also dangerous. Young men who engage in promiscuous sexual behavior are also sending signals that must be interpreted by parents. They may have immediate importance or be very significant to the young man's future sex and married life.

Experimentation is often a message in male promiscuity. Males go through the same transient period of sexual exploration as female teenagers. The signal and the message are no different. The time line is the same. Most importantly, parental response MUST not differ either. Why the emphasis on this? Because for years, it has been the parents of the young girls who have felt the need to teach responsibility to their daughters while too few parents of teenage males bothered to do the same. If the girl "gets into trouble," it's "her own fault." Nothing could be further from the truth. The young man must learn to be a responsible member in the sexual partnership, asking sensitive questions, being prepared with birth control devices of his own, considering the feelings and consequences of the sexual act on his partner. This is not only an essential preparation for his adolescent encounters, but a vital aspect of his training for a successful relationship in marriage.

When sixteen-year-old Herbie came into the office with venereal disease for the third time, it was appropriate to question him in depth about the frequency of his sexual activities. He willingly disclosed an overly active and random sex life. As he talked, it became apparent that his sexual activities had a compulsive nature about them. "Why the driving need to be so active at so young an age?" we inquired. Herbie was direct and honest. "Everybody in my crowd screws around a lot. It's what's expected of me." It is not unusual for the message in the promiscuous sex life of a young man to be the need to conform to what he perceives as the expected norm. He is living up to the expectations of his group. Actually, in probing further into Herbie's lifestyle, he willingly admitted that, more often than not, he pushed himself beyond his inner sexual drive. He was having sex far more often than he wanted to. The message in Herbie's case is the message of so many promiscuous young men: "Being like everybody else." Conforming to the expected norm—whatever the youngster thinks this is —in the area of adolescent sexuality. Actually there *is* no expected norm. And it was important for Herbie to understand this. He had to learn that he could be his own man. This is a lesson that parents must try to teach their teenagers. "Be yourself," "Do not feel the need to follow the crowd," "There is no model to copy," "Each person moves to the beat of his own drummer." Such independence should be the expected norm of our sexual society. Teaching this to our young people will often eliminate the signal of sexual promiscuity.

Adolescence can be an extremely confusing time for a young man. He is slowly developing his sexual identity at a time when the sexual stimuli within our society are intense and the sexual demands of his own teenage group are great. There no longer appears to be time for teenagers to ease comfortably into their own sexual identity; they are shoved into confronting themselves sexually far too soon. Often this creates fear and concern in the teenage male about his own masculinity. He feels that he must prove something—not only to the world around him but also to himself. Frequently the adolescent seeks the easy way out: "I'll show them by screwing everything in sight." Crude but accurate. This is the Don Juan syndrome of the adolescent male. The young man who feels insecure about his sexual self proceeds to demonstrate his masculine capabilities physically by engaging in promiscuous sexual behavior. At first he feels satisfied that he has shown the world who and what he is. But gradually a gnawing doubt creeps into his thinking because he knows that he has not completely convinced himself. Sex with strangers so often frightens even the teenager. The expected rewards may vanish like smoke, leaving behind the same self-doubts and the occasional consequences of venereal disease and failure to develop a single lasting female friendship.

How can parents prevent this signal of promiscuity? The message is the teenager's need to find his sexuality too fast. The parents can make the adolescent years less hurried and traumatic if they can teach their son that masculinity is not measured by sexual prowess. Helping the young man to realize that sexual awareness need not happen overnight or at the same rate in every teenager will allay many of the fears that precipitate the sexual acting out. Developing as a *person* rather than just as a sexual being should be the key idea that the parent tries to instill in the growing adolescent. A future life of reward and love will be offered to the child who is taught that sex is a form of communication, the highest expression of feeling when it takes place in sharing and intimacy. Without these deeper feelings, sex is empty, carnal. Your child will have to find his sexual self as he or she grows up, but the journey can be helped by frank and open talk with both parents.

The parents need not "discover" unexpectedly that their child is sexually active. They should prepare for the possibility. An early anticipatory talk with a teenager which goes something like this might open the doors to future sharing: "You're starting to date now. I know the question of sex will come up sooner or later. Would you like to talk about the important things you will have to think about when you make that decision?" The key words, of course, are "Would you like," which offers the young person the option, and "when you make that decision," which clearly indicates that the responsibility is ultimately the teenager's. This may avert the future signal of excessive sexual activity in your child.

The promiscuous teenager is not the stereotypic "whore" or "stud" of our yesterdays. He or she is a young person sending out signals of underlying problems that need analysis and very sensitive parental help.

25

Serious Signals—
The Emotionally Disturbed Child

"Help me, please! I can no longer control myself."

Struck by the numbing shock of these words, you are confronted by the reality of your fears over the last two years. You finally— and clearly—have read the signal. The underlying message is despair. Your child has a runaway train in his head that is careening toward an emotional collision. He has lost his controls. He is emotionally ill.

You stand facing the child, bewildered, repeatedly asking yourself, "Why?," as if the repetition could help you understand. You feel frustration, anger, rage—then fear. The painful "Why?" finally stops, but you remain frightened and desperate. "What now?" "What can I do for my disturbed child?" "Where can I take him?" "Who can help me?"

A parent faces the ultimate problem in decoding the signals of emotionally disturbed children. The realization that a child has serious emotional problems and may need long-term care that could require hospitalization crosses the parent's troubled mind. Fortunately this extreme situation is not common. But none of us, as parents, are immune. It could be any of us. How would you start the process of getting help for your child?

The parents who face this traumatic realization usually need some self-help before they can be totally effective in making appropriate decisions for their child. There are feelings with which the parents themselves must learn to deal in order to remain cool and objective. Myths about emotional illness must be abandoned by the family. Parents have to calm down, view their child objectively, and restore their own equilibrium. Then, and only then, can they act rationally in getting the proper help for their child.

One of the major problems parents have to face is their own feelings of guilt. Today's generation of parents often have grown up on the fable that there are no bad kids—only bad parents. The prevalent caricatures of psychiatrists as Freudian types who urge their clients to "lie back and tell me about your parents" has encouraged the belief that parents somehow cause mental illness in children. Most common stereotypes completely ignore the massive research that suggests biochemical abnormalities in the brains of some emotionally disturbed people; or the wealth of material from the social scientists that indicates that an emotionally disturbed child may *create* an emotionally disturbed family, rather than the reverse.

No, guilt is not needed—or wanted—in the parents with an emotionally disturbed child. They must stop beating themselves with their own mental whips. The child is ill. It has happened. No amount of guilt will reverse the illness. But that child now urgently needs parents who are guilt-free, open, and rational.

If you can attain a stage in your thinking in which you can be relatively free from your own anxiety and guilt, realize that you have a problem that requires rational thinking, and are able to approach the problem of therapy without prejudices, you are ready to help—truly help—your child. Then, and only then, are you ready to ask, "What now?"

Ultimately you will want to have your child seen by a psychosocial professional: a social worker, a psychologist, or a child psychiatrist. How can you find this person? Start with either the school's special education department, or your family's doctor or pediatrician.

If you work with a school system, you probably already know that a school psychologist is available. Also, school files may contain material that would be helpful to a referring professional. Thus a school's referral, through your school principal or the Director of Special Education, may prove to be the most expedient method of securing the help of a good professional.

Many school systems, however, have a waiting list for appointments with their school psychologists. You cannot afford to wait because your child needs help immediately. Your family physician or pediatrician's office is an excellent place to take the child. These doctors know your child, your family, and much of the background history. They can make referrals quickly and effectively. These physicians also can suggest medications, when needed, to stabilize your child until other helping professionals can see him.

After you and your child see the recommended psycho-social professional, you and this professional will have to arrive at a treatment plan. There will be several options.

One option is to keep the child at home, and initiate intensive psychotherapy for him or her in an office or clinic setting. If this treatment course is elected, you must realize that you will be responsible for working with your own family, to adjust to the changes your child will experience. As your child changes through therapy, so will your family; sometimes in healthy ways, occasionally in ways that temporarily appear regressive or harmful. This option can be a stormy voyage for your family. You should take into consideration the strengths or weaknesses of the other family members and their ability to survive a continually changing person in their midst.

If your child is young, verbal therapy may not work well; the therapist may function best in a play therapy situation. If the child is older, the therapy may be verbal, but the setting may be startlingly different from your expectations. Much modern therapy is performed in groups, with members of the group acting as therapists for each other. Individual therapy is often administered in informal settings; in recreation areas, on hikes or cook-outs, or in "rap sessions."

Often a child's therapist will ask you, the parents or entire family, to enter therapy. Consider this recommendation seriously. Remember that your child may have been sick a long time, and you and the rest of the family have learned to react to the illness in set ways that may need to be changed.

Another reason for entering family therapy is to understand how your child's illness was *reinforced* by your family behavior patterns. No, not caused—reinforced. The family has to learn how this occurred in order to solve the existing problem and prevent it from happening again.

A request by a therapist to enter family therapy usually brings forth once more the guilt of the parents. Again, try to confront and dispel your guilt and anger. Entering therapy does *not* mean you are sick. It means, in this case, that you are trying to create a healthy environment for your child through your own understanding of your family's dynamics.

Another option is for treatment in cooperation with a public or private special education school system. This can occur at the same time that individual or group therapy is being undertaken. Many school systems now have special classes and rooms for emotionally disturbed youngsters, and teachers equipped to work with these special children and with the child's therapist. This option has the advantage of placing the disturbed child in a therapeutic environment during regular school hours, and takes the pressure off the family for dealing with the child between therapy sessions. A further advantage of this option is that parents can observe their child in the classroom and, by so doing, learn better techniques of working with him. Most knowledgeable families prefer this option *if* their child is stable enough to tolerate it, and *if* the school system has properly trained people and facilities. It is more common to find the first condition met than the second.

A third option is for treatment in a public or private residential school or hospital. This option is usually selected when the child needs constant attention and intensive therapy. It means that the child will actually leave the family, become part of another—the nuclear family of the hospital—and then face returning to the natural family. The process will be painful alike for the parents, the other family members, and the child. But if this option becomes necessary, it can be managed wisely and well. The parents can prepare the other family members and the child for the separation, work out arrangements for communication during the separation, and prepare themselves for the "reentry" process when the residential care is over. When this choice is made, the family must never feel that they "turned over" their child to the hospital. They must work to keep the sick child's image alive in the family. Planning must be started for the child's return into the family. The family must follow the child's progress, and prepare themselves for his or her changes.

In the hospital setting, your child will be assigned his or her own doctor and/or therapist. There will be a team of professionals caring for—and observing—your child around the clock. Your child will be cast into a setting of new acquaintances, new environments, and new expectations. Your family routines may be completely foreign in this setting. The child—and you—will have to adjust to this different, strange situation. But you should realize that, in the long run, this change is best for your child.

Three major challenges confront the parents of the hospitalized emotionally disturbed child; accepting the separation; working with the hospital staff; and making the reentry of the child into the family situation one of smooth transition. Cooperation with hospital staff is really no different from the "working together" that will be outlined in reference to teacher-school therapy or outpatient professional psychological help. The only difference is your child's separation from the home. It is the reentry into the home that is uniquely challenging. You have to help both your child and your family to make this difficult transition. And you do it by obtaining all the information you can from the personnel at the hospital. Because your ultimate goal is for your child to get well and return home, you will have to make dramatic readjustments. You yourself may need therapy to help you see the necessity of these changes within your home.

Despite many immediate and long-term discouragements, your child can, and usually will, become emotionally well. But when embroiled in the midst of intensive therapy, hospitalization, or family therapy, it is often hard to see the major gains—to rejoice over parts of the therapy that prove successful. There are, however, certain signs of progress you can look for.

Watch for increased communication between yourself and your child. Do not settle for a greater *quantity* of talk; instead, try to search for a better *quality* of communication. Talk about the child's world rather than your own or the family's. Talk about common interests. Talk about mutual plans and ambitions. Ease into shared problems, adjustments, and the future. But *talk*—communicate—no matter the degree of pain that sometimes accompanies these conversations. When you can achieve open and honest communication with each other, you have reached a starting point to good mental health.

Watch for a lessening of communication with the therapist. As the child becomes more able to verbalize his or her problems and solve them independently, the therapist will be withdrawing contact. Next, the therapist will give the child a chance to try things. The child will become less dependent on the therapist. Then, sooner or later, the child will break with the therapist. As your communication with your child increases, the child may transfer some of his or her communication back from the therapist to you. This is a very positive sign. But remember you are not the therapist. You are the parent. As such, you can listen and give advice only when asked. But parental input is invaluable to the therapist.

A word of caution needs to be inserted here, however. It is possible that you may *not* find the relationship with the therapist diminishing; you may *not* find the therapist in easy communication with your child; you may *not* find a therapist explaining to you what is happening with your child, and offering help in understanding the child's problems. In an unfortunate number of cases, parents may not pick the "right" therapist for the child. Perhaps the parents had no choice; a school psychologist or a hospitalization plan psychiatrist was assigned to your child—and the "fit" was not good. With a growing sense of panic you realize that the therapist is wrong for your child. What can you do?

Whatever you do must be done quickly, firmly, and decisively. Stop that therapy if you are not getting the answers you need.

Look for another therapist, or insist on a conference with that therapist's superior. Have the child examined by another therapist for a second opinion. Ask others who have used that therapist about results. *Do not accept any therapist as the right one for your child.* Much of therapy is an art, not a science, and the artist must have the right skills and materials in order to communicate with his audience—your child. After giving the therapist a reasonable time, you must either decide to stay or change. But do not remain for the sake of ease. Your child and your child's therapist must WORK at getting better; and you must witness that struggle, even participate in it. The therapist must be someone you trust to take care of your child as *you* would—he or she is that important.

Finally, strive to solve problems together with your child. When this occurs, you have once again resumed your true role as the parent. You are communicating in order to share concerns. The child is trusting you, rather than the therapist, with the frightening task of helping him or her to make decisions. You have become important to your child once again. The child's new healthy signal is trust and confidence.

If you "lose" your child to emotional disturbance, you may think that child is gone from your life forever. You expect the worst; you are faced with the prospect of "putting your child away," or providing him or her with long-term and expensive therapy. You will learn, however, that, in this day and age a child can be "found" again—often very quickly. You should work for, and look forward to, walking hand in hand once again beside your mentally adjusted child, talking about shared dreams and planning for both your futures.

PREVENTION

26

Preventive Parenting

As parents, we struggle for a definition to start us on the road of preventive parenting. Although we find no such definition, we know that we would rather *prevent* a child's problems than have to face them and treat them.

Can we honestly put together what spells out the aspects of good preventive measures during our parenting period? A definition could be attempted, but while it might come close to the essence of what we mean, it would remain only a series of words strung together on paper. For prevention is a constant, continuing, process! Preventive parenting by its very nature entails dynamic actions, reactions, or lack of actions.

However, we are not prepared for our role as parents by courses in school, seminars in college, or educational television programs, nor do we have any idea of how well qualified we are to be parents. We are often literally tossed into the stormy waters of parenthood and told to sink or swim. Frequently we resort to the models set by our own parents, even though we recognize that we were not, as youngsters, satisfied by their parenting techniques. Usually we act by reflex and out of desperation. We need to do something when a parenting crisis arises. And we revert back to the only methods we know—those of our own parents. This is why we so often lament, "I'm doing the same thing my father did—and I can remember resenting him for doing it." The victim in this directionless parenting is, of course, your own child.

As parents, we need directions for action—a map that tells us how to prevent unhealthy signals in our own children. Clearly there are actions and options that can be taken by parents, and these form the basis for preventive parenting, the ultimate in sensible, sensitive child rearing.

Familiarize yourself with the following ten key preventive parenting activities. Use them as a guideline for your daily encounters with your children. We hope they will prepare you to deal most effectively before rather than after a childhood crisis. Try to make these suggestions your commandments for parenting.

1. ESTABLISH A SPECIAL DAILY "ATTENTION TIME" FOR THE ENTIRE FAMILY

An attention time is a period in which the whole family can be together and participate in open and free discussion. For many families, the "attention time" is at the evening dinner table. For others, this special period might be at breakfast, before bed, or right after school or work. Whatever the time, it should be a period always set aside with the understanding that children *and* parents usually will be present. Often the parents will want to use this period to set family rules, but such business should be kept to a minimum. This period should really be one of family sharing, when children can speak freely. "What happened today?" is a good starting question. The "attention time" is a period when the parents really get to know their child better. The parents can listen "between the lines" and discover the fascinating world of their child. And, likewise, the parents can share some of their own daily frustrations or joys. It is a time for discovery—of each other. The quality of the time spent is infinitely more important than the quantity.

2. LISTEN AGGRESSIVELY TO YOUR CHILD

Listening is a word with which you are familiar, but do you know how to listen aggressively? The process of listening aggressively is difficult for the average parent, who is harassed by many demands on his time, the noise from children and friends endlessly marching in and out of the house, and a lack of the privacy necessary for listening to someone else. However, you must find ways of initiating this listening if you want to learn all you can about your child and his world. When you listen aggressively to your child, you look directly at him and maintain eye contact. You listen until the child is finished and then you let the child know that you have heard. How? You can restate what he has said in your own words, or you can ask questions for clarification. The second action is usually better, because it allows you, the parent, to find any subtle messages that you might have missed. Often a simple, "How do you feel about that?" will open up hidden meanings to the child's message. There will be many times when aggressive listening with your child is not possible, but it should be practiced constantly.

3. KNOW YOUR CHILD'S FRIENDS

As difficult as it may be, particularly during your child's adolescence, you must get to know your child's friends in order to know your child. Friends have influence, often control, over some aspects of your child's life. Knowing friends can give you insight into the daily pressures faced by your child. Encourage your child to invite his friends into your home whenever possible. Encourage "at home" birthday parties so that you may meet your child's peers. Include your child's friends in some of your family's activities: dinners, outings, vacations, sports. Through school or community meetings, you may meet these children's parents and learn other facts about your child's friends, but your most important prevention activity is to know your child's friends personally. There will be many friends whom you do not like; you will worry about them as friends for your child. Try to put off judgment until you have some real reasons for this dislike. Do *not* point out negative traits about his friends in front of your child, or you will be excluded from meeting the important people in his life. Later if you still have negative feelings about any one of your child's friends, talk it over with your child privately. As a parent, you will be entering your child's world in a manner that says to the child, "I care."

4. ESTABLISH A SYSTEM OF PUNISHMENTS AND REWARDS

Any child needs to be rewarded and punished at various times. It is often helpful to both child and parent to know the consequences of any act, whether positive or negative. Essentially, the parent is establishing a "social contract" with his child that lays down the rules, the rewards and the punishment. This provides the child with a secure feeling of knowing the rules of the game. Too often the child is only aware of the punishments for misbehavior. Rewards for accomplishments also can be determined in advance. As you see your children mature, give them the privilege of determining the rewards and punishments for some of their acts. Often they are harder on themselves than you would be. By permitting this self-decision process, the youngster enters into negative or positive activities with a fuller responsibility for his own actions. This is a vital preparatory step toward adulthood.

5. SHARE EXPERIENCES WITH YOUR CHILD

Certainly you and your child have experiences together. But do you really share them? Do you talk about them together? Do you recall them often? Do you compare them to other experiences you have had? The prevention message is to talk about shared experiences in great detail. The objective is to build up good methods of communication between you and your child. And when you do this, you also offer the child a feeling of belonging. This bridge of communication will be needed often during the childhood years. Such belonging will hold the child closer to the mainstream of your family's lifestyle and values. Sharing can be a rich preventive measure.

6. **ASSIGN YOUR CHILD TASKS THAT INCREASE INDEPENDENCE**

One of the marks of his or her maturity is the child's ability to assume more independence. The parent must help the child prepare for this responsibility by asking him or her to perform tasks that lead to less dependence upon the parent. Naturally, you should exercise restraint in the amount of responsibility you demand of a child, but there are many small tasks that can be assigned early. How many times have *you* paid the cashier at the diner? When shopping with the kids, does each select his own foods? How often do *you* fill your own gas tank at the self-service gas station? Who reminds the family of telephone calls that need to be returned? If you, as a parent, do all of these things yourself, and you have children over seven years old at home, you are missing opportunities to assign them greater responsibility. Simple tasks such as these allow a child to move along the road toward independence. Certainly there are risks in assigning a child responsibility, but these risks can be anticipated—and if a child makes a mistake, you are there to remedy it. Increased responsibility will prepare the child to become the independent adult.

7. **LOOK AT SITUATIONS POSITIVELY AS WELL AS NEGATIVELY**

In every dilemma, every problem, and even every success, there are positive and negative elements. Harassed parents often find themselves seeing only the negative aspects of every childhood problem. They do not allow themselves the luxury of two-sided thinking about the normal stresses of growing up. In other words, they have difficulty in saying, "Well, here is the obvious side of the story; now, what could be the other side?" The parent who is concerned with prevention *must* ask the two-sided question. Finding positives in all situations can lighten the tense atmosphere of childhood problem solving. Positive statements will help you talk more easily with your child; he will not feel as negative about the solutions to his own problems. "Two-sided thinking" also can open up new insights that will produce better and healthier ways of dealing with the child's concerns or problems. Constant negative thinking gives most youngsters a "hopeless" feeling about their abilities to cope. Think positive. A good slogan to follow is that of a major child-serving agency: "Catch a Kid Doing Good."

8. OFFER YOUR CHILD ANTICIPATORY GUIDANCE

As your child experiences the frequent problems of normal growth and development, he or she will encounter many expected problems for which you already know the answers. Adolescent dating, competing on the sports field, obtaining a driver's license—all these problems can be softened for a child if he has some guidance which you can offer in advance. Guidance that merely says "do this" or "don't do that" is usually unheeded by the child. This is not really guidance—it's a command. But guidance that anticipates the situation the youngster may have to face can be more readily followed and used by him. "When I first got my driver's license, I was really scared," can initiate the first part of the anticipatory guidance when your child is about to take his driver's test. "When I went to that first window and was sent into the driver's examination room, I wasn't sure I was going to make it. Then I was given this eye examination. . . ." The young person listens attentively as you simulate the entire experience. Guidance is being given in an anticipatory way, and it is being heard and received. You are practicing good prevention.

9. **ALLOW LOVE AND AFFECTION IN YOUR HOME**
How strange that sounds! Every one of us firmly believes that we open our doors to allow love within the four walls of our lives. But do we? Do our children know that our homes contain the emotional and physical warmth that comes from love and affection? Part of this process is the ability openly to express to your child and your spouse the words, "I love you." So many other ways are available to us to permit our youngsters to feel the glow of mutual affection permeating their environment. For the young child, a bedtime hug. An arm around an older boy's shoulder as you walk down the street. An unexpected smile that shows caring between you and your child. Holding your daughter's hands during a difficult moment. A surprise gift to your spouse or your child. Working side by side with your child on his or her favorite project. A touch during a meaningful moment. These are subtle expressions of love and affection. It is extremely important that we learn to tell each other physically how much we care. Too often we are embarrassed to touch, hug, kiss. How often children want that open display of our devotion. And how meaningful it is for them to see a brief, loving display of affection between their parents to give them the security and the model of a loving home. Have your children ever seen you kiss, hug, or touch in front of them? If not, why not? Fathers must not feel ashamed to show love to their sons physically. There is nothing "sissified" in a father hugging his son spontaneously. If we expect our youngsters to grow up believing in the importance of love in a relationship, whether marriage or parenthood, we must

give them positive examples. Only then can our children mature into their own future relationships, understanding the continuing process of love, affection, and security.

Another subtle way of expressing love is the willingness of a parent to say, "I was wrong and I'm sorry." How often have your children heard you say this? Only people who truly care about each other can share their errors as well as their successes. Admitting a mistake, particularly when it applies to something you said or did to your child, draws you and your child closer together. This is part of the expression of love.

10. TAKE INVENTORY OF YOURSELF AS A MODEL PARENT

A major aspect of prevention is the presentation of a good model for adulthood to your child. The best and most accessible model should be you. Have you ever thought how you present yourself as a model to your child? It is wise to consider seriously your own personal characteristics, for they could form the basis of your child's personality traits.

Test yourself on the following rating scale. Answer the questions honestly, then determine if you feel comfortable about the things you are teaching your child *merely by being yourself.*

Each "Yes" earns you 10 points:

A. *Moral Values*

1. Do I think about the morality of my actions?
2. Do I live by an established, consistent set of values?
3. Do I reassess my values periodically and change them when appropriate?
4. Do I share my values with my family and NOT force them upon the others?

5. Do I accept the values of others if they differ from my own?

In this area, you should score 50. These are essential parts of good parent modeling behavior.

B. *Behavior*

1. Do I always act like an adult?
2. Do I try to solve problems in a mature, thoughtful way?
3. Do I try to see all sides of a problem?
4. Am I rarely impulsive?
5. Is my temper usually under control?

None of us is perfect. Often we explode or regress because of external pressures. However, your score should not be lower than 40 in this area or you are modeling immature behavior for your child.

C. *Temperament*

1. Am I a person who can solve problems by reasoning?
2. Can I control my anger and frustration?
3. Am I predictable?
4. Can I accept criticism?
5. Do I get along easily with other people?

Again, as human beings, we often err on the emotional side of life. Therefore we must be somewhat lenient on ourselves. A score of 40 is quite acceptable. Anything less may suggest that you are setting an example of confusing unpredictability for your child.

D. *Flexibility*

1. Can I easily handle new information?
2. Can I accept the fact that I have been proven wrong?
3. Can I see both sides to an argument?
4. Can I modify my rules as the need arises?
5. Am I successful at coping with obstacles?

Here is an area that often creates the basis of many

parent-child conflicts. Rearing children requires the flexibility of a contortionist. You're going too far if you bend over backwards and hit your head on the pavement. But you should try to score 50 on this part.

E. *Tolerance*

1. Can I accept the company of people whom I do not like?
2. Can I accept the fact that someone else has different philosophies?
3. Can I accept the existence of lifestyles other than my own?
4. Can I tolerate rebellion in my spouse or my children?
5. Can I accept other people's solutions to problems, even when they differ from my own?

This is the "zinger" in the battles between adolescents and their parents. A lack of tolerance sets the parent up as the "heavy" in the new teenage society. Tolerance does not mean to encourage, condone, or assist. Tolerance signifies the ability to ACCEPT the situation that exists and deal with it. If you want to be both the proper model for your teenager and also the appropriate counsellor, you should do your best to reach 50 on this series of questions.

F. *Consistency*

1. Am I consistent in administering punishments and rewards?
2. Are my rules always the same?
3. Do I follow through on promises and threats?
4. Do I ask the same things of my children that I expect from others or myself?
5. Do I keep my cool when challenged by difficult child signals?

Consistency provides the element of security in every child's life. Children usually understand the "rules of the game." Life should not change for them daily. Consider how you would feel if you went to work each day not knowing what was expected of you and totally dependent on the whim of an unpredictable boss. This is the way a youngster feels in an inconsistent home environment. Don't perpetuate such inconsistency in your child. If you don't reach the magic number 50 when you score yourself here, then try your best to improve.

Administer this inventory to yourself frequently. It is extremely important for prevention that you feel satisfied with yourself as an adult model. If not, seek help for change. Your child will someday become like you. Are you satisfied with that prospect?

Prevention is a part of parenting that every parent must understand and practice. Preventive parenting lessens the chances that your child will send you a signal that means serious trouble. Preventive parenting earns results. It can also be creative fun! The end results are mature and emotionally stable men and women who, years before, stood as your children at the crossroads of their lives. That is reward enough.

THE
PROFESSIONALS

27

The Teacher

Parents frequently encounter a signal that appears to be harmless but is quite puzzling. Who knows your child almost as well as you do and can help you to decide whether your child is signalling or merely going through "another of his phases"?

The teacher is a valuable resource who can add many important clues about childhood signals. If you can talk openly to your child's teacher, you may be able to discover new facts about how well your child is adjusting to the outside world. She is aware of some of the daily stresses faced by your youngster about which you have no knowledge. The teacher can reflect upon whether your youngster's behavior is different from that of his or her classmates. His ability to be accepted by schoolmates can be her contribution to the solution of the puzzling signal.

If the teacher is such an important resource, you might ask, why don't parents ask for help more frequently in working through the meaning of their child's signals? Perhaps the teacher is not asked because the parent is in awe of the school. After all, the school has always been an "authority figure" to students. Parents may have been brought up on the philosophy that the school could not be questioned because it was always "right." What your parents thought about you when you were a student was governed all too often by the grades and comments on your report card. Careers and futures hung in the balance as a result of classroom rankings and grade point averages. Many parents themselves became scarred in the competitive battle for grades and silently vowed never to trust the educational system again. Even as adults, this fear and distrust may prevent them from communicating with their children's teachers.

Another possible reason why the teacher is underutilized as a resource in unraveling children's signals is that the parents do not realize that the teacher has been trained in such signals. When most parents were of school age, the faculty appeared larger than life and, as a result, insensitive to and oblivious of their needs. Some of this may have been fact; more often, much of it was childish folklore. However, such parents have carried the concepts of the punitive teacher "establishment" into their own adulthood. The truth is just the opposite. Today's teachers are trained to be very different from the teacher in this long-standing myth. They are trained to know a child and his world.

Parents often hesitate to talk to their child's teachers because they do not want to admit that they don't know everything about their child. They sense an underlying competition with the teacher for the child's attention. These parents subconsciously do not want to give the teacher the edge in this misconceived competition. They would prefer to hide from the child's teacher the fact that they are not "perfect" parents. Parents should understand that the child's teacher is often forced to be aware of many of their internal family problems. Teachers overhear children's conversations or learn the intimate secrets of families because they are openly shared during "show and tell" sessions in the classroom. And teachers understand; they, too, have their own personal problems, not dissimilar to those of the children's families. In addition, they also have similar problems in dealing with the very same children. So they know and share many of the parent's feelings.

A good teacher does *not* want to become a surrogate parent. They would much rather help *you* become a better parent. In this way, the teacher can reduce your child's signals, which may be disrupting their classroom teaching time.

As difficult as it might be that first time, the parent should visit the child's teacher. Set up an appointment aside from the scheduled parent-teacher evening sessions. These are busy times, when the teacher is pressured by too many parents and too little time to give special consultation. The parent should visit on a scheduled day when the teacher has the time to talk. He or she will gain a far clearer picture of his child and how he functions with classwork and classmates from such a visit than from any amount of psychological testing, doctor or nurse observations, or long talks with the child.

There are certain questions that can be asked of a teacher which help prepare a parent to perceive and interpret a child's signals better.

* *What is there about my child that the other children in the class like . . . and dislike?* This question can elicit answers that paint an objective picture of your child's functioning in a social situation that is totally removed from home base. You will probably learn more new things about your child from this question than you imagined possible. The teacher's observations will allow you to see your child in his or her "other" life, the one at school. This different perspective may have little relationship to how your child is adjusting in your home or neighborhood.

* *In what ways is my child more mature or less mature than other children in the class?* The answers to this question will provide you with important facts about your child's level of emotional growth. In addition, you may learn that your child is not as different as you imagined. The teacher can help you better understand the unusual but normal behavior patterns of children at various ages. As a result, you will be secure in knowing that some of your child's impulsive actions are within the expected range for his or her age. And you will also know when to *stop* tolerating unacceptably immature behavior.

* *Is my child a leader or a follower with his classmates?* Many signals of childhood are merely signals copied from

others. When a child conforms to the pressures of his peer group to a large degree, he may adopt behavior patterns that are not his own. When parents observe unexplained actions, they need to know whether this perplexing behavior belongs *exclusively* to their child and, therefore, represents a true signal of distress. However, if the parents learn from the teacher that the child's activities are mere copies of his or her classmates' behaviors, the signal being sent is one of conformity.

* *Does my child usually appear happy or sad? Tense or relaxed?* If the teacher comments that a child is often anxious or sad, the chances that he is sending serious signals is far greater than if the child seems comfortably well adjusted in her classroom. Children who can express themselves in a relaxed manner rarely resort to signals. If your child's teacher says your youngster is not at ease and open in the classroom, you should be alert that a serious signal is being sent. The child must, in some way, communicate his unhappiness in an effort to mobilize someone to help him solve the problems leading to his sadness.

* Finally, the parent should ask the teacher, *In what ways does my child need to improve?* If your child is using signalling as a method of telling you something, that signal probably will be related to what he sees as his or her greatest deficiency areas. The teacher can help you realize what the youngster seems to perceive as areas of worry and concern. This gives you a vital clue to the basis for your child's signal.

With the help of the teacher's answers to these important questions, the parent will be well equipped to interpret many of the messages sent by the child's signals. However, talking to the teacher can give a parent more than just information about a child's signals. A productive conversation can also enlist an ally to help work out some of the painful messages contained in these signals. You should remember that the teacher controls the majority of your child's day and, therefore, exerts a dynamic influence on your child. For example, if you receive a signal of friendlessness, the teacher can help to remedy the situation by assigning your child to work with other youngsters known for their friendly, open attitudes. Likewise, frequent physical complaints at home that have been shown to have no medical basis can be unrewarded at school and help to diminish the repetitiveness of these signals. The teacher can also help to uncover the reasons for frequent aches and pains and, at the same time, work to minimize the signal. Whatever the message behind the child's signal, the healing response by the parents can be reinforced in the classroom—if a parent takes the time to talk with the teacher.

The teacher can be a valuable, helpful professional to you, one who is available to you free of cost and who is well trained to interpret and work with children's signals. The teacher is often an untapped resource. Use this well of information about your child—for that child's sake.

28

The Pediatrician
and Family Physician

After receiving your child's signal, you may feel the need to talk to someone outside the family. The messages may appear somewhat confusing and you want someone objective to help you sort them out. You might need advice about the seriousness of the signal. Who is the first person to whom you should turn? Your family doctor, whether he is a pediatrician or a general practitioner.

Very likely, no other professional knows your family as well as this person. He has seen your child over a long period of time, often since birth. Even though your visits to his office have been intermittent, he has seen your child and your family over time and has developed his own personal and professional viewpoints about how your family works. He usually knows the inner dynamics between parents and between parents and their children. This knowledge can be tremendously helpful in pinpointing the possible messages buried within a child's signals. Often the signal may not come as any major surprise to him; in fact, he may be better prepared for it than you were. Your doctor has records on your child that detail many of the physical and emotional aspects of growing up, details that may provide clues to help decipher the sudden signal.

Often there are serious questions as to whether a signal represents an actual physical or emotional illness. The physician is in the position of listening carefully and doing a thorough physical examination to eliminate any possible organic causes. Follow-up laboratory tests or X-rays may be necessary to rule out the medical possibilities completely. Certainly in signals such as bedwetting, soiling, refusal to eat, hyperactivity, sleeplessness, and frequent physical complaints, complete physical examinations are essential.

Often, as parents, you become upset by a signal. You jump to conclusions, and want to act upon your instincts impulsively. It becomes very difficult to step back and patiently work through the background and current state of affairs so that the message contained in the signal can be understood and dealt with. Being objective after the shock from a disturbing child signal may be too much to ask of any parent. But the child's doctor can sit back and be objective, analyze the information, and help you decode the meaning behind the signal. He is your front-line resource in this regard. Use him in this manner.

Give the family doctor all the information he requests. Only when he is armed with all of the details, even the embarrassing and painful revelations, can he begin to assist you in putting the pieces of the puzzle together. Even though the material you must share may be very personal, share it with your physician. He will keep it confidential. He will not make judgments about you or your child. Your family doctor should not be your judge. He listens objectively to the unusual stresses and strains that create family and personal illness, whether physical or emotional. He will not be shocked or angry; he will simply listen and use what you tell him to try to interpret the signals being sent by your child.

Remember that your child probably has developed confidence and rapport with his doctor over the years. Their open communication might help to unravel the problems. Encourage your youngster to chat with his doctor privately. Do not become alarmed when the doctor or the child suggests this. There are many things troubling the child that he will feel more comfortable sharing with this friend who is not a member of his family. The doctor often will ask your child for permission to share with you certain bits of information which the child has given to him. Sometimes the child refuses. The doctor must honor the youngster's confidence. In no way will this seriously hamper a clever physician from helping your child and you. It will only tax his ingenuity to help you help your child without destroying his own relationship with your child.

Certain signals require medication as part of the process of therapy. Hyperactivity associated with minimal brain damage is a good example of one of these; bedwetting could be another. The family doctor is best qualified to begin the appropriate medication and to evaluate the success of the medicine.

In many of the situations being signalled by your child, the child's doctor can act as a child and/or family counsellor. Listening to the problems with you, pointing out the facets that appear to have relevance to the case, gently bringing you to realize your own role in the development or response to the signal or message —all can be the first step in effective counselling. When the problem stems from the failure of you and your child to hear each other, to communicate, the doctor can invite both of you into his office; he can stimulate the key issues to be discussed and point out the answers and angers being verbalized by everyone in the room. He can be a mediator, possibly a referee, who has a real interest in the successful outcome of these discussions. When the signal deals with death, divorce, or illness in another individual, the family physician can help your child to accept and assimilate these traumas. Sometimes the family doctor will want to see you, your child, or both for short periods of time to offer concrete advice, help with plans of change, and to work with you or your child to accept the real and unchangeable in the healthiest way possible.

Your child's signal may have more serious significance and require the help of other professionals, such as medical consultants, social workers, psychologists, or psychiatrists. Your doctor will tell you if this consultation is needed. He is aware of the best local experts in these fields and can become a referral source for the necessary outside help. In addition, the doctor will receive feedback from these specialists on a regular basis, and help you when you do not understand what the other professionals are telling you in technical or behavioral terms. But parent and child are the final judges here.

Frequently the school is intimately involved in the signals your youngster is sending. After careful interpretation of the signal, the message, and the therapy needed, the physician can give school officials the necessary information and advice to work with you and your child in overcoming the problems behind the signal. You will want to know that the doctor will share *first* with you the information he is transmitting about your child to the school. This should be part of your stated contract with your doctor from the moment you walk into his office.

Often the doctor's nurse—or the school nurse—will know your child equally well. There are times when she can work easily with your youngster. She may have more time. She will not have hordes of sick children to distract her from the task of working with you and your child; the telephone will not interrupt her so constantly. The professional nurse has received much of the same training in child development and childhood problems as the doctor. She is professionally equipped to work with your youngster in specific situations decided upon by the doctor and herself and agreed upon by you.

What has been outlined above are the expectations that all parents should have of their child's personal physician. You need the doctor as your initial helping hand when that signal begins to alarm you or disrupt you or your child's life. If you cannot honestly see your child's physician performing these tasks, then you have placed your child in inadequate healing hands. Think it over. If he or she fails the test, you must change doctors. Search until you find a doctor for your child who can and will be the resource you need when the going gets rough. Then you can rest easy that you have a friend and expert in your corner, who can and will work to find out what your child is really telling you.

29

The Child Psychiatrist,
Psychologist, and Social Worker

"Good morning, Mrs. Jones." His smile was open as he walked across the room toward her, his arm outstretched in greeting. "I'm Fred Evans, if you haven't guessed by now." His eyes wrinkled pleasantly as he took her hand. "Please come into the office where we can talk." He guided her through the doorway into a small, slightly cluttered office, where he pointed toward a comfortable, modern easy chair. Fred Evans took a notepad from the desk, seated himself next to the woman, and prepared his pen. Then he looked up and smiled once again.

"This is your first time in an office like this, isn't it?" he asked gently. As she nodded, he noticed that she was uneasy. "I'll bet you're looking for the couch." This time she smiled, a bit self-consciously, as she moved her head in agreement. "Most people do," he sighed. "But my Aunt Agatha was the only person I ever knew who had one of those couches. I slept on it once as a little boy." He paused and mused for a second, then spoke directly: "No, we conduct business in this office in a vertical position."

He could sense the tension slowly leaving the woman's body as he continued in an easy, conversational tone. Fred Evans knew that a first visit was always alarming. This mother would be fearful of talking about her problems with her child. She would want to know if she were to "blame" for the child's problems. Mrs. Jones needed some reassurance that she had acted in her child's best interests, even if incorrectly. She would have secret guilt feelings about every past action that could have hurt her child, every unkind word directed to him. To Mrs. Jones, this office visit probably signified her defeat and her failure. She finally had to visit a "shrink." Her child was out of control.

Gradually, she appeared more at ease; her body curved into the chair, her arms relaxed, her hands rested loosely in her lap. Her answers to his questions became more spontaneous. She began to speak more freely and with honest feelings.

Fred Evans picked up his pen, looked at her, and said quietly, "I know if we continue talking like this, we'll be good friends in an hour. But both you and I have a job. We need to talk about helping your son, Darrell. Tell me—who is Darrell?"

She looked astonished. "Why . . . why, Darrell is my son . . . my twelve-year-old." She stopped, waiting for the next question.

"No," he said gently, *"who* is Darrell?"

"Do you mean, 'What kind of a person is Darrell?' "

"Who is Darrell?"

She took a deep breath and looked at him with frightened eyes. She was prepared to describe Darrell's problems. She could use the diagnostic terms she had learned from books and magazines. The conversations with Darrell's pediatrician came into her mind. But describe the real Darrell? Her Darrell? She fought a moment of panic, bit her lip and began.

"Darrell is . . . a . . . boy . . . a little boy . . . a smaller boy than others his age. Darrell is a . . . a frightened boy. He's a child afraid of power or anger. Darrell is a hurt boy, a quiet boy who doesn't show that he's hurt. Darrell is quiet so that nothing shows. Darrell is a quick kiss when you don't expect it. He'll chuckle into a private book, but keep quite silent during a funny TV show. Darrell is . . ."

Mrs. Jones began to immerse herself in the picture she was painting. She was beginning to see Darrell as a person. She trusted the professional sitting across from her enough to describe the boy's weaknesses as well as his strengths.

Fred Evans, taking notes of her descriptions, wrote in the margin that Mrs. Jones never called Darrell the one thing she could have—the reason Darrell had been referred to him—a "chronic liar."

Mrs. Jones was seeing a professional child helper. In the example you have just read, that helper could have been a child psychiatrist, a child psychologist, or a social worker. All of these helpers have one trait in common. They *must* establish a trusting, communicating relationship with the child needing help and with his or her family. All of these professionals know that when parents are first referred to them, the family feels itself in serious trouble. These helpers realize that people are reluctant to probe their deepest feelings with a stranger. So the child psychiatrist, psychologist, or social worker must build up confidence and trust. The problems—all of the problems—must be unraveled gently. The first few sessions are always exploratory periods: exploration of the child's problems, the family problems, and the problems of communication between child, family, and professional. The interview with Mrs. Jones is a good example of the way a professional helper should work with a parent. Fred Evans was informal, pleasant, a good listener, and then a good questioner. He established communication quickly and learned Mrs. Jones's feelings about Darrell. He would be prepared to explore the meaningful areas behind Darrell's problems when he interviewed him.

Suppose Fred Evans had been a child psychiatrist. What could Mrs. Jones have expected of him after this initial interview?

A child psychiatrist is a physician who has had training in the psychotherapy of children. A referral to this kind of helper is often made by another professional who feels that a child's problems require medical attention. Perhaps these referring professionals want to rule out a chronic illness or a neurological condition as a possible cause of the problem. Or they may feel that a child will have to be given medication before he can be helped to solve his signalling behavior. Whatever the reason, a referral to a child psychiatrist will coordinate both the psychological aspects of the child's problems and any related medical problems or treatments.

Parents can anticipate that the child psychiatrist will want all previous medical and psychological records. He may give the child a medical examination. He probably will *not* administer a prolonged battery of psychological tests, but he may ask some informal questions in order to pick up overall clues about the child's behavior. If he needs extensive test data, the child psychiatrist will often refer the child to a psychologist.

The child psychiatrist may engage in psychotherapy with the child, but the parent should not be surprised if the therapy situation is unique or unusual. Psychotherapy can take place in a playroom, on the street, or in groups. It is often very difficult to work with a child in the barrenness of a regular office. The child can become easily bored; his or her attention will lag; the seat becomes uncomfortable and the surroundings are unfamiliar and frightening. Psychotherapy must be brought into the child's world, particularly in the case of the young child. The psychiatrist may play with the child, work with the child, or simply watch the child. Talking directly may not give the needed responses. Therefore, the psychiatrist must use whatever therapy the child can relate to and understand, so that, as a consequence, he (or she) reveals himself and his problems.

The therapy of a young and uncommunicative child may have to be effected through you, the parents. You may be the key patients being seen in the child psychiatrist's office. Why? Because the young child's world is his home. So you may be asked to help the child by changing the home routines, the reactions between your child and your family, or your physical environment. You, along with the child psychiatrist, will be keeping a mental log of your child's progress, remembering which methods fail and which succeed.

What if Fred Evans had been a child psychologist? What could Mrs. Jones have expected from this professional?

The child psychologist frequently is the individual to whom the other therapists turn for further psychological diagnosis. The signals and the messages may be extremely complex or, perhaps, hidden altogether. The child clearly has problems, but the other professionals cannot find easy explanations. Clearly, more in-depth psychological probing is needed.

The child psychologist is prepared to do an intensive analysis of the child's psychological make-up—his thinking and feeling states. With batteries of tests and scientific observations, the child psychologist attempts to perceive the child's actions from that child's perspective. The child psychologist tries to re-create the child's world, find the disturbing elements, and interpret these to the parents and the other professionals. The insights of the child psychologist, particularly in the case of children with complex problems, are invaluable to child psychiatrists and social workers and are often requested routinely before, during, and after a course of psychotherapy.

Child psychologists can, themselves, provide psychotherapy to a child. They are trained in comparable settings and under similar supervision as child psychiatrists. They can provide similar varieties of psychotherapy in different settings. Thus, when medication or medical problems do not seem to be a deterrent to successful psychotherapy, a child psychologist and a child psychiatrist are equally appropriate. The parent has a choice.

And what if Fred Evans had been a social worker? What could Mrs. Jones have expected then?

Parents are usually referred to social workers when the problems of a child are perceived as being rooted in the family, the community, and/or society in general. The social worker or his specialist colleague, the psychiatric social worker, has studied the effects of poor communities, difficult family situations, and a rejecting society upon the actions of children. Part of the social worker's training has been to learn techniques to correct the disturbed behavior patterns of children, even those kids who live in a "sick" community or a "sick" family. A social worker, therefore, is a professional who fits best as a child and family therapist when the signals sent by the child indicate that the source of his problems are external to the family and the child as well as internal.

A social worker often sees the whole family in therapy. He may visit the home or neighborhood to observe the environment in which the child lives. The child may be placed in a therapy group or he may receive individual counselling from the social worker. Sometimes a combination of group and individual therapy is recommended. Whatever the treatment choice, the social worker will be working with the child's *outside* world as well as his *inside* world. This is often the characteristic that makes the social worker different from the child psychiatrist or the child psychologist, both of whom are more intensively trained in therapy related to a child's inner world.

When does a parent seek a referral to one of these psycho-social professionals? *Any time a signal persists for too long a period. Whenever a signal cannot be understood or interpreted by parents, teachers, or pediatricians. And whenever a signal sends a message of potential harm, either to the child or to others.*

How do you find the right professional? The usual way of finding the name of the "right" psycho-social professional is through another professional—one who knows your child and possibly your family. Often your pediatrician or family doctor fulfills this role. Sometimes your minister, priest, or rabbi makes the referral. But if none of these persons can help you, almost every city or county has a mental health center, a family counselling center, a hospital with a psychiatric component, or a school system with a department of special services. Any of these places will help you find a competent psycho-social professional. Most of these professionals or agencies will give you the names of more than one person to contact.

Ask for more information about these referrals. Ask if any of the individuals has been used by the referring person in the past. Ask about particular patterns or styles of diagnosis or therapy. Ask if the individual is known for special skills with a particular problem. Ask about credentials, experience, and training. In other words, try to find out as much as you can about a helping professional *before* you see him. Establishing a therapy relationship with a helping professional is difficult and time-consuming. You may not have the luxury of "shopping" for different psycho-social therapists as you might for a minor medical problem. You should always try to pre-select the best one for your child.

How much should you know about your child's therapy? Everything you want to know. You should know why the psychiatrist, psychologist, or social worker is doing what he is doing as therapy for your child. You should know what kind of progress to expect and in what length of time. In other words, you should ask to— insist on—becoming part of the treatment team for your child. Most professionals welcome parental help that is rational and objective. Listen to your professional and understand his or her methods. Then ask how you can help. Go no further than he or she requests. Observe progress or lack of it in your child, and report it to the therapist. You both must work together toward helping your child solve his problems.

A word of warning: to remain with a child therapist who is not helping a child and/or his family is wasteful and potentially dangerous. Valuable time is being lost while the child's symptoms and the family's and child's needs for understanding decrease daily. The frustrations felt by the child can result in signals recurring or changing into more serious ones. The signal of a worsening symptom while the child is in therapy may have a new message: Change therapists! As difficult as it may seem, new signals must be heard —and obeyed.

Because the child psychiatrist, psychologist, and social worker are all persons trained to help children and parents work through difficult problems, they are competent interpreters of complex signals. Unfortunately, many parents have been led to believe that consulting one of these professionals is the same as openly admitting that their child has a serious mental problem. As a result of this fear, if a parent is reluctant to consult such a professional when he cannot understand or interpret a signal from his child, he is delaying the process of gaining insight into what may develop into a serious problem.

You can be one of the enlightened parents. Be aware that the child psychiatrist, psychologist, and social worker are available to help you unravel the complexities of an obtuse or distorted signal. They are easy to locate by asking the proper people or agencies. These professionals can save parents years of child problems. They are professionally trained to identify, and treat, troublesome and persistent signals.

PARENTING
BY SIGNALS

30

Troubleshooting Your Child's Problems

Signals, messages, analysis, interpretations. Helping professionals. Prevention. Acceptance. What do all these words mean to a parent who has a child in trouble? How do they all fit together? How can you use the concepts of this book to "troubleshoot" problems with your child?

The problems described by this book have no "cookbook" answers. The interactions between a child and his or her family and friends cannot be categorized or treated in simplistic terms. The intelligence of parents and the integrity of the authors would be offended if you were told, "If this happens, then do that."

What this book tries to offer is insight: a heightened ability to look at a child's actions and determine what the child is *really* telling the parent. The parent then must react to the signal and/or the message behind the signal in the most rational manner possible. When the signal cannot be interpreted within the family, the parents are given advice in finding outside professionals to help. But it is the parent who must decide the importance of the action —the parent who must decode the signal—the parent who ultimately must cope with all the problems and consequences affecting the child.

How well have you, as a parent, gained some insight into your child's problems? Compare the next two cases. How well did these parents read Sandra's and Henry's signals? How well would you have reacted to the messages if you had been the parent of either child?

CASE A: SANDRA, TEN YEARS OLD

In the first three grades of school Sandra had been a "model" student. Not only did she receive "A's" and "B's," but the notes on the bottom of each report card glowed with warm comments about her excellent attitude.

When Sandra entered the fourth grade, she encountered a young teacher, new to the school, fresh out of college, and driven to prove herself up to the job. She was determined to push her students to their maximum.

Sandra soon realized that she had to study harder than during any previous year. She had to establish a study routine at home which interfered with her favorite television shows and her play-time with the neighborhood children. Her frustration grew to anger and tears as her first report carried her usual "A's" and "B's," but also the terse note: "Sandra is a bright child who can do better."

Sandra changed her study routine. She would bring her books home, take them immediately to her room, and close the door. She would emerge at dinnertime stating that she had completed her assignments. Her parents praised her concentration and diligence.

At the second grading period, however, the family received a great shock. Sandra brought home a report card with three "C's" and one "D." A frantic call to her teacher revealed that Sandra had turned in almost no homework assignments that semester, had seemingly studied very little, and was on the verge of complete failure in one subject.

A long, tearful conversation between Sandra and her parents revealed that Sandra had *not* been able to study during those hours after school. Yes, she had opened her books, but she usually fell asleep while trying to read them. She was chronically tired. She could not work at school. She knew she was falling further behind, but she could not help herself. "I'm so dumb!" she cried, as she fell sobbing into her mother's arms.

Sandra's father called school the next day and set up an appointment with Sandra's teacher. He confronted the teacher with the story of the night before.

Sandra's teacher felt that Sandra was lazy. "She's capable of doing the work, but doesn't want to give up playtime and exert the additional effort to make better grades," was her response. She fully intended to push Sandra to her top level of achievement.

Sandra's father and mother were stunned. That was not the signal at all. Sandra had never been lazy in any other area of her life. She was anxious, frightened, tired, but certainly not lazy. They tried to interpret this signal to Sandra's teacher; the young woman would not listen.

Sandra's father abruptly terminated the meeting, and set up another—with the principal of the school. He asked for a meeting in several days. He wanted a "cooling-off" period.

At the meeting with the principal, he calmly explained Sandra's signal, sudden school failure, and the message behind it: "I am being overly pressured." He explained the history of Sandra's schooling, the family routines of encouragement, and her dramatic confession of failure. He asked that the message be answered by, "You can achieve at your own rate."

The principal understood. And he agreed with Sandra's parents. He talked to Sandra's teacher, but found her attitude impossible to change. So he transferred Sandra to another class. The pace in the other class allowed Sandra to learn and study without stress. Her grades got better but the greatest improvement was in her attitude. She felt better about school and about herself. Sandra returned to school a happier and more productive child. And the next year, the young teacher's contract was not renewed.

CASE B: HARRY, FOURTEEN YEARS OLD

Harry was the third of four children. He was a fourteen-year-old boy of average ability. In appearance, he could only be described as plain. He had grown to the ungainly stature of the early adolescent—his pants and shirt always too small and his body lanky and awkward. He had trouble making the junior varsity teams because of his awkward teenage coordination. Every club or activity seemed to have "no more room" when he applied. He moved as a singular, lonely figure through the high-school halls.

Harry was fortunate to have been born into a family with warm, understanding parents. They loved him as they loved his three brothers. They tried to let him know this, but even they had trouble communicating their message to Harry. When they could praise one child for being a football hero, another for his high marks in school, and a third for obtaining leading parts in every school drama production, it was extremely difficult to praise the fourth for a "sweet and gentle personality." All they could do was continue to repeat, "We love you," to him, knowing that their words had a hollow ring.

The week before his sophomore year, he bicycled by himself over to the nearby shopping center. About two o'clock the phone rang in his father's office. "Mr. Hanson, this is the store detective at Farbinger's. Do you have a child named Harry?"

With a sinking feeling in the pit of his stomach, Harry's father replied shakily: "Yes. Is something wrong?"

"Something *is* wrong, Mr. Hanson—very wrong. I just caught your child shoplifting a sweater. It's Farbinger's policy to prosecute, so I'm calling the police. May I advise you to get over to the police station?"

"Yes, of course," Mr. Hanson replied in a stunned voice as the detective hung up the phone. His Harry? He didn't need a sweater. He had never stolen anything before. He wasn't dishonest. *Why?*

Harry's father called his wife and told her. She gasped: "Oh, God. I knew something like this would happen to Harry."

Her husband frowned. "Why?"

She sighed over the phone. "Well, he's so different from the other boys. And he's so alone all of the time." When he hung up the phone, Harry's father was suddenly struck by an insight. Harry was nothing unless he did something dramatic. He had to win attention by some forceful means in order to compete with three over-achieving brothers. He was achieving in the only way he could, through an antisocial act. His signal was clear: "I'm getting left out of everything in life." His message was even more forceful: "Pay attention to *me!* I need to be somebody." Now, everyone *had* to pay attention to Harry.

Harry's father met his son at the police station with an attorney. Together they convinced the magistrate not to penalize Harry for his shoplifting. Harry was told to pay the store for the sweater within a week. His father set up several tasks at home for Harry that would permit him to earn the money.

And the Hansons sat down to have a long talk with Harry. "What do you do well, son?" his father asked. The boy lowered his head and finally muttered, "Nothing." Mr. Hanson did not blink. "What do you like to do?" he continued. Harry paused and looked up at his father. "I like sports. But I haven't found one I can play well, even a little bit." Mr. Hanson thought for a minute. "You know, I used to like playing tennis. I've let my game go to pot. Would you like to join me in picking it up again?" Harry nodded enthusiastically. Mrs. Hanson interrupted: "You know what just occurred to me. We're always asking Harry to take pictures when we go on vacation. I bet he could become a really good photographer." The boy's dull eyes began to take on an inner glow. "Is there a photography club at school?" she asked. Harry nodded. "Well, work around the house. After you pay for the sweater, you can save for the photography equipment. Dad and I will match what you earn. It shouldn't take very long." Harry was beginning to see the light out of the long, dark tunnel of his isolation and loneliness.

The Hansons had interpreted Harry's signal correctly, responded to the message, and taken positive steps to eliminate the need for Harry ever to send such a serious signal again.

You have just read two cases of successful parenting—successful because the wise parents listened to the child's signals, correctly interpreted the messages behind the signal, and took positive actions.

How are the stories different? The children are of different ages, and different sexes. They sent signals of different types. The reasons for the signals were external in Sandra's case—her teacher put her under stress; and internal in Harry's case—he had lost his sense of worth and identity.

As parents you can also learn by comparing the *similarities* of the cases:

* Both cases were climaxed by dramatic signals, behavior that was totally unexpected and out of character. The children were driven to send explosive signals that said they were being "boxed in" by impossible situations. The stresses on them were great, they could not verbalize their problems, and they knew that they could not solve their problems by themselves.

* Sandra and Harry had sensitive parents who did not label their child's behavior. Sandra's parents did not call her a "failure" when her grades were low. Harry's father would not call Harry a "thief," even when his son was caught shoplifting. Both sets of parents were willing to look at the surprising, unusual behavior as a signal with an explicit message rather than as a label of inferiority.

* Both Sandra's and Harry's parents calmly and rationally thought through their child's signal to reach the meaning of the messages. They summarized all the facts they knew about their children, their families, schools, and friends, before reaching any conclusions about why the signals were sent.

* When both parents recognized the signal *as a signal,* and discovered what the child was really telling them, they acted upon that message with firm and aggressive determination. In Sandra's case the message said: "I need help in school," and school changes were made. In Harry's case, he needed a way of finding new horizons. His parents helped him discover what these new vistas might be.

* The parents of both children perceived the signals and acted upon the underlying messages with speed and understanding. Both children responded: the signals

stopped. "Happy endings" are the rule rather than the exception with perceptive parenting.

You have read how two sets of parents could "troubleshoot" their child's signals. You have also considered the principles of perceiving, and acting upon, signals and messages that will help your child through the rough spots of his or her childhood.

In order to illustrate these principles, let us consider a few challenging problems. Take a test of parenting by signals.

CASE 1

Billy has begun to stutter. He is four years old and whenever he is excited, he has difficulty in finishing his words. Except for the frustration of his halting speech, he seems to be a relaxed, imaginative little boy. Which of the following would you do if you were his parent?

(a) Recognize his stuttering as a signal.
(b) Take him immediately to the pediatrician for a speech referral.
(c) Wait patiently for his normal phase of poor speech coordination to pass.
(d) Assist him in finishing his sentences and urge him to try to control his speech.
(e) Allow him to finish his words by himself without impatience on your part.

The perceptive parent will immediately recognize the first principle of parenting by signals, which is (a): *"Recognizing the signal."* In addition, the parent will also put (c) and (e) into effect because, having picked up the signal and correctly interpreted it, he understands that the underlying message and problem are benign and usually time-limited. Overreactions as in (d) would be wrong in responding to Billy's signal. If you selected (a), (c), and (e), you have the first basic principle clearly in mind.

CASE 2

Millie, who is four, plays by herself a good deal of the time. She works happily on puzzles alone and holds excited tea parties with her doll collection. She will play with her cousins quite well when she visits but prefers to remain by herself when she is at home. How would you react as her parent?

   (a)   Decide that Millie needs more friends because she is becoming withdrawn.

   (b)   Refuse to label Millie with any terms but watch for the meaning of her signal.

   (c)   Take Millie to the local mental health clinic.

   (d)   Offer Millie the opportunity of a preschool play group for part of the day.

   (e)   Observe whether Millie is unhappy because of her lack of friends.

The second principle to be followed in the parenting by signals process is noted in (b): *"Do not label an unusual behavior until you know more about what it means."* To begin to decipher Millie's message, you will want to analyze (e). The initial steps in helping Millie balance her social life will be taken in (d). So (b), (d), and (e) are the correct actions in this case.

CASE 3

Six-year-old Artie has started to wet the bed again after having had no problems of this type for four years. You stand looking at the wet sheets and wonder what to do next:

   (a)   Punish him immediately.

   (b)   Wake him before you go to bed and take him to the bathroom.

   (c)   Carefully consider all the possibilities for Artie sending you the signal of bedwetting.

   (d)   Make an appointment with your pediatrician to rule out medical causes.

(e) Indicate to Artie that you want to help him stop this uncomfortable problem.

The third principle in dealing sensitively with signalling behavior can be found in (c). *"Think through the child's reasons for sending a signal. What message could the child be sending you?"* After you have stepped back, remained calm, and thought through the situation, you can then move on to the next appropriate actions. Both (d) and (e) fit into this child's problems as part of the beginning toward a solution. To arrive at these two actions, however, you must first be able to see and deal with the importance of (c).

CASE 4

Your fifteen-year-old daughter has just lost her part in the school play. This is the latest in a series of major disappointments for her. When you clean her room, you find her diary open and notice the words written in bold black letters: "I wish I were dead. I think about doing it all the time." You stand, stunned. What should you do?

(a) Realize that teenage girls can be hysterical and dismiss the problem from your mind.
(b) Attempt to reassure your daughter that there will be successes as well as failures in her life.
(c) Ask her best friend to find out if she really means it.
(d) Recognize that this signal is a potentially serious one.
(e) Because of the emotional and complex nature of the possible underlying messages, seek outside professional help as soon as possible.

In this instance, you would be dealing with a signal of extreme urgency that goes beyond your capability as a parent to handle as quickly and expertly as necessary. Failure to do the correct thing could lead to serious complications. Therefore the next principle of signal parenting is found in the combination of (d) and (e):

"Answer all messages. Recognize the potentially serious message and act upon it immediately!" If the signal has ominous overtones or if the underlying message is too complex or too emotional for a parent to handle, the parent must *seek outside help.*

CASE 5

Jenny has always been a moody child. You have become accustomed to her high points and her low periods. But since her twelfth birthday, she seems especially volatile, her states of excitement almost unnerving and her low periods close to depression. Should you do any of the following?

(a) Be alerted that there has been an increase in the level of Jenny's behavior and consider this to be a signal.

(b) Be sensitive to every mood swing to detect extremes.

(c) Remain hopeful about finding out the underlying messages in her moods.

(d) Seek the proper professional advice from teacher, physician, and psycho-social therapist if needed.

(e) Realize that once you have interpreted Jenny's signal and worked with her to solve the message (her underlying problems), you have an excellent opportunity to help her become a well-adjusted child.

The final principle of parenting by signals is contained in ALL of these answers. *"Be always alert. Never stop looking for messages."* Statements (a) through (e) are the essence of parenting by signals. They are the preliminaries to the final concept: "You can perceive your child's signals. You can answer his or her messages. You CAN be the front-line defense for your child facing these problems."

Being a parent and guiding a child through the complex and challenging years of childhood may well be the most difficult job you will undertake during your entire life. To make this responsibility end happily for you and your child, you must always be aware of what your child is REALLY telling you. Knowing and interpreting the signals along the way will ensure that your child will reach his or her final destination—as a mature, emotionally adjusted, and contented adult.

Index